Drugs, Prisons and Policy-Making

For my father
and
in memory of my mother

Drugs, Prisons and Policy-Making

Karen Duke
Senior Lecturer in Criminology
Middlesex University

palgrave
macmillan

First published 2003 by
PALGRAVE MACMILLAN
Houndmills, Basingstoke, Hampshire RG21 6XS and
175 Fifth Avenue, New York, N. Y. 10010
Companies and representatives throughout the world

PALGRAVE MACMILLAN is the global academic imprint of the Palgrave Macmillan division of St. Martin's Press, LLC and of Palgrave Macmillan Ltd. Macmillan® is a registered trademark in the United States, United Kingdom and other countries. Palgrave is a registered trademark in the European Union and other countries.

ISBN 0–333–98203–7

This book is printed on paper suitable for recycling and made from fully managed and sustained forest sources.

A catalogue record for this book is available from the British Library.

Library of Congress Cataloging-in-Publication Data
Duke, Karen.
Drugs, prisons and policy-making / Karen Duke.
p. cm.
Includes bibliographical references and index.
ISBN 0–333–98203–7
1. Prisoners–Drug use–Government policy–Great Britain.
2. Prisoners–Drug use–Great Britain–Prevention. 3. Prison administration–Great Britain. I. Title.

HV8836.5D85 2003
365′.66–dc21

2003043146

10 9 8 7 6 5 4 3 2 1
12 11 10 09 08 07 06 05 04 03

Printed and bound in Great Britain by
Antony Rowe Ltd, Chippenham and Eastbourne

Contents

Preface

In her analysis of imprisonment around the world, the prominent penal reformer, Vivien Stern, has argued, 'it is impossible to talk about crime, prisons and prisoners without coming to the question of drugs' (Stern, 1998: 121). In Britain, the current government has become obsessed with what they perceive to be a direct link between drugs and crime. Millions of pounds have been committed to its fight against drug-related offending. The aim is to provide interventions at each stage of the criminal justice process – arrest, bail, sentencing, imprisonment, and community supervision (see Home Office, 2001). However, this emphasis on the interconnections between drugs, crime and punishment has not always been so pronounced, particularly in terms of the discourses and policies around drugs and prisons. This book traces the history of the development of prisons drugs policy in England since 1980 and exposes the processes by which the drugs 'problem' shifted from being a concealed and relatively invisible issue to one which occupies an important and significant place on the penal policy agenda.

When I first became interested in the interface between drugs and prisons in the mid-1990s what struck me was the paucity of research in this area and also the lack of attention paid to policy development and the key actors involved in these processes. Drugs and prisons are politically sensitive research areas, and for many years access to conduct research on these topics was virtually denied (Pearson, 1990). As the drug 'problem' in prisons was acknowledged and more explicit policies began to develop, the focus of much research was on the prevalence of drug taking before, during and after imprisonment; the extent and nature of HIV risk behaviour; the results of mandatory drug testing and the monitoring and evaluation of various strands of policy. Within this context, there was clearly a need for the research gaze to capture those who are in the powerful positions of 'making' and influencing policy in order to understand the conflicts, contradictions, uncertainties and politics inherent in the policy process. This study was therefore based on semi-structured interviews with key policy actors, including civil servants and representatives from drug agencies, penal reform groups, and professional associations, and an analysis of documentary materials. In particular, it examines the activities of policy networks around drug issues in prisons and their involvement in agenda setting, lobbying and influencing the policy process within the wider political, economic and social contexts.

The book is based on the construction of a series of four case studies which correspond to the key phases in prison drugs policy development since 1980: 1980–6; 1986–93; 1993–7; and 1997 onwards. It explores the policies around drug treatment and throughcare, HIV/AIDS, supply reduction activities, and security and control measures. The development of policy has hinged upon complex patterns of conflict, contradiction and convergence between treatment and punishment. Throughout the phases, particular policy networks have evolved around drug-related issues within the penal system, expanding and becoming more complex in their structure and operation over time. They have attempted to contain, balance and negotiate the contradictions and tensions within policies. The book seeks to explore the different forms this 'balancing act' or 'containment' has taken and examine how it has been shaped by the following processes or forces: the way in which the drug problem has been framed and defined; the role of research, evidence and knowledge; and the impact of wider social, political, policy and institutional contexts.

Chapter 1 begins by exploring the statistical indicators of drugs use and offending within the prison population. It outlines the interconnected themes which will run through the book, including the role of the policy network, the shifting conceptualisations of the drugs 'problem', the role of research and evidence, and the impact of wider contexts. The chapter also explains the research design and methodological framework employed in the study.

Drawing on documentary and interview data, Chapters 2 to 5 form the core of the analysis. Chapter 2 considers the period from 1980 to 1986 and examines the initial collusion around drugs within prisons. It explores how a small policy network began to emerge which lobbied for changes in the way prisoners with drug problems were treated. Given the constraints of the prison context during this period, it is argued that the policy network adopted a pragmatic approach by pressing for service provision on release, rather than tackling the problem internally from within the prison environment. This phase laid the foundations for later policy developments. Chapter 3 focuses on the period 1986–93 and explores the impact of HIV on the development of a more explicit drug policy within the prison system. However, it argues that the policies which emerged were inadequate and failed to fully embrace the concept of 'harm minimisation' and the public health agenda which were successfully operating in the community. Such initiatives were constrained by the unwillingness of the Prison Service to consider radical policies, the inherent conflict between treatment and punishment, and the pressure to adopt a hard-line, abstinence-based approach. Chapter 4 considers the period from 1993 to 1997 and explores how the populist punitive rhetoric around drugs and prisons and the new managerialism impacted upon policy development. It demonstrates how the drugs issue in prison was increasingly framed as a problem of order and control. The response in both political and policy terms was to 'get tough' and take control of the problem by implementing a defined prison drugs strategy in 1995 which emphasised mandatory drug testing and security measures. As the contradictions and tensions between treatment and punishment intensified, the chapter explores how a policy network began to form which attempted to re-balance the strategy towards treatment and care. The focus of Chapter 5 is on the revised 1998 prison drugs strategy and the key changes which have occurred since New Labour's victory in the 1997 general election. Although these reforms mark an attempt to rebalance the strategy towards care and treatment for prisoners, it is argued that the basic punitive framework for delivering the strategy has remained intact and the emphasis on the discourses of 'security', 'control' and 'punishment' has endured. Moreover, in the process of attempting to rebalance the new strategy towards treatment, the policy network around prison drug issues has been reshaped with drug agencies entering into more formalised, contractual partnerships with the Prison Service.

The book concludes in Chapter 6 by reconsidering and summarising the developments within prison drugs policy from 1980 in relation to the key research questions, themes and debates outlined in Chapter 1. It then discusses the significance of the research findings for the future development of prison drugs policy and the activities of policy networks. In particular, it focuses on the growing incorporation of a core part of the policy networks, namely the drug agencies, and questions whether these processes are inevitable.

****

I am indebted to many people for their guidance and assistance with this book. I would like to thank all of the people who were interviewed during this research. They must remain nameless as I promised to protect their anonymity, but I would like to express my gratitude to them for being so generous with their time and sharing their experiences, knowledge and contacts with me.

My colleagues and students at Middlesex University have been supportive and helpful in developing ideas. I have benefited considerably from the constructive comments, guidance and inspiration of Susanne MacGregor. I am very grateful to Sarah Neal for reading the various versions of the chapters and for her valuable suggestions, support and friendship throughout the research and writing process. Thanks also to Nigel South, Betsy Thom and Tony Cutler for their comments and encouragement to publish. I am grateful to Heather Gibson, Briar Towers and Jennifer Nelson of Palgrave for their editorial support.

Thanks are also reserved for the library staff at Middlesex University Library (Enfield), Senate House, University of London Library, the Home Office Library, and the Institute for the Study of Drug Dependence (now Drugscope) for their expertise and help in locating and ordering references. I am grateful to the Prison Service, the Home Office and the UK Anti-Drugs Co-ordination Unit for responding to my requests for documents and other information. The Tables which appear in the Appendix are reproduced with the kind permission of the Home Office.

Finally, this book would not have been attempted or completed without the ongoing support and encouragement from my parents, Donna and Claude Duke, and my brother, Scott Duke. I am also grateful to my friend, Lorna Klose for all her supportive emails and sharing her experiences of writing with me. My greatest thanks go to Hugh Giles, who lived through the process with patience and understanding, commented on the various drafts and provided useful advice at each stage. Very special thanks are reserved for Scott Duke-Giles, who appeared during the writing phase and provided a wonderful distraction. Without them, the project would never have been undertaken or finished.

Karen Duke
Middlesex University
November 2002

List of Abbreviations

ACMD	Advisory Council on the Misuse of Drugs
ACPO	Association of Chief Officers of Police
ACOP	Association of Chief Officers of Probation
ADFAM	The national charity for the families and friends of drug users
ADSS	Association of Directors of Social Services
AIDS	Acquired Immune Deficiency Syndrome
CARAT(s)	Counselling, Assessment, Referral, Advice, and Throughcare Service
CCTV	Closed circuit television
CDCU	Central Drugs Co-ordination Unit
CDPU	Central Drugs Prevention Unit
CFI	Central Funding Initiative
DARI	Drug Addiction Research Initiative
DAT	Drug Action Team
DDAC	District Drug Advisory Committee
DHA	District Health Authority
DH	Department of Health
DPAS	Drugs Prevention and Advisory Service
DPI	Drugs Prevention Initiative
DRG	Drug Reference Group
DTTO	Drug Treatment and Testing Order
EMCDDA	European Monitoring Centre for Drugs and Drug Addiction
GP	General Practitioner
HIV	Human Immunodeficiency Virus
HMP	HM Prison
ISDD	Institute for the Study of Drug Dependence
KPI	Key performance indicator
LGDF	Local Government Drugs Forum
LDPF	London Drug Policy Forum
MDT	Mandatory drug testing
NACRO	National Association for the Care and Resettlement of Offenders
NAPO	National Association of Probation Officers
NHS	National Health Service

PGA	Prison Governors' Association
POA	Prison Officers' Association
PRS	Parole Release Scheme
PRT	Prison Reform Trust
RAP	Radical Alternatives to Prison
RAPt	Rehabilitation for Addicted Prisoners Trust
SCODA	Standing Conference on Drug Abuse
TDT	Tackling Drugs Together
UKADCU	UK Anti-Drugs Co-ordination Unit
VIR	Viral Infectivity Restrictions
VTU	Voluntary Testing Unit
WHO	World Health Organisation
WIP	Women in Prison

1
Analysing Prison Drugs Policy: Problems, Networks and Contexts

Introduction

The drug issue in prisons is a global phenomenon and has become a policy concern in many countries. There are several groups which can be identified in relation to drugs within the prison population: those who are imprisoned for drug offences and who may also be drug users; those who are imprisoned for non-drug offences, but who are drug users; and those who begin using drugs during their prison sentences. The proportion of prisoners serving sentences for drug offences has increased dramatically over the last two decades. Reflecting the 'war on drugs' and introduction of mandatory minimum sentences for minor drug offences, the percentage of the federal prison population in the United States serving sentences for drug offences has more than doubled over the last 20 years from 25 per cent in 1980 to 55 per cent in 2001 (Federal Bureau of Prisons, 2002). In England and Wales, the percentage of male prisoners serving sentences for drug offences increased from 2 per cent in 1980 to 15 per cent in 2000. The percentage of women prisoners serving sentences for drug offences has increased even more sharply from 5 per cent in 1980 to almost two-fifths (37 per cent) in 2000 (Home Office Prison Statistics, 2001). One factor which helps to explain this rise is the increasing number of foreign national women convicted of drug-trafficking offences (see Green, 1996).

In comparison with the general population, there are high rates of drug use and drug dependence amongst prisoners both prior to imprisonment and during their sentences. In the US, over half of all prisoners (56 per cent) were found to have a diagnosable drug use disorder (Robins and Reiger, 1991). In the European Union, problem drug users and/or injecting drug users represent up to 50 per cent of the prison population in some countries (European Monitoring Centre for Drugs and Drug Addiction, 2001). In England and Wales, over half of male (51 per cent) and female (54 per cent) remand prisoners were assessed as drug dependent. Although cannabis is the most frequently used drug both inside and outside prisons in England and Wales, one-fifth of male sentenced prisoners (19 per cent) and female sentenced prisoners (20 per cent) had used heroin in prisons, with women being more likely to report opiate dependence than men (Singleton et al., 1999). More than one-third (36 per cent) of male sentenced prisoners and one-fifth (18 per cent) of female sentenced prisoners who had used heroin reported their first use of the drug in prison (Singleton et al., 1999).

Patterns of drug use vary between the different groups within the prison system, but a typical profile of a drug user in a European prison would include the following characteristics: very socially deprived; poly-drug use; previous prison sentences; several treatment attempts; high incidence of relapse; and severe health damage (including irreversible infectious diseases) (see EMCDDA, 2001). Due to the secrecy surrounding drug use within prisons and the reluctance of prison authorities to fully embrace harm reduction principles, prisons are also the setting for high-risk behaviours such as unsafe injecting practices (Strang et al., 1998). Drugs are in great demand within the prison environment due to the number of existing drug users and also because they provide a means of escaping from the deprivations of prison life.

In Britain, official interest in drug issues within the penal system is relatively recent, with formal policy only beginning to develop from the mid-1990s. The prison system was included in national drugs policy for the first time in 1995. The increasing interface between drugs and penal policy has prompted interest in this area from various perspectives including the Prison Service in its strategies to combat drugs in prisons (HM Prison Service 1995a; 1998b), the former Conservative and current Labour governments in their national drugs strategies (HM Government, 1995; 1998a); the Department of Health in their review of services for drug users (Department of Health, 1996); the Home Affairs Select Committee (1999) and the Advisory Council on the Misuse of Drugs (1996) in their reports on drugs and prisons; various voluntary agencies working with prisoners and drug users; and the media. Increasing amounts of government expenditure have also been directed at the prison drugs 'problem'. For example, during 1996–7, £4.2 million was made available to cover the costs of implementing mandatory drug testing. For the three years commencing 1999/2000, the Prison Service received an additional £76 million to fund a new framework for drug treatment within the prison system (DPAS, 1999).

Despite the increasing interest in the relationship between drugs and prisons, this area has attracted very little research attention. This neglect is related to the difficulties around gaining access to conduct research on this sensitive topic within prisons. Until the early 1990s, politicians, government officials and prison governors were reluctant to publicly acknowledge that there was a drugs 'problem' or even that drugs were being used within the prison system. The research which was eventually conducted in this area was focused mainly on the nature and extent of drug use amongst prison populations (see Maden et al., 1990; 1991; 1992) and their patterns of drug use and HIV risk behaviour (see Dolan et al., 1990; Dye and Issacs, 1991; Turnbull et al., 1991; 1994; Bird et al., 1992; 1993; Strang et al., 1998). These studies have highlighted the extent of drug use prior to and during imprisonment, the problems and risks associated with continued use and the lack of treatment services within the prison system.

With the implementation of the 1995 and 1998 prison drug strategies in England and Wales and the more open acknowledgement of a drug 'problem' within prisons, there now appears to be greater willingness to allow researchers to undertake research and evaluations in this area. The Prison Service commissioned its own evaluation research to examine the effectiveness of the strategies (see Edgar and O'Donnell, 1998; Farrell et al., 1998; PDM Consulting Ltd, 1998). Other studies exploring the impact of particular aspects of the policy in individual prisons (see Seddon, 1996; Gore et al., 1996; Keene, 1997a; Bird et al., 1997; Hughes, 2000) and the experiences of women drug users in prisons have been conducted (Malloch, 2000). Although some of the studies have been policy related and provided some critique of the evolving strategy, they have not focused on the dynamics of the policy process itself. This lack of research highlighted the need to trace the contemporary origins of the 'problem' of drugs in prison and to explore the processes involved in the development of policy.

Policies and initiatives must be viewed as not just a reaction to the current situation, but as historically and culturally framed. One important theme emerging from both analyses of drugs policy and penal policy is the complex relationship between medical and penal forms of control. There has been a long history of debate regarding the locus of responsibility for the social control of drugs. British scholars have generally concluded that policy has been shaped by an accommodation between medical and criminal justice concerns (see Berridge, 1978; Smart, 1984; Stimson and Oppenheimer, 1982; Pearson, 1991; Dorn and South, 1994). As Smart (1984: 31) has argued, 'the drug user is in the unique, although unenviable position of occupying the locus of attention of several different modes of regulation; legal, moral and medical. Whilst these analytically distinct modes overlap in their concentration on the drug user, they are also frequently in conflict'. The conflicts between these forms of control manifest themselves within the values and ideologies of practitioners and professionals, in the decisions regarding policy options and also at a structural or institutional level where there has been historical tension between the key government departments (i.e. the Home Office and Department of Health). Analyses of drugs policy indicate a balancing act between medical and penal forms of control or between treatment and punishment. This balance has changed over time and is influenced by the nature of addiction or the drugs 'problem' as well as the social, political and institutional contexts. Within policy there is an enduring tension between 'whether the addict is to be termed sick and a fit subject for medicine, or bad, and a subject for penal control' (Berridge, 1996b: 302).

Similarly, the competing paradigms or discourses of 'rehabilitation' and 'welfare' versus 'punishment' and 'justice' are important components of penal policy development. Several analyses have illuminated these tensions and the problems of containing and managing these contradictions (see Garland, 1985; 2001; Cohen, 1985; Adler and Longhurst, 1994). However, other observers of contemporary policy argue that a 'new penology' has emerged which involves a shift away from the individual towards the aggregate (Feeley and Simon, 1992; 1994). Its goals are managerial rather than transformative. The new penology is not concerned with rehabilitation, treatment, interventions or even punishment for the individual offender, rather it emphasises managerial processes and 'techniques to identify, classify and manage groupings sorted by dangerousness' (Feeley and Simon, 1992: 452). Interestingly, Feeley and Simon (1992) argue that drug use has become a major feature of the contemporary penal landscape and the new penology. Drug use is treated as a risk indicator for re-offending and employed as a criterion to classify offenders. The new initiatives around drugs are often represented in the language of the old penology with its focus on individuals, reform and rehabilitation; however, in practice greater emphasis is placed upon drug testing than drug treatment. In effect, testing fills the gap left by the decline of other treatments, interventions and programmes. As Feeley and Simon (1992: 462) argue, 'by marking the distribution of risk within the offender population under surveillance, testing makes possible greater coordination of scarce penal resources.'

The tensions and contradictions between medical and penal forms of control manifest themselves in their most acute form where drugs and prisons interface or within the development of prison drugs policy. For example, Berridge (1999: 274) notes that the prison doctors who gave evidence to the Rolleston Committee in the 1920s adopted a much harsher approach to dealing with drug addicts in prisons compared to their colleagues in the community by subjecting their patients to abrupt withdrawal rather than maintenance prescribing. At the end of the 1980s, MacGregor (1989b: 199) points to the lack of attention paid to the prison system in drugs policy and service development, arguing that 'this neglect is the real hidden scandal of the 1980s'. By the mid-1990s, the prison system was becoming much more of a focus in drugs policy discussions. For example, in relation to the 1995 prison drugs strategy, Berridge (1996b: 304) highlights the growing convergence between medical and penal responses: 'the penal aspect of the health response as well as the health aspects of the penal approach are once more on the agenda.'

This book presents a case study of the development of prison drugs policy in England from 1980, involving documentary analysis and interviews with key policy players including civil servants, directors of drug agencies and penal reform groups, and spokespersons from professional associations. It explores policy development through the prism of the 'policy network'. The policy network approach has become one of the dominant approaches to studying policy-making (Dowding, 1995), but has rarely been applied in analyses of drugs and penal policy. In relation to prison drugs policy, important questions which needed to be addressed were: why did policy begin to develop, why did it develop in a particular way, who was involved in this development, and how did they shape policy outcomes?

Since the early 1990s, drug issues in prison have become increasingly important in drugs and penal policy debates leading to the development of very explicit policies in 1995. Since 1980, prison drugs policy can be divided into four main phases of development: 1980–6; 1986–93; 1993–7; and 1997 onwards. A central contention of this book is that this policy development has hinged upon the complex patterns of conflict, contradiction and convergence between treatment and punishment. Throughout the phases, particular 'policy networks' have evolved around drug issues within the prison system, becoming more complex in their structure and operation over time. It will be argued that these networks have played key roles in containing, balancing and managing the contradiction between treatment and punishment and that their activities have been influenced by (a) how the drug problem in prison has been framed and defined; (b) research, evidence and knowledge; and (c) wider contextual features. This research therefore aims to address the following questions which are interlinked:

How influential have the policy networks around drug issues in prison been in the development of policy? When have they been most influential and why?

How have these networks attempted to contain the contradiction between treatment and punishment in policy development?

How has this 'containment' been shaped by changes in the way in which the drug problem has been framed and defined, new research, evidence and forms of knowledge, and the impact of wider political, policy, social and institutional contexts?

I am using the term 'treatment' to cover a wide range of therapeutic activities which involve 'caring' for drug users such as detoxification, maintenance prescribing, harm reduction measures, drug-free wings, drugs counselling, throughcare and aftercare services, and practical help and advice. The term 'punishment' refers to those activities which involve 'punishing' or 'controlling' drug users such as mandatory drug testing and the associated sanctions, and security measures including cell and body searches, CCTVs, use of sniffer dogs, intelligence gathering, and targeting visitors. However, it is important to note that 'caring' and 'controlling' measures often converge. Control and punishment can also be viewed as methods of 'caring' for prisoners. For example, creating a drug-free prison environment can be viewed as caring for prisoners. Similarly, care and treatment measures can be viewed as methods of 'controlling' and 'punishing' prisoners. Examples include the practices of abrupt withdrawal, coerced treatment, and withdrawing privileges for positive drug tests.

The next sections will outline the main features which will underpin the analysis which follows in Chapters 2, 3, 4 and 5. A number of themes and concepts will be explored: dimensions of policy and policy analysis; the role of the policy network and the institutional context of policy development; the framing of the drug issue in prison; the relationship between research and policy; and the impact of shifts in wider contexts and related policy subsystems.

Towards a framework for analysing prison drugs policy

Key dimensions of policy

There is a lack of consensus as to what constitutes 'policy' and how the term should be defined. Hill and Bramley (1986) suggest that policy should not be treated as a self-evident, concrete or constant phenomenon. They argue that any attempt to define policy will be artificial in that what we are trying to define is contested. Similarly, Gordon et al. (1993: 8) suggest it is misleading to view policy analysis as the study of 'identifiable things called policies which are produced, or crystallise, at a particular stage in the decision process'. Thus, policy should be conceived of in more fluid and dynamic terms. It is helpful nevertheless to place at least some loose parameters around the term and outline some of its key dimensions. Jenkins (1978: 15) offers one of the most useful working definitions of public policy:

> A set of interrelated decisions taken by a political actor or group of actors concerning the selection of goals and the means of achieving them within a specified situation where these decisions should, in principle, be within the power of these actors to achieve.

This definition has a number of strengths encapsulating several key dimensions of policy (Hill and Bramley, 1986). It emphasises that policy is more than a single decision, but involves a series or pattern of decisions extending over time. So, rather than focusing on one particular shift in prison drugs policy, I have adopted a more longitudinal approach by exploring a series of policy decisions extending over a period of nearly two decades. The term 'political actors' could be expanded to include officials, politicians and other policy influencers. This is important in the analysis of prison drugs policy because several groups have been engaged in decision-making. The definition stresses that both means and ends are involved in policy. The means by which the drugs policy was pursued were, arguably, of equal significance to the end result of the policy. The definition emphasises that policies are contingent in that they refer to or depend on a specified situation. Prison drugs policy has been shaped by a wider political, social, institutional and policy context. Policy is restricted to that which can be achieved or those 'matters over which the state has authority, and to actions/results which are practically feasible' (Hill and Bramley, 1986: 3). Decisions taken in relation to the development of prison drugs policy have been restricted to what can be feasibly or practically achieved within the authority of the state. However, in the arena of penal policy the exercise of state power is often pushed to its limit. An indication of this is the number of successful challenges that there have been to various aspects of prisons policy before the European Court of Human Rights.

Another important feature of the definition is that it also allows for the possibility for inaction or the decision not to move (Jenkins, 1978). Policies can therefore refer to what is not being done (Heclo, 1972). The absence of policy is also defined as a 'policy'. In a similar vein, policies can serve symbolic purposes. They are often created only to give the impression that action is being taken by government in order to maintain political support, but leaving the particular problem untackled (see Edelman, 1964; 1971; 1988). In many cases there can be barriers to some policy issues or problems becoming public. Therefore, political activity may be mainly concerned with maintaining the status quo and resisting challenges to the existing circumstances (Ham and Hill, 1993). As we will see in later chapters, this was the case with the drug issue in prisons for many years. There was no official admission that drugs were a 'problem' in the penal setting which meant that the issue was not being addressed by formal policy. A public acknowledgement that drugs were problematic would have been a tacit admission of the failure or non-existence of policy.

Policy analysis

Wildavsky (1979: 15) emphasises the 'art' and 'craft' of policy analysis which involves imagination, thought and creativity. A range of activities are involved in analysing policy. Hogwood and Gunn (1984) identify several approaches to policy analysis including studies of policy content, policy process, policy outputs, evaluation studies, information for policy-making, process advocacy, and policy advocacy. My analysis best fits into their category of studies of the *policy process* which are concerned with exploring the various influences on the development of a policy issue and how this development unfolds over time. However, it can also be classified as a study of *policy content* in that I seek to describe and explain the origins, changes and developments within prison drugs policy.

It is difficult to locate policy analysis within existing disciplinary categories. It is a field which is composed of various models, theories and disciplines. Analysts of public policy often find it useful to adopt an open and multidisciplinary approach to their subject which draws on several different disciplines. For example, Ham and Hill (1993: 11) argue that policy analysis must be a multidisciplinary pursuit and its purpose is 'to draw on ideas from a range of disciplines in order to interpret the causes and consequences of government action, in particular by focusing on the processes of policy formulation'. Similarly, Hogwood and Gunn (1984: 30) stress that policy analysis must develop 'an integrated, or interdisciplinary approach, which will combine in a synergistic manner elements from many disciplines'. It became clear during the course of my research that an analysis of drugs policy development in prisons failed to fit neatly into any one disciplinary category. The 'problem' of drugs in prison has several dimensions. It can be viewed as a drug issue, penal issue, legal issue, public health issue, medical issue, community issue, crime issue, political issue, economic issue and so on. It follows that the subject of prison drugs policy can be viewed through a variety of different disciplinary lenses including criminology, sociology, law, political science, public administration, history, medicine, and so on. In my analysis, I have therefore found it useful to adopt a multidisciplinary approach which draws on the ideas, theories, concepts and research from a variety of social science disciplines including social policy, criminology, sociology, political science and public administration. The literature from the area of 'policy studies' or 'policy sciences' provides a useful overarching theoretical and conceptual framework for this study.

Policy networks

Analysing policy networks has become one of the dominant approaches to studying policy-making in the UK, Europe and North America (Dowding, 1995). Various case studies have demonstrated the relevance and utility of the 'policy network' concept in describing the policy process in different sectors (see Marsh and Rhodes, 1992; Wilks and Wright, 1987; Smith, 1993; Berridge, 1996a; 1997; Thom, 1999; Ryan et al., 2001). Policy network approaches emphasise the interaction and patterns of association between various actors in particular policy areas. The type of relationships that form between civil servants, politicians, group representatives and others are seen to shape policy outcomes and explain policy change. Rhodes and Marsh (1992a) characterise policy networks as meso level concepts which provide the link between the micro level of analysis dealing with the role of interests and the macro level of analysis dealing with the distribution of power within society. Policy networks both influence the policy process and reflect the relative status and power of the various interests in particular areas of policy (Rhodes and Marsh, 1992a).

Policy networks have been conceptualised in a variety of ways (see Rhodes and Marsh, 1992b; Sabatier, 1988; Hajer, 1993; Wilks, 1995). Wilks and Wright (1987) offer a model which stresses the need to disaggregate to subsectoral networks and places emphasis on interpersonal relationships. They draw distinctions between 'policy universe', 'policy community' and 'policy network'. The *policy universe* refers to the large population of actors or potential actors who share a direct or indirect interest in policy and may contribute to the policy process on a regular basis. Under their typology, *policy communities* are more disaggregated systems of actors drawn from the *policy universe* who share a common interest in a particular policy area and interact with one another to shape policy. The *policy network* is the linking process or the outcome of the interaction within a policy community or between a number of policy communities over particular policy issues, problems or functions (e.g. budgeting, auditing, or planning). In effect, policy issues, problems and functions provide the occasion for a policy network.

Wilks and Wright (1987) argue that their model, which treats the concepts of 'community' and 'network' as separate, has several advantages. First, policy subsystems always generate policy communities but these do not always generate networks. Second, it recognises that the members of a policy network can be brought in from different policy communities within the same or different policy areas. Third, it enables researchers to identify those members of a policy community who are excluded from a policy network. Finally, their model also stresses that all policy issues in a subsector are not necessarily dealt with by one network, thus allowing comparison of membership, function, and characteristics of networks whose membership is drawn from the same policy community (Wilks and Wright, 1987; Wright, 1996).

Policy networks at the sectoral level often play a role in shaping the membership, values and outcomes of subsectoral policy networks (Cavanagh et al., 1995). In relation to drugs policy during the 1980s and 1990s, Berridge (1996a; 1997) identifies a drugs policy community consisting of revisionist doctors, researchers, drug agencies and civil servants. Similarly, Wilson (2001) examines the activities of key players in the penal reform community. Drawing on the model offered by Wilks and Wright (1987) emphasising the subsectoral level, I am concerned with intersection between drugs and penal policy and their respective policy communities, the emergence of policy networks around prison drug issues and how these have changed and evolved over the various phases of policy development from 1980. Over time, policy networks have interacted over several different issues such as release and throughcare, drug treatment and detoxification, HIV/AIDS and harm reduction, security and control issues, and mandatory drug testing (see Table 1.1).

Although the network approach has been widely applied, it has been subject to various critiques (see Atkinson and Coleman, 1992; Kassim, 1994; Dowding, 1995; Blom-Hansen, 1997). In particular, the network approach fails to provide an account of why relationships form and change between the various actors and how power is exercised. It also fails to provide an adequate account of the role of the state and institutions and the impact of political discourse, ideology and cognitive frameworks of network members (Atkinson and Coleman, 1992; Kassim, 1994). There is often no clear indication of boundaries delineating where networks begin and end or who is excluded and included (Kassim, 1994). Most analyses of networks have tended to focus on whole policy sectors, thus neglecting the subsectoral level of policy. Moreover, issues tend to overlap with other issues and interact with policy solutions. They tend not to remain within one policy network, but often intersect with the interests and concerns of other networks. Because policy networks change over time, Wilks (1995) has outlined the need to provide more dynamic, longitudinal analyses, rather than snapshot analyses of one particular period.

Atkinson and Coleman (1992) argue that two key questions should be asked in relation to policy networks, namely, who participates and who wields power? My analysis is concerned with the changing membership of policy networks around drug issues in prison. During the course of policy development, key roles have been played by drug

Table 1.1: Policy communities and policy networks (the Wilks and Wright (1987) typology adapted to prison drugs policy)

Policy level		*Policy actors*
Policy area	*Health,Criminal Justice*	Policy universe
Policy sector	*Drugs, Prisons*	Policy communities
Policy subsector (focus)	*Prison drugs policy*	
Policy issue	*e.g. Throughcare* *Treatment* *HIV/AIDS* *Security/control* *Mandatory drug testing*	Policy networks

agencies, penal reform groups, professional associations, the Prison Medical Service, researchers and government departments. The Advisory Council on the Misuse of Drugs (ACMD) has produced two reports dealing with the prison system (ACMD, 1980; 1996). It has been influential in shaping policy outcomes, but also in the development of services and practice. Policy network analyses indicate that some members or organisations will be located at the 'core' of the policy system while others will occupy a position on the margins or 'periphery' (see Coleman and Skogstad, 1990; Marsh and Rhodes, 1992; Smith, 1993). The analysis will therefore focus on which organisations and individuals are included or excluded in the networks, which members gain access to the 'core' or remain on the 'periphery', who has the power to influence and shape policy and practice and how these positions have altered over time.

Network approaches offer only a partial explanation of policy shifts and variation. There is a need to explore how interests, ideas, discourses, institutions and social, economic and political contexts interact and influence how networks operate over time. Several scholars have attempted to bridge some of the gap between network approaches and institutional arguments (see Skocpol, 1985; 1992; Smith, 1993; Pierson, 1994; Blom-Hansen, 1997) and this work provides a starting point in addressing some of the criticisms of the network approach discussed above. For example, Smith (1993: 2) argues that the impact of groups depends on the interests of state actors and the types of relationships between groups and the state – policy networks – which exist in specific policy areas. Similarly, the 'new institutionalists' assert that institutions and patterns of governance matter by setting the parameters for action and establishing the rules of the game, by shaping group identities, goals, and choices and by enhancing the bargaining power of some groups while devaluing others (Skocpol, 1992; Pierson, 1994). Skocpol (1992) has cogently argued that politicians and civil servants are actors in their own right who are enabled and constrained by political organisations and possess the ability to make independent contributions to policy development. This capacity of the state to act autonomously is dependent on the fiscal, judicial, and administrative capacities (Weir and Skocpol, 1985). However, it is often the case that governments need groups to develop and implement policy so they 'exchange access to the policy process for co-operation and thus establish a policy network' (Smith, 1993: 59). Policy networks are therefore a means of increasing state autonomy. Smith (1993: 6) describes the reciprocal relationship between the state and groups in the following terms: 'group power depends on state recognition and state power depends on the support of groups'.

Drawing on the work of the 'new institutionalists', this research is concerned with the impact of institutions, structures and state actors in the development of policy networks and prison drugs policy. The key state agencies or institutions involved in this area have changed or been reorganised over time and include the Prison Service, the Home Office, the Central Drugs Co-ordination Unit (1995–8), the UK Anti-Drugs Co-ordination Unit (1998–2001) and the Home Office Drugs Strategy Directorate (from 2001). The degree of state autonomy will also be explored by examining the discourses, interests, activities and influence of state actors – politicians and civil servants – over time. However, this is not to suggest that the state has a set of unified interests: policy may be the outcome of conflict between state agencies (Smith, 1993). The institutional contexts of other groups participating in the policy networks such as drug agencies, penal reform groups and professional associations are also significant in my analysis. The ideological foundations of these groups are important as these are brought to the policy network fora by their representatives. Their ideas and discourses play a central role in how the drug issue in prison becomes defined, how policy alternatives are framed and placed on the agenda, and how policy is implemented (see Duke, 2000).

The particular focus of this book is to assess the role, influence and power of policy networks in prison drugs policy and to explore their role in containing the central contradiction in policy development between treatment and punishment. This containment has been shaped by several processes such as how the drug issue in prison has been framed and defined; the relationship between research and policy; and the impact of shifts in the wider social, political and institutional context and related policy subsystems. These processes appear more or less dominant in the different phases of policy development. Each of these processes will be discussed and elaborated upon below.

Framing the drug 'problem' in prisons

The way in which the drug 'problem' has been perceived, defined and redefined over time is an important influence on policy development. Analyses have shown that who the drug addict or user is becomes significant in how the problem is defined and understood (see Berridge, 1999; Harding, 1988; Lart, 1998; South, 1999). In particular, race, gender and class are important factors influencing the construction of drugs 'problems' and the types of policy adopted. Equally important however are the data on the real extent and nature of the social phenomenon which include indicators such as the size of the drug problem, its social and physical location, and the characteristics of the drug users (MacGregor, 1999a).

The way in which the drug issue in prison has been defined and framed has shifted over the various phases of policy development and influenced policy outcomes. Defining social problems and framing policy agendas continues throughout the policy process. In order to understand a social problem, we must explore the process by which it came to be identified and defined as a problem (Becker, 1966). From a social constructionist standpoint, 'problems' are created by society and viewed as the outcome of a political process where certain groups are labelled by the powerful as 'problematic' or 'deviant'. In relation to drugs policy in prison, a key role has been played by policy networks in defining policy issues and problems. However, as Jock Young (1997a) has argued, the social constructionist perspective attempts the impossible in that it tries to explain the reaction against deviance separately from the deviance itself or the formation of social problems separately from the problems themselves. Thus, the reaction against drug use in prison cannot be bracketed off from the phenomenon itself. In left realism, the two sides of the dyad – action and reaction, the signified and the signifier, rule-making and rule-breaking – interact and shape each other (Young, 1997a). In my analysis, I will integrate these two processes by examining the reaction, framing and definition of the drug problem in prison as well as the nature and extent of the problem itself.

Rein and Schon (1993) offer a useful framework for analysing policy discourse which integrates facts, values, theories and interests. In their view, policy participants construct and make sense of problematic policy issues through a process of 'framing' which is defined as 'a way of selecting, organising, interpreting, and making sense of a complex reality to provide guideposts for knowing, analyzing, persuading, and acting' (Rein and Schon, 1993: 146). Policy issues are often framed in terms of severity, incidence, novelty, proximity and crisis (Rochefort and Cobb, 1993). These dimensions influence whether they will be placed on the policy agenda. Severity refers to how serious a problem and its consequences are perceived to be. It often helps if an issue affects a large number of people or has a devastating impact on a few people. Incidence refers to the number of people affected or at risk of the problem and whether the problem is perceived to be growing, stable or declining. Novel, unprecedented or trailblazing issues have the capacity to win attention quickly. Proximity refers to whether the problem is perceived to be personally relevant or of general social concern. Problems which have reached 'crisis' or emergency proportions are also given priority on policy agendas. However, the distinction between 'problem' and 'crisis' is not always clear. Advocates often use the rhetoric of crisis to stress the urgency of an issue. This is particularly the case in relation to the areas of prisons and drugs. References to the 'penal crisis' and the 'drugs crisis' have become enduring features within these policy lexicons.

The populations affected by the problem are also defined. In particular, distinctions are drawn between populations who are perceived to be deserving versus undeserving, legitimate versus illegitimate, worthy versus unworthy, familiar versus strange, and sympathetic versus threatening (Rochefort and Cobb, 1993). Characteristics such as race, gender, class and age are also considered. Often, 'deviants' and other excluded groups do not receive equivalent considerations. In definitional terms, it could be argued that drug using prisoners are labelled as doubly 'deviant' in that they are viewed both as criminals and drug misusers, and therefore defined as undeserving, illegitimate, unworthy, strange and threatening. Moreover, the discourse of 'less eligibility' has always influenced the development of penal policy and ensured that the conditions and services available to prisoners are not superior to those available to the working classes or they will not be deterred from committing crime (Melossi and Pavarini, 1981). The way in which drug users in prison are perceived by policy-makers and the public are therefore crucial in terms of determining the balance between treatment and punishment in policy design.

Policy issues and problems are malleable and open to competing interpretations, definitions and solutions. Each framing of a particular policy terrain is likely to select and name different features of the problematic situation which may lead to conflicting frames. Rein and Schon (1993) argue that the 'institutional embedding' or the structural location of the different policy actors will affect the way in which a policy issue is framed. Each professional group within the penal system have their 'own jurisdiction, career structure, interests and ideologies' (Garland, 1990: 182). In relation to prison drugs policy, the 'institutional embedding' of the various participants will influence their framing of drug issues, the nature of their discourses and the types of policies and courses of action advocated. Framing could highlight issues around treatment, harm reduction, release and throughcare, security, control, punishment or drugs testing.

It is important to examine the naming and framing of policy issues over time in order to identify 'frame shifts' (Rein and Schon, 1993). It will be clear from the analysis which follows that four frame shifts can be identified over the phases of prison drugs policy development. In broad terms, as the extent and nature of drug use in prison became officially acknowledged by civil servants, politicians and prison governors, the framing of the issue shifted from being defined primarily as a medical issue and a problem of treatment for individual prisoners to a control, order and enforcement issue and a problem for the institution.

Role of research, evidence and knowledge

Research can play an important role in sensitising policy networks to new issues and turn what were regarded as 'non-problems' into 'problems' (Weiss, 1977b: 16). This book is therefore concerned with the role of evidence, research and knowledge in the recognition, definition and framing of drug issues in prison and in the development of policy, implementation and change (see also Duke, 2001). Carol Weiss (1986) argues the term 'research utilisation' is associated with a variety of different meanings and interpretations. She identifies seven different models of the research–policy relationship: knowledge-driven, problem-solving, interactive, political, tactical, enlightenment and research as part of the intellectual enterprise of society.

The *knowledge-driven model* is derived from the natural sciences and assumes a linear application of research findings. Here, basic research highlights an opportunity, applied research is conducted to define and test these findings, appropriate technologies are then formulated, and finally application occurs. It assumes that the existence of knowledge will drive it towards development and use. Few examples of the knowledge-driven model can be found in the social sciences (Weiss, 1986). The *problem-solving model* also offers a linear account of research utilisation. Here, research directly influences policy choices and decisions by providing evidence, information and knowledge which help to solve and illuminate a particular policy problem. This can be achieved by drawing on existing research, data and information or by commissioning new research to fill gaps in knowledge. Although this model is the most common perception of research utilisation, it is rare to find examples of research having such a direct effect on policy decisions (Weiss, 1986).

Within the *interactive model*, information is sought not only from researchers, but from a range of actors in the policy process including politicians, civil servants, journalists, interest groups, practitioners, planners, and clients. There is no linear relationship from research to policy decision, instead the process consists of a 'disorderly set of interconnections and back-and-forthness that defies neat diagrams' (Weiss, 1986: 35). Members of policy networks pool their knowledge, intelligence and perspectives in order to define and make sense of the problem. Research is but one element of a process which involves political insight, experience, pressure, technology and judgement (Weiss, 1986). In this model, researchers can play an important role in promoting and acting as partisans for their research (see Donnison, 1978; Booth, 1988; Bartley, 1996). Tizard (1990: 438) argues that researchers need to ensure that their findings and ideas progress through crucial 'gateways' if they are to come to the attention of policy-makers and influence the policy process. It is therefore important to recognise the 'micro-political activism undertaken by many scientists, regardless of their policy orientations at the macro level' (Bartley, 1996: 23).

In many cases, various interests and ideologies coalesce to predetermine the positions of policy-makers on particular issues or problems. Under the *political model* of research utilisation, new research and evidence is therefore unlikely to influence or change these positions. It therefore plays a legitimisation or justification function for particular policy decisions. Research which confirms the existing arguments is used by advocates as 'ammunition' to attempt to neutralise opponents and persuade those who doubt their position (Weiss, 1986). The political model often masquerades as the problem-solving model (Tizard, 1990). For example, in analysing the clinical trials of heroin and methadone prescribing in the 1970s, Berridge and Thom (1996) argue that this research did not determine policy, but provided justification and legitimation for policy changes which were already underway. They conclude that the research–policy relationship is influenced by policy networks, civil servants, the historical context and the local traditions in particular policy areas. Another example within penal policy is the research which indicated that 'nothing works' in terms of treatment and rehabilitation in prisons in the 1970s (see Martinson, 1974). This provided further justification for the decline of the rehabilitative ideal and the shift in policy towards the justice model.

A variant of the political model is the *tactical model*. Here, the findings of research are unimportant, rather it is mere existence of research or the notion of 'research in progress' which is considered paramount. When faced with demands for action on particular issues, governments are able to delay responses by playing the 'research card' (i.e. they are awaiting the results of research). Social researchers and the research they produce can also be used to deflect criticism away from government in relation to unsuccessful policies (Weiss, 1986). As Tizard (1990) argues, employing research as a tactic results in many research reports remaining unread and collecting dust on the shelves of government departments.

Research can also enter the arena of policy through a process of 'enlightenment' or 'indirect diffusion' (Weiss, 1986). Within the *enlightenment model*, single pieces of research or even a body of related studies do not directly impact upon policy, rather it is the effect of cumulative research and information over time which sensitises policy-makers to new issues and shapes the way in which problems are defined and framed. However, the role of research through the process of enlightenment can have a dramatic impact and can help to redefine the policy agenda. Although the enlightenment model often corresponds most closely to the way in which research informs policy decisions (see Weiss, 1980), it does have several limitations. For example, there is no filtering process by which inadequate or invalid research is screened out. Many research findings will also fail to penetrate the policy arena, while others take such long periods that they are out of date or irrelevant by the time they are considered. Finally, the more research conducted on a particular issue, the more complex the implications become for policy decisions. The direction for policy therefore becomes less clear.

Research can also be viewed as *part of the intellectual enterprise of society*. Here, research is not viewed as an independent variable affecting the policy process, but rather as a dependent variable. As Weiss (1986: 39) argues, 'social science and policy interact, influencing each other and being influenced by the larger fashions of social thought'. Policy interest often sets the parameters of research, influencing which social issues or problems are studied. One of the barriers to exploring the relationship between research and policy is that they are often treated as separate and self-contained activities. Smith (1992) also emphasises the reflexive relationship between policy and research and argues that research and policy are processes which constantly interact and shape one another.

It is important to acknowledge that different types of research correspond to different types of models (Tizard, 1990). In my analysis, I aim to draw on the various models discussed above to explore 'research utilisation' within the phases of prison drugs policy development. The penetration of evidence into the policy-making arena is not automatic and depends on various factors. These factors have been discussed by various commentators and include the nature, type and quality of the research, the characteristics and institutional location of the researcher, the characteristics of the policy-making apparatus, the extent of the gap between the worlds of the researcher and policy-maker, and whether research is discovered and publicised (see Bulmer, 1978; 1982; Finch, 1986; Booth, 1988; Tizard, 1990; Petersilia, 1991). The political, economic and social context of research utilisation is also important.

During the period under review, research in all areas of public policy was influenced by the 1971 Rothschild report which established the distinction between the roles of client and research provider and a reorientation towards planning, efficiency and relevance. By the 1980s and 1990s, reflecting the market values imposed by the Conservative government, research had become a commodity and there was growing pressure for more accountability and tighter project management. This has had serious consequences for the production of independent research and new knowledge (see Samson and South, 1996; Shove, 1996; Walker, 1989). Due to changes in research funding and the way research is now commissioned and conducted, researchers are under pressure to ask particular questions and produce research which intersects with a particular research programme or agenda (Bartley, 1996). Much research has become atheoretical and preoccupied with existing policies, rather than concerned with discovering and theorising about new problems. Although there were increased opportunities for criminological research in the 1980s, the attempt to integrate research with wider theoretical frameworks declined, leading to the rise of what Young (1986) has characterised as 'administrative criminology'.

The impact of related policy subsystems and the wider context

The way in which the drug issue in prison is framed, debated and the setting out of policy options is influenced by wider forces. Rein and Schon (1993: 154) emphasise that the framing of a policy issue always occurs within a 'nested context'. In this view, policy issues emerge in connection with governmental programmes, which exist within a wider policy environment, which is part of a broader political, social and economic setting, which is situated within a historical era. Features of this context shift and impact on each other, often resulting in the reframing of a policy issue. Rein and Schon (1993) distinguish between four nested contexts: internal, proximate, macro and global.

The *internal context* refers to the policy program itself and changes in its own personnel, sponsors or clients. In this analysis, changes within the internal structure and organisation of prison drugs policy and the membership of policy networks will be explored. The *proximate context* refers to the changes in the policy environment in which the particular program operates (Rein and Schon, 1993). Prisons drugs policy can be viewed as the outcome of interaction between three main public policy subsystems or sectors: penal policy, drugs policy and social policy. The distinction and separation between these areas of policy is artificial as they overlap in both practice and theory. Traditionally, penal policy and the criminal justice system have not been included in the realm of social policy, but have been placed in a separate and distinct category of public policy (Hudson, 1993). Similarly, drug issues have tended to be the province of the medical-scientific community and have therefore occupied a marginal position within social policy (MacGregor, 1998b).

There are aspects of the penal system which are concerned with the general welfare needs of prisoners, such as probation, specialist services delivering drug treatment and counselling, as well as other agencies providing services in prison and on release. Hudson (1993) has illustrated the cleavage and continuity between social and penal policy and argues that the same ideological and material forces affect the development of both sets of policies and that they deal with the same 'client' groups – the poor, the disturbed, and the addicted. Similarly, MacGregor (1998b) shows how the development of drugs policy in Britain, once the domain of the medical community, has also begun to converge and intersect with other areas of policy. As drugs have become 'normalised' within communities, policy responses have become more congruent to the way in which other 'social problem' groups are dealt with. Thus, the concept of 'policy spillovers' is useful to explain the process where new principles, ideas or policies are transferred or spill over to adjacent policy areas (Kingdon, 1995). Although my analysis concentrates mainly on the impact of developments and changing discourses within penal and drugs policy, the growing overlap between these areas with wider social policies is also important. It is also concerned with the reverse process or the extent to which developments in prison drugs policy have impacted upon or been transferred to adjacent policy areas.

The internal and proximate contexts can also be shaped by 'policy transfers' or policy convergences between countries. Garland (2001) argues that the languages and practices in crime control between the

USA and UK are converging due to the fundamental structural and cultural changes occurring in late modernity. However, Jones and Newburn (2002) argue that both the role of structural factors and human agency are important in understanding the nature of policy convergences and divergences within and between nation states. For example, in his analysis of programme development at the Home Office, Rock (1994) notes how civil servants who had previously held posts in North America began to channel North American models, policies and practices into the Home Office. In the case of prison drugs policy, policy initiatives from the United States, such as drugs testing, certain types of treatment programmes and drugs courts, have played important roles in influencing policy development. However, these transfers have not been direct, but mediated through key actors and organisations involved in the policy networks around drug issues in prisons.

The *macro context* refers to wider changes in the overall direction of policy and social, economic, political and institutional change, while the *global context* refers to those at the broadest level such as changes in the historical eras in which reframing may occur (Rein and Schon, 1993). From 1979 to 1997, significant changes took place in prison drugs policy under the Conservative governments of Thatcher and Major. This development has occurred within a broader context of turbulent political, historical, economic and social change heavily influenced by the ideologies of the New Right. Thatcherism was underpinned by a combination of neo-liberalism emphasising the free market, freedom, choice, liberty, limited state, and the primacy of the individual, and neo-conservatism emphasising authority, order, stability, tradition, the family and morality. The ideologies of the New Right informed Conservative policy, but often in inconsistent and contradictory ways (see Brown and Sparks, 1989; Atkinson and Savage, 1994). For example, in some policy areas such as welfare provision, controls on public spending and minimal state intervention were advocated, while in other areas such as law and order, resources and state intervention increased.

Since 1979, developments in public policy have challenged the traditional 'public administration model' of welfare delivery based on a bureaucratic structure, professional domination, accountability to the public, equity of treatment, and self-sufficiency (Butcher, 1995). Under the Conservative governments, there was increasing emphasis on a more managerialist and consumerist orientation to public sector organisation. The 'new public management' which emerged emphasised value for money, a performance-based culture, the disaggregation of large bureaucratic organisations, promotion of greater competition through the use of market-type mechanisms, and customer orientation (Butcher, 1998: 25). Cutler and Waine (1997: 6) outline the key dimensions of public sector managerialism which include an hierarchical approach where targets are set and monitoring is controlled from the top; an assumption that the structure is universally valid and can be applied to both the private and public sectors; the need for performance monitoring and the assumption that it is possible to develop valid management information; and tension within professional practice as a result of the hierarchical approach.

Initially, the criminal justice system was believed to be safe from these managerialist tendencies. It was not subjected to the large-scale reforms of health and education. This was related to the increase in expenditure on law and order during the 1980s, the opposition and power of key professional groups such as the judiciary and chief constables, the dispersal and lack of co-ordination between the various agencies in the criminal justice system, the lack of alternative providers in the market, and the absence of 'consumers' (i.e. there was no prospect of reconceptualising offenders as 'consumers') (James and Raine, 1998; McLaughlin and Muncie, 1994). However, the managerialist agenda was soon applied to the problems of crime and punishment in the form of financial controls, performance monitoring, and organisational design. For example, several prisons were contracted out, contracts were awarded for prison escort duties, the operation of prisons and the administration of the Crown and County Courts were hived off into Next Steps agencies, partnership and multi-agency structures were established, aggregate monitoring systems were introduced, and management by objectives or performance indicators were introduced across the whole criminal justice system. A common theme emerging from the literature is the notion that managerialism is not concerned with the individual or the overall purpose of the criminal justice system, but with the management of crime, punishment and criminals (see Feeley and Simon, 1992; Garland, 1996; James and Raine, 1998).

The principles of partnership, crime prevention and involving the community in drugs and crime control are also prominent themes in policy. For example, Drug Action Teams consisting of senior representatives from various local agencies were established in each health authority district in 1995. A distinctive feature of these partnership structures is the closer alliance between the criminal justice system and other agencies. Other policy subsystems and the 'community' have therefore been drawn into the management of the contemporary drug problem. As Garland (1996) argues, the managerialist trends intersect neatly with the partnership principle, multi-agency approaches, and the rise of the community where the state seeks to activate action on the part of non-state agencies and organisations to take responsibility for controlling crime.

It is within this context that prison drugs policy began to be developed and formulated in a more explicit way, taking on the attributes of managerialism. Shifts within these nested contexts will be an important feature in the framing and reframing of drug issues in prison. However, Rein and Schon (1993: 155) also argue that the 'reframing of issues can shape the contexts on which that reframing is dependent'. This links into the arguments of the new institutionalists which emphasise the role of 'policy feedbacks' or the ways in which previously established policies or inherited policy structures shape subsequent political processes (Skocpol, 1992; Pierson, 1994). In this view, policy is treated as both an independent and dependent variable. Skocpol (1992: 58) argues that policies have feedback in two major ways. First, policies transform and expand the capacities of the state or alter the administrative possibilities for future initiatives. Second, new policies affect the social identities, goals and capabilities of the groups involved in politics. In some cases, groups will have a stake in the expansion and continuation of particular policies while in others, groups may seek to repeal or reorient policies (Skocpol, 1992).

Themes in contemporary drug policy have powerful historical antecedents (Berridge, 1989). For example, Stimson and Lart (1994) argue that the discourses of harm minimisation, risk reduction and public health during the late 1980s were not so unusual and have a long history within past drugs policy. Pearson (1991: 169) concludes 'there is a persistent thread of continuity through which the 'British system' retains the possibilities of a flexible and adaptable approach to drugs problems'. Similarly, prior to the 1990s, several commentators recall a sense of continuity and pragmatism within penal policy development (see Rock, 1995; Garland, 1996; Faulkner, 1996). Policy proposals contained a history and links with existing policies and programmes. However, the penal populism and policies advocated by the Home Secretary, Michael Howard, in 1993 indicated a very sudden and radical change in penal policy leading to a 'remarkably volatile and ambivalent pattern of policy development' (Garland, 1996: 449). Since the election of the New Labour government in 1997, a sense of stability has been restored with the continuities and similarities between Conservative and Labour penal policy (see Brownlee, 1998; Morgan, 1999). The policy feedback dynamic underlines the importance of taking an historical approach in order to explore how prison drugs policy has unfolded over time.

These interconnecting themes will run through my analysis: the role and influence of policy networks in containing and managing the contradictions between treatment and punishment and the way in which this process of containment has been shaped by the framing of the drug issue in prison; research, evidence and knowledge; and wider contextual features. The framework employed to develop these themes and concepts draws upon the policy sciences literature. Although this literature has been used extensively in other areas of public policy, it has rarely been applied to the areas of drugs, penal and criminal justice policy. The next section will elaborate on the research design and methodological framework which were employed to investigate the role of policy networks in the development of prison drugs policy.

Research design and methodology

Existing research on drug issues and prisons has tended to focus on the *prisoners themselves*, emphasising prevalence issues, risk behaviour and their 'performance' in relation to the new rules, tests and regulations of the most recent prison drugs strategies. Although criminologists are beginning to examine the activities and cultures of the professionals working within the criminal justice system (see Rock, 1986; 1990; 1994; 1995; Reiner, 1991 and Ryan et al., 2001), the tradition within criminological research has been to concentrate on offenders and 'deviant' populations. Similarly, drugs research has been dominated mainly by studies of drug users (see for example Becker, 1963; Young, 1971; Rosenbaum, 1981; Pearson, 1987a; Parker et al., 1998). With the exception of several analyses of drug markets and law enforcement (see Dorn et al., 1992; Collison, 1995), the focus of research has rarely been on those in positions of power such as the police, Crown Prosecution Service, Customs and Excise, and the probation and prison services or those involved in the formulation of the policies drug users are subject to. The focus has tended to be on the 'objects' of policy, rather than on the policies themselves or the policy-makers and professionals working within this area.

In the case of drugs and prisons research, there was therefore a need to impose scrutiny on those who were in positions of power in relation to the processes of policy-making. In order to explore how policy developed over time, which factors influenced this development and the role and influence of policy networks in this process, a qualitative case study was viewed as the most appropriate design. The main methods employed in the case study were semi-structured interviews with key actors in the policy process and an analysis of policy and other documents.

Documentary analysis

Documentary records have great significance in contemporary social settings, particularly within the policy arena. Here, many of the key actors are involved in the production and consumption of written records and other types of documents (Atkinson and Coffey, 1997). However, documents represent artificial or partial accounts which cannot be taken at face value and require critical assessment. Documentary materials should be approached for what they are and what they are used to accomplish through an examination of their role in organisations, their type and form, and the cultural values attached to them. It is therefore important to attempt to get below the surface of documents by probing and analysing their construction, production and consumption. In relation to drugs policy, Spear (1995: 13) argued for a fundamental rethink and the need to progress beyond the 'glossy government publications' and their associated political rhetoric. Within a context of increasing managerialism, Morgan (1997a) also notes how prison policy documents have become briefer and glossier over time, containing less meaningful information. Such documents tend to reduce the complexity of policy issues to very simplistic and crude levels.

In the area of prison drugs policy, there are several related types of documents which can provide a source of data at the national level. These are mainly 'official' documents which have been either written or influenced by those involved in the policy networks around prison drug issues. Under the typology of documents created by Scott (1990) which focuses on dimensions of authorship and access, 'open published documents of State origin' were the key ones employed in my analysis. The main documents selected were those relating to prison drugs policy, penal and criminal justice policy, national drugs policy, and ACMD reports. Where available, I also collected and analysed annual reports and other relevant documentation produced by penal reform groups and drug agencies to explore the role of prison drug issues in their work. Statistics relating to the prison population, drug addict notifications and drug offenders also formed part of this analysis in order to explore the extent and nature of the 'problem' of drugs in prisons over time through the use of 'official' indicators. Although these statistics have a number of limitations, they are used by policy-makers as one of the indicators of the extent of the drug 'problem' (Mott, 1994).

In order to understand the system of production, exchange and consumption of documentary materials, one needs to consider authorship and readership. When using official government documents, it is often impossible to determine the identity of those responsible for their production or the authors (Scott, 1990; Atkinson and Coffey, 1997). This anonymity is part of their 'facticity' and the official production of documentary reality. Although there may be an implied ownership of a document within a particular government department or agency, official documents do not usually have visible human agencies who express feelings, opinions and beliefs. As Atkinson and Coffey (1997: 59) argue, 'the absence of an implied personal author is one rhetorical device that is available for the construction of 'authoritative', 'official', or 'factual' accounts. It implies a reality that exists independently of any individual observer, interpreter or writer.' Within my analysis, I was interested in exploring the contribution of policy networks in the construction and production of the key documents relating to prison drugs policy.

In analysing the content meaning, the focus is upon the relationships within the text or its parts to each other, the relationship of the text to other texts, and the relationship of the text to those who participated in its construction (Ericson et al., 1991: 48). It is therefore important to look beyond separate texts and analyse how they are related. Atkinson and Coffey (1997) refer to these relationships between texts as 'intertextuality', a term derived from the field of literary criticism. Within my analysis, I was interested in examining the temporal dimensions of documents, the relationships between the various key documents and in exploring any shifts in the discourses around penal and drugs policy over time. In particular, I was interested in exploring how the 'problem' of drugs in prisons had been framed and defined within documents over time; the variations and changes in the conceptualisation and operationalisation of the concepts of treatment and punishment over time and between documents; how the tensions between these concepts were managed within the documents and if this had changed over time; the role of research in proposals for policy changes and the influence of the social, political and wider policy context. By analysing documents at the broader sectoral level (i.e. documents relating to drugs, penal and criminal justice policy), I was also able to explore the influence of and interface between developments in wider policy subsystems and those in prison drugs policy.

The consultation lists of government departments are often used in research on policy networks as the key data source to explore membership and influence. As Cavanagh et al. (1995) argue, this method is problematic and reveals little about the frequency and quality of the consultations. In order to operationalise policy networks and assess their influence, it is therefore necessary to interview both civil servants and interest groups. In this research design, semi-structured interviews were also conducted with key actors in the policy process, some of whom had been involved in the construction of policy documents. Documents can be used alongside other forms of data so that the biases of each can be understood and compared. For certain research questions, the public record and documentation is insufficient (Useem, 1995). Entering the worlds of those involved in the policy networks and engaging them in discussion was the only way to generate rich and detailed data on their perceptions and experiences of the 'problem', the policies and the processes involved in their development. In the interviews, respondents did refer and speak either explicitly or implicitly about the documents which were included in this analysis. The methods were therefore interconnected with the documentary analysis informing the direction and focus of the interviews and providing historical and contextual dimensions to the interview data, while the interviews influenced further analyses and explorations of the documents.

Semi-structured interviews

The fieldwork involved a total of 37 interviews with a wide range of policy actors including fifteen civil servants working in government departments involved in the formulation and implementation of the 1995 prison drugs strategy; 12 representatives of drug agencies developing and providing treatment services within the prison system; 6 directors of penal reform groups lobbying for reform within the prison system; and 4 spokespersons for professional associations. Although policy is shaped and influenced by others including government ministers, members of both houses of parliament, journalists and the prisoners themselves, these groups were not interviewed. Those selected for interviews were considered to belong to a central core of influence in the policy process. This group can be defined by their knowledge of prisons and drugs, their role as mediators within policy development and their regular interaction with one another over time. The rationale for interviewing civil servants is that they play a central role in the formulation, implementation and management of the policies; liaise between Permanent Secretaries and their Ministers and other outside interests; and play a key role in steering between conflicting models of development. Drug agencies were considered important as they deal with the day-to-day realities of delivering care and treatment to drug users within the prison environment. Penal reform groups provided a perspective on the control of drug users within a wider penal reform agenda. Professional associations represent the interests of those involved with the day-to-day implementation and delivery of policy.

The principles of snowball sampling were used. Each respondent was asked to identify others they felt should be interviewed. This helped to identify members of the policy network and those who were considered to be 'key' players. The network of individuals involved in prison drug issues is extremely small. For this reason, it is necessary to withhold specific details about the organisation, agency, or department of each respondent in order to ensure that information is non-attributable. A striking characteristic of those interviewed was their varied backgrounds and experience in both the drug and penal fields. Many had been involved with different jobs and responsibilities over time relating to the areas of prisons and drugs. The main criterion for selecting the respondents was seniority. They needed to be in a position within their organisation to influence policy formulation, implementation and development. Of the 37 interviewed, 27 were men and 10 were women. In terms of ethnicity, all respondents were white. For a more detailed methodological and reflexive discussion of the key dilemmas of researching those in positions of power in policy networks, see Duke (2002).

The main focus of the interviews was to explore how the respondents viewed the development of policy in this area and the processes and factors influencing its development; how they defined the 'problem' of drug issues in prison, the methods used to manage it, why these methods were used, the appropriateness and effectiveness of these methods, and what they believed could work more effectively. The interviews were retrospective in that they included discussions of the origins of prison drugs policy. It was difficult to access individuals who had been involved in policy-making in the very early stages as some of them had retired, changed jobs or died. In the final sample, over half (i.e. 21 respondents) could be described as having long-standing involvement in some aspect of the area under study. Most of this group had experience and knowledge dating back to the early 1980s which enabled them to reflect on the development of policy.

Interviews were conducted between September 1997 and March 1998. This period was marked by a number of political and policy changes which affected the research. After Labour won the general election in May 1997, a series of new policies were in the process of being formulated and implemented. For example, an anti-drugs coordinator was appointed in October 1997 whose mandate was to guide and coordinate the new national drugs strategy which was launched in April 1998. The prison drugs strategy was also in the process of being revised and was launched in May 1998. The timing of the fieldwork was important as prison drugs policy was on the cusp of change and entering a new phase. Respondents were therefore positioned to both reflect back on the previous strategy and comment on the proposals for the new strategy. Other significant developments during this period included calls for a Royal Commission to explore the possibilities around drugs legalisation, the campaign in the Independent on Sunday newspaper for the legalisation of cannabis and the Home Secretary's son found dealing cannabis. These issues and events permeated the interviews through informal discussion and provided further insights into the politics and dynamics of the policy process.

Sabatier (1988; 1991) argues that longer term studies of the policy process covering a time perspective of at least a decade are needed for three main reasons. First, this usually allows for policy to complete at least one formulation/implementation/ reformulation cycle so that the success or failure of a policy can be assessed. Second, the 'enlightenment function' of research stresses that the cumulative effect of research findings impacts upon the policy process gradually (Weiss, 1977a), thus requiring a longer time period to assess its influence. Third, in order to understand the significance of particular innovations in policy, policy-oriented learning, and the importance of changing socio-economic factors, policy analysis should be conducted over longer time periods. In order to assess the influence of various forces influencing the development of prison drugs policy, this research has therefore adopted a time perspective of approximately eighteen years from 1980 to 1998. The study begins in 1980 because this year marked the first formal documented interest in drug issues in prison with the publication of the first ACMD report on drug dependants within the penal system (ACMD, 1980). The main focus of the research revolves around the 1995 prison drugs strategy which involved fundamental shifts and changes in the way that drugs were dealt with in prisons. One of the key difficulties in researching the contemporary policy process is that it is continually developing and expanding. This causes problems for researchers in terms of choosing a cut-off point for their analyses. Moreover, as policies evolve and time passes, interpretations and analyses often develop and change (Berridge, 1994). My analysis ends in 1998 which marked the reformulation of the 1995 strategy. Through my interpretations of the main policy documents and interviews with key policy actors, it became clear that the development of prison drugs policy could be divided into four main phases: 1980–6; 1986–93; 1993–7 and 1997 onwards. At the time of writing, the last phase continues to evolve and develop.

Chapters 2, 3, 4 and 5 deal with the phases of prison drugs policy development chronologically. Each of these chapters broadly conforms to the same pattern. They begin by introducing the particular phase of policy development and highlighting the main features of the period. This is followed by a brief discussion of the drugs and penal policy contexts during the particular phase. The chapters then explore how the 'problem' of drugs in prison was defined and framed. This is followed by an analysis of the policy response to the drugs 'problem' in prisons during the period under review. The chapters draw upon the key policy documents, reports and relevant research, as well as data generated through the interviews conducted with key actors in the policy process. Chapter 6 reflects on the analysis of developments in the various phases by re-visiting the questions, concepts and theories outlined above. This final chapter concludes by exploring the significance of my findings for the future development of prison drugs policy.

2
1980–6: Prelude to Policy Development

Introduction

The period from 1980 to 1986 marked the beginning of external interest in drug issues within the penal setting. In 1980, the Advisory Council on the Misuse of Drugs (ACMD) published its report, *Drug Dependants within the Prison System in England and Wales*. This was the first document which dealt with drug issues in the prison system. During the early 1980s, there was no public document which outlined the Prison Department's policies for dealing with drugs and drug users in prisons. This is in marked contrast to later phases of policy development where there was an explicit prison drugs strategy document which specified clear aims and objectives for tackling the drug 'problem'. However, this does not mean that there was not a 'policy' on drugs during the early 1980s. As discussed in Chapter 1, the absence of policy can be defined as a 'policy'. Moreover, drug users in the prison system were treated in a particular way and this practice can be defined as 'policy'. Policy was therefore implicit rather than explicit, unstated rather than stated, informal rather than formal, and private rather than public. During this period, there was increasing pressure from various sources for a more explicit and defined prison drugs policy. This phase could be viewed as a 'transitional' period or a 'prelude' to more formal policy development. The drugs 'problem' in both the community and the prison was changing, the type of person using drugs was changing, definitions of drug takers were changing, the location of drug use was changing, and the groups and professionals involved in dealing with drug users were changing and expanding. Furthermore, the election of the Conservative party under the leadership of Margaret Thatcher in 1979, along with the ascendancy of

New Right ideas, altered the political and public policy landscape dramatically.

The Thatcher government embarked on a strategy which involved radically restructuring the British economy, dismantling the welfare state, breaking the power of trade unions, reducing public expenditure and minimising state intervention. Thatcher had placed 'law and order' issues at the centre of her election campaign and committed the government to additional resources for the criminal justice system. The Conservative party focused almost exclusively on crimes which caused public anxiety such as public order and street crimes, particularly mugging (Hall et al., 1978). The existence of certain populations who were perceived to be dangerous, including black youth, 'welfare scroungers', drug addicts, and football hooligans, were used to justify and legitimise increased surveillance, regulation and punitive sentencing (Brake and Hale, 1989). In the areas of criminal justice and penal policy, the discourses of punishment and just deserts tended to prevail over those of welfare, help and treatment. Welfare agencies contracted, while penal agencies expanded (Hudson, 1993). However, the Conservative package of social and criminal justice policy reforms implemented in the early 1980s failed: crime rates continued to soar; poverty, homelessness, unemployment and ill health increased; industrial disputes continued (notably the miners' strike in 1984), and a number of riots occurred in various inner-city areas including Brixton (south London), Toxteth (Liverpool), Handsworth (Birmingham) and the Broadwater Farm Estate (Tottenham, north London) (Reiner and Cross, 1991).

This macro context provides the background, framework and setting for changes within drugs, prisons and ultimately prison drugs policy during 1980–6. The chapter begins by exploring the drugs and penal policy contexts during the period under review and then examines the drugs 'problem' in prison and the responses to it.

Drugs policy context: the heroin 'epidemic' and shifting political and policy landscapes

By the late 1970s, the drug dependency units established during the 1960s had become less central in the treatment of drug use (Stimson, 1990a). The heroin problem had stabilised and the proportion of newly notified addicts under the age of 21 had begun to decrease (Home Office Statistical Bulletin, 1984). The clinics were treating only a small proportion of drug users, mainly heroin addicts, while the voluntary sector and general practitioners were beginning to play increasingly important roles in helping polydrug users, particularly those who were using barbiturates, tranquillisers, amphetamines and opiates (Jamieson et al., 1984). In 1971, a national co-ordinating and representative body for drug services called the Standing Conference on Drug Abuse (SCODA) was established which provided a voice for the growing voluntary sector in drugs policy development. Many of the key assumptions underlying drug treatment were being challenged in the late 1970s and early 1980s. For example, therapy and rehabilitative techniques such as therapeutic communities and counselling were becoming increasingly important; the appropriateness of maintenance prescribing was being questioned; the limitations of 'physical' treatment were recognised and a wider social approach was advocated which took into account housing, employment and training, and child care; and significantly a distinction was beginning to be made between the drug 'addict' and other patterns of drug use (MacGregor and Ettorre, 1987). The ACMD (1982) recommended that the terms 'drug addict' and 'drug dependant' should be replaced with the label 'problem drug taker' who would be defined in the following terms.

> any person who experiences social, psychological, physical or legal problems related to intoxication and/or regular excessive consumption and/or dependence as a consequence of his own use of drugs or other chemical substances (excluding alcohol or tobacco). (ACMD, 1982: 34)

This definition encapsulated a wider range of drug takers and took the view that drug problems are wide ranging, extend beyond the clinical discourses of dependence and addiction, and require more than just a medical response. The ACMD (1982) viewed the dichotomy of treatment within the clinic and rehabilitation in non-statutory agencies as unhelpful and advocated a broader social approach. Similarly, the House of Commons Social Services Committee (1985: ix) argued that 'overcoming dependency demands more of a social than a clinical approach'. Thus, a more comprehensive and integrated treatment and rehabilitation policy was advocated which stressed liaison, collaboration, co-ordination and co-operation between statutory and non-statutory agencies. Drug advisory committees (DDACs) were established in health authority districts to develop and plan local service provision. They included representatives from the health service, local authority, police, probation and other statutory and non-statutory agencies. It is important to note, however, that prisons were not expected to provide membership to these new structures.

By the 1980s, the era of the specialist in drug treatment was over and generalists in the community were encouraged to get more involved (Stimson, 1990a; Strang and Gossop, 1994). Within this new multidisciplinary framework, new voluntary and non-specialist services in the community were established and there was a new role for the general practitioner in treating drug use. The 1982 ACMD report was influential in establishing new and broader forms of working with drug users around social models of care (Berridge, 1997). There was therefore a shift in balance as the prominence of the specialised medical discourse began to decline (Stimson and Lart, 1994).

Just as some of these new ideas and concepts began to penetrate the official world of policy-making, there was a dramatic increase in heroin use. In the first half of the 1980s, official indicators point to a heroin 'epidemic' with a peak in 1985 and a subsequent levelling off in the latter half of the 1980s (Power, 1994). For example, between the years 1980 to 1986, the number of new drug addicts notified to the Home Office had increased dramatically from 1, 600 in 1980 to 6, 409 in 1985 and then decreased to 5, 325 in 1986 (see Table A.3, Appendix). Moreover, the percentage of new drug addicts addicted to heroin increased by 20 per cent over this period. The number of drug offences had also increased from 17, 158 in 1980 to 23, 905 in 1986 (see Table A.2, Appendix). Although the great majority of these offences were for unlawful possession and involved cannabis, the proportion of offences associated with heroin increased from 4 per cent in 1980 to 12 per cent in 1985 (Home Office Statistical Bulletin, 1987). Research studies conducted in various British cities and towns also indicated a sharp increase in heroin use (see Ditton and Speirets, 1981; Lewis et al., 1985; Pearson, 1987a; Parker et al., 1988). This was linked to the arrival of cheap, high purity heroin in abundant supply from South-West Asia. Furthermore, heroin from this source could be smoked which was perceived as a clean and safe way to use the drug. The stigma of injecting was therefore removed and more people were willing to experiment (Power, 1994; Griffiths et al., 1994).

The response to this 'epidemic' was to focus on heroin almost exclusively and fall back on the old ideas and discourses around disease, addiction and drug addicts. The professional consensus which had been attained around the notion of 'problem drug taking' and the need for multidisciplinary approaches was ignored by policy-makers (MacGregor and Ettorre, 1987). The drug problem had become a highly politicised issue and the prevailing discourse was one of panic, danger and fear. Drugs had become defined as an 'alarming issue, a crisis, an epidemic, even as a plague' (MacGregor, 1989a: 3). There was much concern within political circles that the UK would 'inherit the American nightmare' where drug taking and crime would become a way of life for the 'underclass' in society (MacGregor and Ettorre, 1987). In effect, a 'moral panic' had been created around drugs, drug use and drug addicts (Cohen, 1972). This was neatly characterised by a speech given by the Home Secretary, Leon Brittan, to the London Diplomatic Association in 1983 in which he professed a strategy of eradication:

> Drug abuse is a disease from which no country and no section of modern society is immune ... Stamping it out will be slow and painful ... The rewards are great if we succeed – and the price of ultimate failure unthinkable (quoted in Home Office, 1985: 3)

The heroin 'epidemic' was associated with a younger group of 'new heroin users' who tended to be concentrated in areas with high levels of unemployment, social deprivation (Pearson, 1987a) and established irregular economies for drug distribution (Auld et al., 1986). Heroin use was therefore not a 'national problem', but better understood as a highly localised and scattered phenomenon with patterns of use also subject to local and regional variation (Pearson and Gilman, 1994). For young people who had been deprived of achieving status through employment, heroin provided a 'lifestyle' and a new mode to enhance status and prestige (Pearson, 1987b). There was however the perception amongst the public and politicians that the drug problem was spreading, spinning out of control, and corrupting other social groups. The discourse and debate in the 1980s focused on the integration of certain groups in society and fears of contamination and leakage into the general population (MacGregor, 1989a).

1985 national drugs strategy

The reaction to the drug problem in the 1980s was 'designed to preserve the existing social order' (MacGregor, 1989a: 11). Bi-partisan agreement between parliamentary right and left and the low level of politicisation regarding the problem led to a lack of informed political debate (Dorn and South, 1987). Rather than leaving policy decisions to informed members of the drugs policy community, politicians and central government began to play more active roles in drug issues and policy development. In 1984, a Ministerial Group on the Misuse of Drugs was established with representatives from all government departments who had an interest in drug issues. This represented a 'new division of labour' or 'diffusion of responsibility' for drug issues between government departments (Lart, 1996: 73). The role of the group was to develop and oversee the implementation of the 1985 national drugs strategy which involved activity in five main areas: reducing supplies from abroad; tightening controls on drugs produced and prescribed; making policing more effective; strengthening deterrence; and improving prevention, treatment and rehabilitation (Home Office, 1985: 7). This marked an important shift in emphasis as enforcement measures were given much more prominence in the new strategy with three of the five aims having penal implications.

The expenditure on treatment and enforcement-related activities provides some indication of the balance between these two strands of drugs policy. For example, the total health and welfare drugs-related expenditure was estimated at £25–45 million per annum in the mid to late 1980s, compared to an estimate of £100 million for drugs-related enforcement activities (Dorn, 1990). Although the 1985 strategy stressed enforcement and the relationship between drugs and crime, a government funded survey of drugs research uncovered very little British criminological research in these areas and recommended that future research should be conducted on drug networks at a local level, the question of effectiveness in customs and law enforcement, the relationship between drugs and crime, the effects of sentencing on subsequent drug use, alternative strategies and law enforcement, and drug use in prison (Pearson, 1990).

Treatment and rehabilitation measures within the strategy centred on the Central Funding Initiative (CFI) which was developed to improve services for drug users. Funding over a period of three years was offered on a pump priming basis to statutory and voluntary organisations which provided new services or developed existing ones. Most of the services which were subsequently funded by the CFI were multidisciplinary, community-based and accessible. The initiative was successful in targeting areas which had the most serious drug problems and required drug service development (MacGregor et al., 1991). The thrust behind policy development during this period was 'to attempt to access other resources and bend them to meeting the increased need for services propelled by the increased misuse of drugs' (MacGregor, 1998a: 140). However, the moves to involve 'generalists' such as GPs, social workers, CPNs and others in the provision of services was not wholly successful and the main outcome of the initiative was a new layer of drug agencies and specialists (MacGregor, 1998a).

Prevention activities under the government's new strategy were in the form of high-profile mass media anti-heroin campaigns beginning in 1985. These initiatives were viewed with suspicion by the drugs policy community which warned the government against a national campaign based on fear tactics as this could backfire by stimulating interest in drugs and leading to increased experimentation (ACMD, 1984). As Power (1989) has argued, even a perfunctory review of the literature on campaigns confirms such views and reservations. Despite the warnings, the government went ahead with their plans. Both quantitative and qualitative evaluations of the campaigns were undertaken and confirmed that young people's attitudes against heroin had been reinforced (Research Bureau Ltd, 1986; Andrew Irving Associates, 1986). However, these evaluations have been criticised on methodological grounds due to the sampling design and size (see Marsh, 1986). Moreover, as Dorn (1986) argues, the researcher's conclusions were based on the incorrect assumption that strong anti-drug attitudes will prevent drug use or that a change in attitude will produce a change in behaviour.

Enforcement efforts took the form of new structures of drug enforcement, penalties, surveillance and intelligence. Drug traffickers and dealers were the targets of these efforts and the aim was to ensure that they were 'punished severely and should not profit from their illegal activities' (Home Office, 1985: 14). The National Drugs Intelligence Unit (NDIU) was created under the command of a newly established post of National Drugs Intelligence Officer and regional crime squad drug wings were established to bring a greater degree of co-ordination into the policing of drugs. Following the recommendations of the 1985 Home Affairs Committee, the Drug Trafficking Offences Act of 1986 introduced wide powers for the confiscation of assets of drug dealers. The 1985 Controlled Drugs (Penalties) Act increased the sentencing tariff for trafficking in class A drugs from 14 years to life imprisonment. Greater attention was also paid to international co-operation with regard to drug trafficking through the ratification by the UK of the United Nations Convention Against Illicit Traffic in Narcotic Drugs and Psychotropic Substances of 1988 and by a series of bilateral Mutual Legal Assistance Treaties agreed between the UK and a number of countries. The assumption was that activity on the supply front and the disruption of low level markets would impact upon the demand for drugs by reducing availability and making them more expensive (Dorn and Murji, 1992).

As South (1998: 91) argues, these developments 'placed the police, customs, courts and prisons at the forefront of official rhetoric about responses in policy and practice'. These punitive measures were aimed at the traffickers or the 'corruptors' of drugs, rather than the drug users or the 'corrupted' (Young, 1973). In practice however, Pearson (1991) argues that these enforcement activities coexisted along with harm and demand reduction strategies. Although abstinence was being stressed at the political level, the ACMD (1984) was advocating risk reduction and harm minimisation as the two basic criteria for drugs prevention. There was therefore a clear gap between the 'political' and 'policy community' views of drugs (Berridge, 1991). Similar to previous phases of drugs policy development, a bifurcated policy of control was pursued which now involved life sentences and confiscation of assets for drugs traffickers and improved services, diversion and prevention initiatives for users and potential users (Dorn, 1990). However, enforcement type activity has much more political and populist appeal compared with health-based initiatives which can appear 'too soft'. Politicians and policy-makers were therefore able to stress that tough action was being taken against drug traffickers and other drug 'villains', while drug workers and other professionals were working behind the scenes dealing with 'problem drug takers' or drug 'victims' within a treatment and rehabilitation based framework.

Although medicine remained a central force in drugs policy-making, Berridge (1997) argues that the medical hegemony of drugs policy was becoming diluted. During the 1980s, the policy community around drugs broadened to include a wider professional spectrum as new alliances were developed (Edwards, 1990). For example, the ACMD membership began to change from a mainly medical one, to one which included social workers, teachers, police and probation officers, psychologists, sociologists as well as the traditional psychiatrists and pharmacologists (Edwards, 1990; Berridge, 1997).

Although the 1985 drug strategy was generally viewed as a penal response to the drug problem, the irony was that there was no reference to the Prison Service, the treatment needs of drug using prisoners or to the ACMD report on drug dependants in the prison system published in 1980. Within the prison environment, much of the new thinking regarding drugs and drug treatment failed to penetrate policy and practice immediately. Indeed, for many years, what was occurring outside the prison walls had not impacted on how prisoners with drug problems were treated. There were different discourses around drug issues operating inside and outside the prison walls. The next section will outline the context and main developments within penal policy during the period 1980–6.

Penal policy context: containing and managing the 'crisis'

By the 1970s, the penal system was described by a number of commentators from various perspectives as being in a 'state of crisis' (see Evans, 1980; Hall, 1980; Bottoms, 1980; Fitzgerald and Sim, 1982; Woolf, 1991). Fitzgerald and Sim (1982) argue that the prison crisis is best understood as a series of interwoven crises: the crises of 'visibility', 'authority', 'containment', 'conditions' and 'legitimacy'. The key explanatory factor is the 'crisis of legitimacy' or engaging with the question 'what are our prisons for?'. Since the collapse of the rehabilitative ideal in the early 1970s, which placed emphasis on the treatment, training and reform of offenders (Allen, 1981), policy-makers and politicians have not engaged effectively with this 'crisis of legitimacy'. Instead, they have tinkered with sentencing and parole policy, hoping to have an impact on prison numbers and, when given the choice, they have placed security concerns at the centre of the policy agenda. With the election of the Thatcher government, the rhetoric of 'law and order', 'just deserts' and 'punishment' emerged as the legitimising ideologies of penal and criminal justice policy (Hall, 1980).

In Britain, the emphasis on treatment, training and rehabilitation began to shift following the 'crisis of containment' in the 1960s (Fitzgerald and Sim, 1982). During this period, there was a significant increase in prison escapes, including a number of high-profile criminals, which prompted the government to call for an inquiry. Lord Mountbatten was asked to examine the reasons for the escapes and make recommendations for improved security. The Mountbatten report left an important legacy on the prison system and introduced a new era characterised by an intensification and proliferation of security, surveillance and control across the entire prison estate (Sim 1991; Downes and Morgan, 1997).

By the late 1970s, the prison population had increased dramatically from an average population of 37, 820 in 1975 to 42, 264 in 1980 (see Table A.4, Appendix).This increase led to severe overcrowding with two and three prisoners being held in a cell built for one, degrading conditions and inadequate sanitation (Fitzgerald and Sim, 1982). The 1970s were also characterised by concerns about security, control and containment. For example, the prisoners' rights movement began in 1972 through the National Prisoners Movement (PROP), a series of serious riots took place, and prison officers engaged in an increasingly militant campaign of industrial action over pay and conditions. As Fitzgerald and Sim (1982: 2) note, 'what everyone did agree about was that at the end of 1978 the prison system was in crisis'.

In November 1978, the government responded by establishing a committee under the leadership of Mr Justice May to inquire into the state of the prison service. The May Committee recommended a massive prison building and refurbishment programme to end the practices of slopping out and sharing cells. They also made recommendations in relation to the objectives of the penal system conceding that the 'rhetoric of 'treatment and training' had had its day and should be replaced' (Home Office, 1979: para. 4.27). After much debate, the concept of 'positive custody' was proposed with the hope of developing regimes with a real purpose and objectives. Under this framework, prison authorities and staff were responsible for creating an environment whereby prisoners could respond and contribute to society positively, preserving and promoting their self respect, minimising the harmful effects of prison life, and preparing and assisting them for discharge (Home Office, 1979: para. 4.26). However, the implementation of the May Report became the responsibility of the new Thatcher government and the notion of 'positive custody' was never officially adopted.

Morris (1989: 189) argues that the Thatcher government would never have considered setting up a structure like the May Committee, preferring instead to employ 'high powered individuals from the world of commerce to conduct managerial-style reviews'. During the 1980s, Royal Commissions and standing advisory bodies, such as the Advisory Council on the Penal System, tended to be replaced with official inquiries which were ad hoc, highly specific, short-term, manageable, and internal (Downes and Morgan, 1997). By the 1980s, links between the Home Office and pressure groups were strengthened forming a policy community which interacted over various issues. Although the government often ignored protest from the pressure groups, it also recognised their use in identifying problems, assessing the feasibility of reforms and increasing the legitimacy of the policy process (Downes and Morgan, 1997: 115). New pressure groups emerged on the scene including Inquest which was founded in 1981, the Prison Reform Trust (PRT) in 1982 and Women in Prison (WIP) in 1983. During the 1980s, the penal reform lobby and academic commentators began to press for the recognition of prisoners' rights and timetables for the introduction of minimum standards and conditions

(Morgan, 1997), while the new government began devising strategies for 'managing' the prison system.

The problems of an increasing population, overcrowding, riots, and industrial action by prison officers endured throughout the 1980s. The response by the Conservative government was one of 'penal pragmatism' with no consideration of long-term or overarching goals (Bottoms, 1980: 4) and a contradictory mix of policies. In 1982, the most extensive prison building programme since the nineteenth century was initiated. While the prisons were being built, two techniques were employed to reduce the prison population and overcrowding which simultaneously appeased both the 'law and order' lobby and liberal critics. These included increasing the numbers of short-term offenders eligible for parole and introducing a range of community penalties to divert offenders from custody, while simultaneously increasing parole restrictions for those who had committed more serious and violent offences. Both techniques were part of a bifurcated policy or twin-track approach which distinguished the most serious and dangerous offenders from the less serious and dangerous, ensuring the former received tough prison sentences with restricted prospects for parole and the latter received more lenient measures in the community (Bottoms, 1977; 1980). Such a strategy had great political appeal because it allowed the government to remain tough to appease the law and order lobby and populist opinion, whilst simultaneously appearing soft to liberal critics (Edelman, 1984).

In 1984, the Home Secretary, Leon Brittan, reduced the minimum qualifying period for parole from twelve to six months. This led to an increase in the numbers of grants of parole to short-term prisoners who had committed less serious offences. At the same time, parole restrictions were imposed on those who had committed more violent and serious offences. For example, prisoners serving life sentences for certain types of murder would normally remain in prison for a minimum of 20 years before becoming eligible for parole, unless there were exceptional circumstances. Similarly, prisoners serving more than 5 years for violent offences or drug trafficking were unlikely to be granted parole until just before the ends of their sentences or in exceptional circumstances. The parole policy had two main effects. First, it led to a dramatic increase in the long-term prison population. Second, it removed all incentives amongst long-term prisoners towards positive behaviour and led to much hostility and unrest (Cavadino and Dignan, 1997).

The loss of faith in rehabilitation as the primary purpose of imprisonment and the rising prison population also led to a proliferation of 'alternatives to custody' which reflected a growing disillusionment with the efficacy of prison for reforming offenders and the costs of mass imprisonment. In the early 1980s, such alternatives included community service orders and intermediate treatment for juvenile offenders. The new alternatives to custody were thought to be both more humane and effective. However, the criticism of deinstitutionalisation that developed in the 1970s and continued in the 1980s suggested that these forms of punishment were neither humane nor effective in terms of cost or reducing offending compared with imprisonment (Greenberg, 1975). In fact, it was argued that these forms of decarceration actually widened the net of social control and extended the segregative principle from the institution to the community (Cohen, 1985). The mode of penality had been dispersed throughout society to more locations, agencies and personnel. Throughout this era, the prison persisted and community corrections supplemented, augmented, and replicated the prison rather than replacing it.

By the mid-1980s, the institutional context of policy-making began to shift as increasing emphasis was placed on the financial management of the public sector and drives toward the 3 E's: Economy, Effectiveness and Efficiency. Managerialism began to creep into all areas of public policy and the problems of crime and punishment were no exception. Rather than engaging with the question of legitimacy or 'what are prisons for', the Prison Service became obsessed with the technical and legal requirements of keeping prisoners in custody (Morgan, 1997). The penal strategies of the early 1980s cannot be deemed successful in their practical aims. The prison population continued to rise, overcrowding was still a problem, inadequate conditions prevailed and riots and disturbances were regular occurrences. During the period 1980 to 1986, the average prison population rose from 42, 264 in 1980 to 46, 770 in 1986 (see Table A.4, Appendix). The crisis of legitimacy remained untackled, with no long-term strategy, penal philosophy or overarching goals identified for the prison system. It was within this penal setting and policy context that the issue of drug users in the prison system began to be debated.

Nature and extent of the drugs 'problem' in prisons

It was not until the late 1970s that the issue of drug users within the prison system began to be recognised and debated. Historically, drug users in the criminal justice system, and particularly prisoners, had not been given prominence in discussions of drugs policy. As one commentator argued, 'in the 1970s prisons were regarded as a footnote, albeit a perplexing one, in the treatment and rehabilitation debate' (Runciman, 1996: 4). Similarly, the problem of drugs using prisoners had not been a priority within penal policy. At this time, there was virtually no research or evidence on the extent or nature of the drug problem in prisons and very little external scrutiny (Berridge, 1990; Pearson, 1990). Although there was no official, formal documented policy or strategy which was publicly accessible, drug using prisoners were dealt with by the Prison Medical Service (PMS). There was growing criticism of the practices of the PMS from drugs experts and other professionals in the community. The interest in the issue therefore emanated from external sources, rather than from internal sources within the prison system. In the 1980s, three investigations were conducted which began to examine the treatment of drug users in prison, highlight and define the problem, and question existing strategies. These included the 1980 ACMD report on drug dependants within the prison system, the 1985 House of Commons Social Services Committee Report on the Misuse of Hard Drugs, and the 1986 House of Commons Social Services Committee Report on the Prison Medical Service.

By the late 1970s, the drugs policy community began to show interest in the drug issue in prisons. In June 1977, the ACMD working group on Treatment and Rehabilitation appointed three of its members to examine and report on the treatment of drug dependants within the prison system. Statistical evidence collated by the enquiry indicated a growing number of drug dependants entering the prison system. A sample of male addicts, followed up for five years after their first notification, showed over half (56 per cent) had some experience of custody (Mott, 1977). The report also provided evidence that the majority of prisoners who were considered to be addicts had not been receiving treatment during the year in which they were imprisoned.

Prior to the 1970s, prisoners with drug problems tended to be viewed by both prisoners and prison staff as particularly 'deviant' and on the margins of the mainstream population and culture within prisons. Many prisoners were forced to keep their addiction hidden to avoid mistreatment, bullying and harassment from other prisoners and prison staff. Very few would actively seek treatment and help. During the late 1970s and early 1980s, there was a perceived shift in the prison population in relation to the characteristics of drug users or drug involved offenders. A director of a drug agency who had been involved in drug treatment in prisons during this period suggested there was a shift or crossover emerging between mainstream criminality and drug importation and dealing:

> *People who were coming in with drug problems were considered second class citizens for a long time and were almost in the same category as child molesters. They were seen apart from the criminal population and they didn't really mix very much ... It used to be the case in the 1970s that criminal gangs down in South London wouldn't touch drugs. It was mainly the hippies, degenerates and down and outs. Then what started to happen is that mainstream criminals started to get into drug importation. The whole division started to get more blurred.* (Interview (03) with director of drug agency)

Mirroring what was occurring in the community during the period 1980–6, increases in drug use and drug offences were also represented in the prison population in terms of official indicators. For example, the number of new drug addicts notified to the Home Office by prison medical officers increased from 320 in 1981 to 1, 102 in 1986 with the proportion of all notifications increasing from 14 to 21 per cent during this period (see Table A.1, Appendix). In addition, drug offenders sentenced to custody had increased in number from 1, 676 in 1980 to 3, 928 in 1986, with the proportion rising from 10 to 16 per cent over this period (see Table A.2, Appendix).

Illegal and legal drugs: issues of control and collusion

During the late 1970s and early 1980s, there was increasing concern that prescription drugs, such as tranquillisers, were being used as mechanisms of control and discipline by the Prison Medical Service, particularly in women's prisons (Ryan, 1983; House of Commons Social Services Committee, 1985 and 1986; Sim 1990). In November 1977, the Medical Committee Against the Abuse of Prisoners by Drugging was formed through the National Prisoner's Movement. It consisted of representatives from the National Prisoners' Movement, the National Council for Civil Liberties, the National Association for Mental Health, SCODA, Radical Alternatives to Prison and Release, as well as a number of consultant psychiatrists. The Committee monitored the allegations of drugging and campaigned for a prison health service administered by the NHS (Sim, 1990). By 1986, contradictory evidence was submitted to the Social Services Committee regarding the levels of prescribing. Some submissions pointed to excessive levels and coercive practices, while other evidence indicated that prescribing policy had undergone a radical change with prisoners being subjected to abrupt and inhumane withdrawal (House of Commons Social Services Committee, 1986: xli–xlii).

The use of prescription drugs in controlling prisoners was related to the collusion amongst prison staff around the use of illegal drugs. Evidence submitted to the 1985 Social Services Committee suggested that illegal drugs were available and being used in the prison system. For example, the Association of Police Surgeons reported:

> When the addict goes to prison he will be able to, in most circumstances, continue with drug abuse. While we appreciate the difficulties for the prison authorities with the present state of overcrowding especially in local prisons, it is common knowledge among addicts that drugs are available. (House of Commons Social Services Committee, 1985: xxxiii)

Similarly, the Prison Medical Association argued it was 'difficult to initiate treatment and rehabilitation in long-term prisons where uncontrolled drink and drugs are so readily available' (House of Commons Social Services Committee, 1985: xxxiv). There was also evidence, albeit limited, of the availability of drugs within prisons in the annual reports of the Prison Service. For example, since the 1970s, deaths associated with drug overdoses and misuse had been recorded (Home Office, 1975, 1977, 1978, 1983) and dogs were increasingly being trained to detect drugs (Home Office, 1985b).

Despite these rumours and evidence, the Prison Service was reluctant to publicly acknowledge an 'illegal' drug *problem* in prisons. This collusion was a powerful force which masked the nature and extent of the problem and also had a detrimental effect on initiating research in this area. In a summary of research on drugs, law enforcement and criminology in 1986, Pearson (1990: 142) described the problems of negotiating access on drug issues in prison as 'insurmountable'. A public admission or evidence on the nature and extent of the problem might have forced the prison authorities to initiate some form of action to deal with it. Such a tacit admission would have indicated the failure or non-existence of a drugs policy. Drugs, particularly cannabis, were viewed as functional in that they kept the prison and prisoners quiet and under control, making the job of prison staff easier. As the National Association of Probation Officers (NAPO) argued in their evidence to the 1985 Social Services Committee, 'uniformed prison staff collude with the use of cannabis unless it becomes so virulent that a 'purge' is necessary for credibility to be retained' (House of Commons Social Services Committee, 1985: 48). Those who had been involved in prison drug treatment during this period suggested that the collusion and complacency around drugs use was related to control issues:

> *What you had was a Prison Service – a monolithic organisation – which had a stance that if we don't talk about it, we don't have to do anything about it.* (Interview (10) with director of drug agency)

What appeared to be occurring was a form of 'institutionalised' collusion:

> *There was a complacent attitude – a collusive attitude – by prison personnel. Because with a compliant, stoned population, they were much easier to manage. It was an institutionalised collusion ... It was a lot of turning a blind eye.* (Interview (15) with director of drug agency)

Thus, both illegal and prescribed drugs were used as mechanisms of control within a prison system which was operating in a context of an increasing population, overcrowding, inadequate conditions and unrest. Illegal drugs were condoned and legal drugs were prescribed to minimise disruption and to contain and manage a potentially volatile population which was increasingly made up of prisoners serving long-term sentences with little hope of parole. This collusion prevented the growing illegal drug problem from becoming public and therefore policy in this area was private, in-house and internal. As Heclo (1972) reminds us, policies can consist of what is not being done.

Dealing with drug users in prisons

Paradoxically, it was within the non-treatment, non-rehabilitative and 'just deserts' penal framework which had emerged during the late 1970s and early 1980s and the collusive environment around drugs, that the ACMD (1980: 1) rather naively suggested that a prison sentence should be regarded as an 'opportunity' for drug treatment and rehabilitation. In 1985, this point was reiterated in the Social Services Committee report (1985: xxxiii) on the misuse of hard drugs: 'our greatest concern is that the time so many addicts spend in custody represents a wasted opportunity for tackling the problem of their addiction'.

The role of the Prison Medical Service

During the period 1980–6, the Prison Service had its own system of health care, the Prison Medical Service (PMS), which was separate from the National Health Service (NHS). Prison doctors and medical staff are employed by the Prison Service and are not accountable to health authorities in the outside community. Medical staff within prisons have always experienced an acute conflict between their contradictory roles of caring for the health of prisoners and maintaining control and discipline (Sim, 1990; Ralli, 1994). For example, under the Prison Rules, medical officers have the dual responsibility of providing medical care and ensuring that prisoners are fit for certain punishments, such as solitary confinement and physical restraints. Sim (1990: x) cogently argues that control and discipline have been more central to their roles than health care: 'prison medical workers, rather than operating from a perspective bereft of ideology and politics, have been intimately involved in reinforcing the discipline of penality'. Similarly, in evidence to the 1986 Social Services Committee enquiry into the Prison Medical Service, the Royal College of Psychiatrists urged a review of the prison medical officer's role outside the provision of health care (House of Commons Social Services Committee, 1986: 62).

The Prison Medical Service was central to how drug users were dealt with in the prison system during the 1980s. Drug addiction was defined by the Prison Service primarily as a medical problem and dealt with internally. Drug treatment, particularly withdrawal programmes, were firmly located in the hands of Prison Medical Officers and subject to their clinical judgement. Drugs policy was therefore related to the internal practices of prison medical officers. All prisoners, both those beginning their sentences and on remand, were medically examined by a prison medical officer on admission to prison, providing the main opportunity to identify drug users. The initial assessments, however, were noted to be very brief and often 'perfunctory to the point of uselessness' (House of Commons Social Services Committee, 1986: xi). This was mainly due to the large numbers of new prisoners who had to be processed in a very limited period of time, as well as the prison medical officers' lack of experience and training in working with drug users (ACMD, 1988). As a result, many drug users escaped detection and some actively tried to conceal their drug use due to fear of being sent to a more secure prison, increased chance of cell searches, and a reduced chance of early release (Tippell, 1989). Women prisoners, in particular, are often reluctant to disclose a drug problem, as they fear their children may be taken into care (Nichols and Henderson, 1990).

If prisoners were identified as drug users on reception, they could be offered a short-term withdrawal programme depending on the professional judgement of the prison medical officer.

Historically, the discourse of less-eligibility has underpinned penal policy whereby prisoners should not be seen to be in receipt of services or living in conditions which are superior to those living in the community (Sim, 1990; Sparks, 1996). When this discourse is translated into penal practice however, it has often meant that prisoners receive a standard of service provision well below that offered in the community. The discourse of less eligibility also applies to the treatment prisoners receive for drug addiction and has a long history. For example, the Rolleston report of 1926 defined addiction as a disease requiring medical treatment and legitimised maintenance prescribing. However, the approach derived from the Rolleston report was class based and had been developed for the middle-class addict who was perceived to be 'deserving' and 'respectable' (Berridge, 1989; 1999; Stimson and Lart, 1994). In contrast, the Rolleston consensus was not extended to drug addicted prisoners who were treated by methods of abrupt withdrawal. Berridge's analysis (1999: 274) illustrates how, 'the prison doctors formed a distinct group who always favoured harsher methods, in particular the abrupt withdrawal method of treatment; their addict clientele was distinctively different'.

These distinctions between treatment in the community and prison have continued. For example, the ACMD (1980) argued that treatment in prisons was not congruent to what was being offered in the community and that much of the existing provision was inadequate and dated. Treatment provision in prisons had not kept pace with the new thinking and theories around addiction. The professional consensus which had been achieved in the community around 'problem drug taking', social models of care, and integrated treatment and rehabilitation had not penetrated the prison environment. Within the penal setting, the dichotomy between medical treatment and rehabilitation persisted. The Social Services Committee (1986: xxxix) argued that drug addiction in prisons should be defined as a social service problem, rather than a medical problem.

The ACMD (1980) also criticised the withdrawal programmes in prisons as inadequate, particularly in relation to remand prisoners. Three recommendations were made to improve withdrawal procedures emphasising that they should take full advantage of the techniques developed by specialised units in the NHS; maintenance regimes should be instituted for drug dependant remand prisoners; and the widest possible use should be made by the courts of drug treatment centres, for remanding notified drug dependants on bail for the purpose of obtaining medical reports (ACMD, 1980). However, it was clear the legacy of the practices adopted by the prison doctors of the Rolleston era had endured. In their response to the ACMD report, the Home Office advocated an abstinence-only approach and considered maintenance regimes inappropriate within the prison system (Home Office, 1980). Five years later, in the 1985 Social Services Committee report, submissions indicated that withdrawal programmes in prisons remained inadequate. Although provision varied between establishments, many prisoners taken into custody in police cells, remand centres and prisons were only given one option – abrupt withdrawal. In evidence to the Committee, Dr Akhter of the Royal College of Psychiatrists provided this graphic description of the inhumane treatment drug addicted prisoners received: 'the only treatment that drug addicts get in prison is 'cold turkey'. Nothing is prescribed and they are just given a mattress on the floor'(House of Commons Social Services Committee, 1985: xxxiii).

There were clear contradictions between the public and private discourses operating within the prison system. The public discourse was pushing forward the punitive, anti-drug, abstinence-based approach, while the private discourse was quietly condoning and permitting drug use. The private discourse involved turning a 'blind eye' and collusion to maintain control of an increasingly unstable system.

Drug treatment provision

With the exception of pioneering projects like the Community Drugs Project in London which undertook drugs work with prisoners (see Dorn and South, 1985), drug treatment and counselling programmes were scarce in prisons in the 1980s. The Social Services Committee (1985: xxxv) concluded: 'we cannot but condemn the absence of even rudimentary services for prisoners with a history of drug use, both while in custody and after release'. Despite the growth and diversity in services in the community, there were very few outside agencies undertaking drug work in prisons (Hamer, 1998). Most provision was internal, medically driven and provided on an ad hoc and individual basis. A civil servant suggested that the lack of service provision was related to the failure to acknowledge the problem of drug users within the prison system and the lack of a clear drugs policy at this time:

> *Prior to the 1990s, there was very little clear action on drugs in prison and individual cases were tackled through the medical model. The Prison*

> *Service wasn't really out there acknowledging that it had a large number of drug misusing prisoners or in fact didn't know whether it had or not in any structured way.* (Interview (19) with civil servant)

The ACMD (1980) suggested that the reasons for this paucity in treatment facilities included the shortage of psychiatrists in the Prison Service; failure of the Joint Consultant Programme between the Prison Medical Service and the NHS; opposition to treatment in prisons by some psychiatrists; unwillingness of prisoners to seek treatment; low concentrations of drug users in a single prison to make treatment viable; the range of sentences served by prisoners made it difficult to maintain intensive therapeutic regimes; many therapies were based on a single theory of addiction and were unacceptable to many drug users; prisoners often changed their minds about treatment between remand and return for sentence; and overcrowding and budget cuts made it difficult to initiate and sustain programmes.

In the late 1970s and early 1980s, the few formalised attempts at drug treatment in prisons involved some form of therapeutic community based on a democratic, collaborative, self-help ethos (ACMD, 1980). In such units, no psychotropic medication was available, consultants from the NHS were brought in and prison officers were trained to work within these regimes. The ACMD (1980) described the efforts to provide therapeutic regimes in five prisons: the Holloway Therapeutic Unit, the Annexe at Wormwood Scrubs, Grendon Psychiatric Prison, Pentonville and Feltham. The ACMD recommended that more therapeutic units for drug dependants be established on the model of those operating at Holloway and Wormwood Scrubs and that follow-up studies be undertaken of drug dependants who had received treatment in custody. In response, the Home Office argued that resources were not available for any further units (Home Office, 1980). In 1985, the Social Services Committee was similarly impressed by what they witnessed during their visit to the Annexe at Wormwood Scrubs and reiterated the ACMD recommendation regarding the provision of further similar units.

Overall, the ACMD report received very little attention and did not have a huge impact on the prison system or prison drugs policy (Tippell, 1989; Runciman, 1996; Hamer, 1998). With reference to the 1980 ACMD report, the Social Services Committee (1985: xxxiii) noted that, 'the sad truth is that none of these recommendations have been carried out: this report would seem to have been swept under the carpet.' In order for the report to be taken seriously, the Prison

Department would have had to at least acknowledge a drugs 'problem' and that existing provision was inadequate. It can be argued, however, that the ACMD had some success in highlighting the importance of one of their recommendations – to establish a service to co-ordinate and improve the aftercare provision available to ex-drug dependant prisoners on release.

Release and throughcare: the development of services

Much of the ACMD report focused on the release and throughcare arrangements for drug dependant prisoners which were viewed as both 'the most important and the weakest element in providing this "comprehensive service"' (ACMD, 1980: 7). Drug dependant prisoners have similar problems to other prisoners during the resettlement process, such as housing and employment, as well some specific problems related to their drug dependant status. For example, there was growing evidence that a high proportion of prisoners die from an overdose on release from prison because they cannot tolerate the same levels as they could prior to custody. A study of addict deaths in London between 1970 and 1974 indicated that 10 per cent died within a few days of release from prison (Stevens, 1977 quoted in ACMD, 1980). Prisoners with a history of drug problems were often denied parole because the Local Review Committee was concerned that insufficient support was available in the community (Parole Release Scheme, 1983).The ACMD (1980) highlighted the importance of liaison and communication between drug agencies and prisons so that follow-up arrangements could be made on release. They found evidence that voluntary agencies were experiencing difficulties gaining access to prisons to establish contact with future clients and to undertake throughcare work. The Prison Service often resisted allowing access to these agencies because many drug workers were ex-addicts or ex-prisoners themselves and because the staff turnover rates were high. On the other hand, there was also evidence to suggest that drug agencies and drug treatment centres were reluctant to become involved within the criminal justice system, particularly prisons. In many cases, they may have refused prisoners due to time and financial constraints (Tippell, 1989), but their reluctance also reflected an underlying resistance to become involved in treatment and therapy within a coercive environment.

As a result of the findings and recommendations of the ACMD, SCODA co-ordinated a small working group to plan a service for problem drug users in prison who were eligible for parole (Parole Release Scheme, 1985). The group consisted of representatives from

SCODA, NACRO, non-residential and residential drug services, Inner London Probation Service, and the Prison Service. The impetus for this initiative emerged primarily from the voluntary sector, although the prison and probation services supported it. It was originally envisaged that the service would perform a co-ordinating role between prison and services in the community, but the Home Office advised that funding would not be available for non-residential service (Parole Release Scheme, 1985). As a result, the working group developed plans for a residential facility which would be attached to the service. After several years of planning and negotiation, the Parole Release Scheme (PRS) was established in 1983. The development of the PRS is characteristic of the move away from 'specialists' and towards involving 'generalists' in the work with drug users which occurred during the 1980s. It represented the first dedicated service for drug using prisoners. Adopting a pragmatic and modest approach to its work with ex-prisoners, the scheme began as a small pilot project with three main functions: to link prisoners who were eligible for parole and had a drug history with suitable post-release services; to offer a residential service through its own hostel; and to monitor its work and learn more about drug users in prison (Parole Release Scheme, 1984). In terms of resources, the PRS had four staff, one hostel and an agreement to work with seven prisons in London and the south-east chosen by the Prison Department.

It was originally envisaged that the PRS would work with approximately thirty parolees per year. In reality, however, this was a huge underestimate (Tippell, 1989). As discussed in the previous section on penal policy, changes were announced to the parole system to alleviate the growing prison population in 1984. The length of sentence during which a prisoner would be eligible for parole was reduced. This meant that more prisoners were placed into the parole process and thus more imprisoned drug users were eligible for referral to the PRS (Tippell, 1989). In the first year of operation, the PRS received 124 requests for referral instead of the thirty originally envisaged. By 1986, the PRS had received 404 requests for referral and was receiving 1, 000 enquiries per year from probation officers in relation to drugs and drug services (PRS, 1986).

An emerging policy network

Over the course of the phase 1980–6, it is clear the work of the ACMD and the Social Services Committees on the misuse of hard drugs and the Prison Medical Service began to generate discussion and debate regarding the treatment of drug users in prisons. The drugs and penal policy communities began to recognise that there were important issues which needed to be addressed within prisons regarding drugs. A policy network began to emerge around drug issues in prison which operated at the subsectoral level or at the interface between penal and drugs policy. The main concern for this policy network was the treatment provision for drug using prisoners, particularly on release. Although the Home Office and Prison Medical Service remained at the core of this network, an increasing number of groups and organisations became involved at the periphery including the probation service, SCODA, NACRO, and drug agencies. The drug issue within prisons was gradually becoming exposed and subject to greater external scrutiny and challenges.

This policy network recognised the constraints within the prison system during this period, including the difficult penal conditions and context, the lack of a formalised drugs policy, the collusion around drug issues, the professional power of the Prison Medical Service, the lack of financial resources, and the decline of the rehabilitative ideal. Rather than attempting to tackle the problem on the inside, they pursued a much more realistic and pragmatic approach by developing measures to deal with the problem on the outside through throughcare and release measures. Working within these parameters meant that they would not have to confront the problems, conflicts and constraints internal to the system. The Parole Release Scheme marked the beginning of drug service development in prisons. It revealed a glaring gap in provision and highlighted the lack of understanding around this aspect of the drug problem (Tippell, 1989). In the following chapters, it will become clear that service development preceded policy development in this area. Following the work of the PRS, other drug agencies began to work within prisons and internal interest in the drug issue within the prison system began to increase. It gradually became more acceptable for drug agencies to become involved in the criminal justice system:

> *the prisons started to develop an interest in drugs and drawing in outside agencies. It wasn't really so much through drugs as much as through some of the throughcare issues and pre-release groups. They started to see the value of outsiders. The drug agencies were freaking because you know we were 'right on' and we were a little bit on the edge when it came to criminal justice issues and legality. Many drug agencies shied away [from] working in prison ... gradually they began to see that they could do it.* (Interview (26a) with director of drug agency)

Conclusion

Although very little substantive research or evidence existed in relation to the drugs 'problem' in prisons during the period from 1980 to 1986, statistics on notifications and drugs offences showed increases and several official reports pointed to a growing 'problem'. There were, however, powerful forces masking this increasing 'problem'. Drugs, particularly cannabis, played an important control function within the prison system and prison staff were reluctant to admit that drugs were being used. A form of 'institutionalised collusion' emerged which kept the problem hidden from outside scrutiny. During this period, drugs were seen primarily as an 'individual' problem rather than a problem for the 'institution'. Prisoners who had been identified as having drug problems were dealt with individually mainly through the medical model. However, the treatment they received was inadequate and often inhumane in comparison with community provision, particularly in relation to withdrawal programmes. Various recommendations had been made to improve treatment programmes in prison, yet the government had failed to seriously consider or implement any of them.

During this period, prisons were operating on the periphery of the drugs policy debates, similarly drugs were not central to the penal policy debates. Many of the new ideas in relation to drug users and drug treatment in the community had not penetrated the walls of the prison. Although the tradition of treatment and rehabilitation continued in the community by the caring professions, the discourses of 'law and order' and 'just deserts' were particularly acute within the prison environment.The objectives of drug treatment were clearly in conflict with the aims of penal policy. Moreover, treatment objectives would also be hindered in a system under crisis with its increasing population, inadequate conditions, unrest and overcrowding. The idea that prison should be regarded as an opportunity for drug treatment also conflicted with the fact that drugs, both illegal and legal, were used as mechanisms of control in the prison environment. Those lobbying for change recognised the power of this punitive framework, but rather than tackling the problems on the inside, chose to tackle it in the community on release.

A key figure in prison drugs policy described the early 1980s as a period of 'modest ambitions' in relation to developments in both policy and service provision. Although no concrete prison drugs policy or strategy emerged during the period from 1980 to 1986, it was an important phase in that it laid the foundations for later policy developments. External interest in drugs and drug users in prison was growing and a small policy network was beginning to form around the issue. The Prison Medical Service had always had a monopoly over the control of drug treatment in prisons, but this began to change as more external drug agencies became involved in treatment provision in prisons from the mid-1980s. By 1986–7, drugs policy was increasingly shaped by the HIV/AIDS crisis. The next chapter will explore the impact of HIV/AIDS within the prison system and on policy development.

3

1986–93: The HIV/AIDS Crisis and Fears of Contamination

Introduction

This chapter focuses on the period 1986 to 1993, which signalled the beginning of more explicit policy development in relation to drug issues in prisons. As in the previous phase, the issues of throughcare and treatment continued to be emphasised, resulting in a more formal policy document on throughcare in 1987 (HM Prison Service, 1987) and a manual dealing with guidelines on how drug users should be cared for within the prison system in 1991 (HM Prison Service, 1991). The HIV/AIDS crisis was the key factor precipitating this move towards a more defined prison drugs policy. In 1986, HIV/AIDS first began to be debated in relation to drugs policy in the community (Stimson and Lart, 1991; Berridge, 1996a). In contrast to the earlier phase, the 'denial' and 'collusion' which existed around drug issues in prison were no longer sustainable in light of HIV and the evidence and research base which was beginning to emerge on the nature and extent of the problem. The concern around HIV and injecting drug use within the prison environment resulted in a policy network forming around this issue which began to pressure the Prison Service to acknowledge and respond to the problem.

During the period 1986 to 1993, the macro public policy context continued to be shaped by the reforms and restructuring initiated by the Conservative government. The discourses of managerialism, value for money, privatisation, devolvement, voluntarism, partnership and community were becoming dominant features of the public policy and political landscape. These were evident in the reforms to the NHS, education and local government as well as criminal justice policy. The main thrust behind the reforms and restructuring was to shift the state towards the role of facilitator rather than provider (Atkinson and Savage, 1994). However, as Reiner and Cross (1991: 7) argue, two contradictory trends can be identified: the devolvement of responsibility from official agencies to the community and the enhancement of power and control within central government. These themes and trends influenced the development of drugs and penal policy during 1986 to 1993.

The chapter begins with a brief outline of the major developments in drugs and penal policy which provide the context for the emerging policy on drugs in prisons. It then explores the nature and extent of the drugs 'problem' in prison and how it was reconceptualised by key actors during this phase. The final section of the chapter examines the policies developed around drugs and HIV/AIDS in prisons during this phase. It will emerge that these policies were inadequate, failing to fully embrace the concepts of 'risk reduction' and 'harm minimisation' and the public health agenda which were successfully operating in the community. In effect, it appears that they were designed to appease critics and give the impression that action was being taken (Edelman, 1971).

Drugs policy context: the discourses of 'harm minimisation', 'public health' and 'partnership'

During the period 1986 to 1993, official indicators showed that the drug problem continued to grow. With the exception of a decrease between the years 1986 and 1987, the number of new drug addicts notified to the Home Office increased steadily from 5, 325 in 1986 to 11, 561 in 1993 (see Table A.3, Appendix). The heroin 'epidemic' of the early 1980s, however, appeared to be levelling off, as the percentage of newly notified heroin addicts fell from 91 per cent in 1986 to 78 per cent in 1993. During this period, the number of drug offences increased threefold from 23, 905 in 1986 to 68, 480 in 1993 (see Table A.2, Appendix). As a result of the crack cocaine 'crisis' in the United States during the latter half of the 1980s, there was growing political and media concern regarding increasing use of cocaine in the UK. However, the addict statistics failed to show a significant problem, with the proportion addicted to cocaine accounting for less than 10 per cent throughout the period 1986–93 (Home Office Statistical Bulletins, 1987–94; see also Power, 1994 and Bean, 1993).

By the end of 1985, HIV infection was already established within drug injecting populations in England, Wales and Scotland. For example, 55 cases of HIV infection among injecting drug users were reported in England and Wales and 356 cases in Scotland (Robertson, 1994). Local studies conducted in Edinburgh pointed to a rapidly spreading HIV epidemic amongst the drug injecting population, with sero-positive levels of around 50 per cent (Robertson et al., 1986). This epidemic was associated with a shortage of clean syringes and 'shooting galleries' where as many as 30 drug users would gather to share a single syringe. The way in which the drug problem was framed and defined changed in light of the HIV/AIDS crisis. Injecting drug users were expected to be one of the key groups in terms of heterosexual transmission and therefore seen as a threat to public health. Drugs policy became shaped and reinforced by the advent of HIV/AIDS. The main response was to re-examine harm minimisation policies and to continue the emphasis upon collaboration, co-ordination and partnership between agencies and services.

HIV/AIDS and harm minimisation

The interest and concern regarding the relationship between HIV and injecting drug use were minimal initially. During the early period of the virus, key players in the drugs world were slow to come forward and many lacked expertise in relation to HIV/AIDS. Berridge (1996a: 93) argues that although a liberal consensus had been achieved in mainstream AIDS policy by 1986–7, this was initially difficult to extend to the area of drugs due to problems with political and public approval around harm minimisation techniques such as syringe exchanges, the isolation of drugs policy psychiatrists from public health and clinical medicine, and the traditions of local drugs policy-making. Conflicts and divisions were also rife within professional groups in terms of the choice between abstinence and harm minimisation approaches. However, the epidemic amongst drug injectors in Scotland and the subsequent McClellend Report advocating harm minimisation helped to shape future policy (Berridge, 1996a).

In 1987, the UK government initially implemented three measures to tackle the spread of HIV through injecting drug use including a publicity campaign, provision of extra resources to drug services, and the introduction of 15 pilot needle exchange schemes (ACMD, 1988). The ACMD established a working group to discuss and consider the implications of HIV/AIDS for drug services and to make recommendations on how the problem should be tackled. The group produced three influential reports on the topic (ACMD, 1988; 1989; 1993). They concluded in their first report that 'HIV is a greater threat to public and individual health than drug misuse' (ACMD, 1988: 1). Thus, the containment of the virus was viewed as more important than drugs prevention (Stimson, 1990b; Berridge, 1991). The drugs policy community increasingly recognised that many drug users may not wish to stop injecting and that risk reduction and harm minimisation strategies must be developed to work with this group. Research evidence from the pilot syringe exchanges also indicated that they had been successful in attracting clients and changing risk behaviour, but less successful in retaining clients and attracting women and young people (Stimson et al., 1988).

Policy-makers were eventually persuaded that harm minimisation strategies must be adopted to contain the virus and the threat of leakage into the general population. As Berridge (1996a: 95) argues, the gap between the 'political' and 'policy community' views on drugs policy narrowed and an alliance or consensus developed which was based on harm minimisation rather than eradication or cure. Drugs had become a problem of public health rather than individual pathology (Berridge, 1996b). Harm minimisation was officially adopted as a policy goal and involved the extension of syringe exchange schemes, free distribution of condoms, education around injecting and sexual practices, and increased use of methadone prescribing. The new language of risk reduction, harm minimisation, accessibility, and user friendliness became the 'official' discourses in relation to HIV/AIDS and drugs (Stimson and Lart, 1991).

The HIV/AIDS epidemic and the shift towards greater harm minimisation also brought new players into the field including infectious disease specialists, public health professionals, GPs and a re-shaped voluntary sector (MacGregor, 1998a). Although at one level the response to HIV/AIDS indicated a partial re-medicalisation of drugs policy, the emphasis on involving generalists such as community workers, outreach workers, and ex-addicts in drugs interventions continued (Stimson, 1990b). More funds were made available for drug services. The Central Funding Initiative in the mid-1980s had produced a wide range of new drug agencies which were in place and ready to adapt and respond to the HIV/AIDS crisis. In 1988–9 an extra 3 million pounds and in 1989–90 an extra 5 million pounds were made available for drug services to increase their role in halting the spread of HIV (Home Office, 1990b). Such funding enabled many of these services to survive. However, in order to meet the requirements of HIV funding, many services were bent towards responding to HIV and injecting drug use, to the exclusion of other drugs and other drug users (MacGregor, 1998a). HIV had a profound effect on the way in which drug services operated.

Accessible services which operated outreach, open-door and user friendly policies were developed and big targets such as abstinence were replaced with smaller targets and a hierarchy of goals (Stimson, 1990b). Moreover, their traditional autonomy was increasingly eroded, they were asked to collaborate with other agencies, become part of a wider planning process and accountable for large sums of earmarked finance (Cranfield et al., 1994).

As argued in the previous chapter, drugs policy during the mid-1980s was set within an increasingly penal framework and more focused on enforcement issues than previously. The HIV/AIDS epidemic was seen to have the effect of overturning that policy. However, as Berridge (1996a) argues, the reality was much more complex. HIV/AIDS did not overturn the penal response nor did it introduce brand new concepts into the drugs policy debate. During the period 1986–93, the 1985 national drugs strategy was not revised in any significant way in response to the HIV/AIDS crisis and its five main action points remained unchanged. The bifurcated policy of control endured with punitive enforcement measures targeted towards drug dealers and traffickers and harm and demand reduction measures for drug users. During the late 1980s, policy-makers, politicians and the media became increasingly concerned and preoccupied with the notion that crack would threaten the stability of British communities. They feared that the crack 'epidemic' amongst black people in some inner cities in America would reproduce itself in Britain, particularly in areas where there was a significant black population (Bean, 1993). The panic around crack ensured that the 'war on drugs' continued and provided legitimacy for the existing penal framework.

Two very contradictory discourses – enforcement/punishment and harm minimisation/public health – continued to operate simultaneously and were articulated publicly at the political level. As Edelman (1984) argues much political mileage can be gained by putting forward soft and hard approaches simultaneously. Such a strategy appeases both liberal critics and hard-line law and order advocates. It is possible to draw a discursive distinction between the legitimate, deserving victims and the illegitimate, undeserving villains of drugs, whereby the victims receive treatment and harm reduction and the villains receive punishment and custody (Collison, 1993; 1994). However, as Collison (1993: 383) cogently argues, in practice this distinction is simplistic and the two sides of the 'British System' are frequently dealing with the same groups of people (i.e. low level dealers drawn into the criminal justice system who are also problem drug users).

During 1986–93, there were also indications that drug issues in the criminal justice system, particularly in relation to prisons, were moving into mainstream drugs policy debates. Since their report on prisons in 1980, the ACMD showed a renewed interest in the criminal justice system. In the series of reports on AIDS and drugs (ACMD, 1988, 1989; 1993), the special problems around the link between HIV and drug use in prisons were specifically highlighted. In 1990, the Criminal Justice Working Group of the ACMD was appointed. It explored the various aspects of the criminal justice system in relation to drug users in three major reports dealing with probation, police, and prison (ACMD, 1991; 1994; 1996). Policy networks began to form around each of these issues. The membership of the Criminal Justice Working Group varied according to the subject area, but many of the representatives had continuous membership, including Ruth Runciman who chaired each group. The membership was generally comprised of officials from the Home Office, Department of Health, Crown Prosecution Service, and the Scottish Office, psychiatrists, social researchers, and representatives from probation, police, social services, magistrates and drug agencies.

Although the response to HIV/AIDS was perceived to be radical, this was only possible because of powerful historical antecedents (Berridge, 1991). Harm minimisation was not a new or unusual discourse, but one which had a long history and strong tradition in Britain dating back to the Rolleston era. The response was therefore based on what had gone on before. As Berridge (1996a: 95) suggests, the AIDS epidemic re-emphasised and gave political legitimacy to issues in drugs policy which were already on the agenda within the drugs policy community. Alongside the penal response, drug services had been expanding through the CFI and becoming integrated with general health provision, harm minimisation was advocated, and partnership, prevention and 'community' were being re-emphasised.

The drive towards partnership, community and prevention

During the period 1986–93, there were further calls for improved partnership and collaboration between services and agencies around drug issues, a renewed stress on drugs prevention and moves to involve the community in tackling the drug problem. In 1989, the Home Office Drugs Prevention Initiative was established which involved setting up 20 local drug prevention teams throughout England, Scotland and Wales. The aim of these new structures was to involve all sectors of the community in tackling drugs and assist in the development of community initiatives (Home Office CDPU, 1993). Collaboration between agencies and services at local level also continued to be stressed through the DDAC structures. The interface between criminal justice agencies and other agencies in DDACs was becoming more apparent. For example, it was increasingly recognised that DDACs would have to engage with prisons particularly around HIV/AIDS issues because prisoners were seen to be a key population in relation to the transmission of the disease. The Department of Health (1988) suggested that a framework was required to enable local collaboration with prisons built either around the 'adoption' of prisons by local health agencies for health care services or with prison education services. Similarly, the ACMD (1991) made recommendations that the Probation Service should collaborate with health and local authorities regarding the treatment of drug using offenders and play a role in the preparation of and consultation on community-care plans.

Despite these numerous recommendations and moves towards joint working, the system of collaboration was not working effectively (Baker and Runicles, 1991; Dorn and South, 1994; Howard et al., 1994). Several problems associated with joint working were identified in a report by the London Research Centre and the National Local Authority Forum on Drug Misuse: some areas did not have functioning DDACs; membership was dominated by the health service; irregular attendance was common; support structures were weak; terms of reference were vague; there was little involvement in resource allocation decisions; difficulties arose over non-coterminous boundaries; seniority levels amongst members varied; there were difficulties in ensuring commitments to joint working; social services were not aware of drug issues; and DDACs had not been incorporated into the formal planning machinery (Baker and Runicles, 1991). In 1992, the Department of Health commissioned Roger Howard, an independent consultant at the time (now Chief Executive of Drugscope), to identify good practice and make recommendations for new collaborative arrangements to tackle drugs use. Howard et al. (1994: 9) proposed new partnership structures to replace the existing DDACs and predicted that the role of the criminal justice system would feature prominently in any future collaborative arrangements:

> The criminal justice system remains a key area of change for tackling drugs misuse, which statutory and voluntary agencies will need to address together. The boundaries of what constitutes enforcement and what constitutes prevention, treatment and care are being redrawn

Penal policy context: key attempts at reform 1986–93

During the latter half of the 1980s, the penal crisis continued, culminating in serious riots at Strangeways and other prisons in 1990. This was described by Sparks et al. (1996: 15) as the 'most drastic and public notorious event in the modern history of the prisons of England and Wales'. During the late 1980s and early 1990s, several attempts were made to manage and contain the crisis in British prisons. The emphasis on economy, effectiveness and efficiency continued and the discourses of managerialism and privatisation began to manifest themselves in more concrete and visible ways. For example, in 1987, the Fresh Start initiative was introduced which involved a fundamental overhaul of working arrangements for prison officers and management structures. By the late 1980s, the issue of prison privatisation was also gradually creeping onto the political agenda. In 1989, two remand prisons were handed over to the private sector to manage on an experimental basis. In 1992, Wolds remand prison on Humberside was contracted out. However, before it could be evaluated, an amendment to the 1991 Criminal Justice Act allowed for the extension of privatisation to the mainstream prison population (Ryan and Sim, 1998).

As discussed in the previous chapter, with the decline of the rehabilitative ideal, the 'just deserts' approach to sentencing moved to the forefront of penal policy (von Hirsch, 1985). Penal policy during the late 1980s and early 1990s was in the direction of making punishment proportionate to the gravity of the offence, making 'fair' punishment the main penal aim rather than the reform or rehabilitation of offenders, reserving imprisonment for serious offences, and substituting community penalties for short prison sentences for non-violent crimes (Hudson, 1993). During the period 1986–93, two central themes were operating within the discourse on justice: 'just deserts' and 'punishment in the community' (Collison, 1993). These themes and trends underpinned the Green Paper, *Punishment, Custody and the Community*, and the White Paper, *Crime, Justice and Protecting the Public*, culminating in the 1991 Criminal Justice Act which marked a significant shift in penal policy and a pragmatic response to the prison population crisis. The Act can be viewed as the outcome of careful deliberation and refinement of the relevant issues by civil servants who had consulted widely and engaged key interest groups in the debates (Faulkner, 1996; Downes and Morgan, 1997). By the late 1980s, the penal lobby was growing increasingly sophisticated in its structure and organisation and could not be ignored by policy-makers. For example, the Penal

Affairs Consortium (PAC) was formed in 1989 and consists of an alliance of diverse organisations including penal reform groups such as the Prison Reform Trust (PRT), NACRO, Howard League and Women in Prison as well as professional associations including the Prison Officer's Association (POA), the Prison Governor's Association, and the National Association of Probation Officers (NAPO). As Downes and Morgan (1997: 114) comment, such a combination of interests was 'previously unthinkable'.

1991 Criminal Justice Act

The 1991 Criminal Justice Act put forward a new sentencing framework which placed emphasis on proportionality, just deserts, retribution, incapacitation, and protecting the public. Prison would be reserved only for the most serious offenders, as it was considered ineffective in reforming the majority of prisoners and an 'expensive way of making bad people worse'(Home Office, 1990a: 6). The overall aim of the 1991 Criminal Justice Act was to reduce the use of custody, rather than tackling the 'crisis of legitimacy' which had been plaguing the penal system. As Hudson (1994: 294) argues, the 1991 Act prioritised 'acts' over individuals and legal facts over social facts as rehabilitation professionals lost power and sentencers moved to the forefront of the penal response.

With regard to drug offenders, the Act pursued a bifurcated approach allowing for harsh punishments for drugs traffickers and treatment and diversion from custody for less serious offenders with drug problems. Sentencers were enabled under the Act to attach an additional requirement to probation orders – that the offender should undergo treatment for drug or alcohol dependency. In theory this meant that more drug users would be brought into contact with the treatment services, thus locating this group of less serious drug using offenders outside the general framework of 'punishment in the community' and 'just deserts', by prioritising drug problems over crime problems (Collison, 1993).The Act also put forth new arrangements for local funding and partnership whereby local probation services were expected to develop agreements with the independent sector and other agencies on best practice in dealing with offenders in the community. Funding of voluntary organisations, some of which deal with drug issues, would be passed from the Home Office to local probation services. As a result, probation services would have more of a role in commissioning. However, research conducted by Lee (1994) suggests that within the first six months after commencement of the 1991 Act, very few conditions of drug treatment were made and it was debatable whether those which were imposed were actually being used as alternatives to custody. Various factors could have contributed to their low take-up rates including their lack of credibility amongst sentencers as a sentencing package for more serious offenders and the competition between the various types of community punishments; the financial constraints of both probation services and drug agencies; the problems around assessment and disclosure of drug problems amongst offenders and questions regarding the motivation of offenders towards treatment (Collison, 1993; Lee, 1994). In practice, the welfarism and treatment orientation of the 1991 Act was abandoned for increasing repression, punishment and criminalisation of addicted offenders and drug-related crime (Collison, 1993; Henham, 1994). Women, particularly foreign nationals working as drug 'mules', have become the victims of such policies as more and more are sentenced for drug-trafficking offences (see Green, 1991; 1996).

The Woolf inquiry

After the riots at Strangeways and other prisons in 1990, Lord Justice Woolf and Judge Stephen Tumin were called upon to conduct an inquiry into their causes. Although Woolf concluded that there was 'no single cause of riots and no simple solution or action which will prevent rioting' (Woolf, 1991: para. 9.23), he identified three requirements that must be met and balanced if the prison system was to remain stable: security, control and justice. The programme of change involved 12 main recommendations including improvements to prison management, new standards relating to overcrowding and sanitation, emphasis on prisoners maintaining links with their families and communities and improved standards of justice in prison. The report was greeted favourably across the political spectrum resulting in a consensus amongst politicians, civil servants, the media, most academics and penal reform groups. The report had 'transcended the divisions' between these groups and united them on the 'ideological terrain of penal reform' (Sim, 1994: 42). Others argued that Woolf's analysis was consistent with contemporary penal practice and discourse and did not offer any radical analysis of the prison system (see Hudson, 1993; Sim, 1994). In particular, Woolf failed to address the problems in women's prisons and the racism inherent within the system (Carlen and Tchaikovsky; 1996; Hudson, 1993). In addition, he failed to address the purposes of imprisonment in any comprehensive or detailed way. However, Woolf had placed the notion of 'justice' at the centre of his conceptual framework in an attempt to resolve the crisis of legitimacy within the prison system (Sparks, 1994: Sparks and Bottoms, 1995).

In terms of implementation, Woolf made it clear that his recommendations had to be taken together as one package. The Home Secretary, Kenneth Baker, announced some immediate reforms to letters, telephone calls, visits, home leave, and sanitation on receipt of the report in February 1991. The official response to the Woolf Report was contained in the White Paper, *Custody, Care and Justice* (Home Office, 1991c) which claimed the government had accepted all of Woolf 's proposals with the exception of parliamentary control on overcrowding which would be dealt with after the 1991 Criminal Justice Act was fully operational. However, the timetable for implementation was vague in relation to the main recommendations. In the summer of 1991, Baker announced that Woolf's agenda would take approximately 20 to 25 years to implement and made it clear that no extra resources would be devoted to implementing his recommendations. It is evident the government responded to the proposals in a 'pick and mix' fashion rather than comprehensively as Woolf had intended. Cavadino and Dignan (1992) identify their response as a two-speed approach with security measures, such as x-ray machines and metal detectors, in the fast lane and reforms such as improved regimes, the end of overcrowding and the adoption of enforceable standards in the slow lane.

Changes to the Prison Medical Service

As we saw in the previous chapter, the Prison Medical Service (PMS) had been long criticised as inadequate and often inhumane in its medical treatment of prisoners. It had been the subject of several official reports which called for urgent reform (Home Office, 1964; 1990c; 1990d; 1990e; House of Commons Social Services Committee, 1986; Woolf, 1991). In particular, medical treatment in prisons was not considered to be of a comparable standard to that provided in the community.

In April 1992, the Prison Medical Service was renamed the Health Care Service for Prisoners. The aims of the new service were to provide a total system of care dealing with the whole person and to promote general health rather than being solely focused on ill health (HM Prison Service, 1992). The new health service for prisoners was to be delivered through a multidisciplinary approach and to encompass physical and mental health, treatment and cure, training and education, conditions and regimes. This shift towards a more 'health' based service and the greater emphasis on multidisciplinary approaches provided the framework and context for the way in which drugs and HIV/AIDS were dealt with in the prison system. The opening up of the prison to outside agencies in the community had the potential to challenge the monopoly prison medical officers had over the care and treatment of prisoners with drug problems. Before exploring some of these issues, the next section will first examine the nature and extent of the 'problem' of drug use in prisons and how it was reconceptualised during the period 1986–93.

The end of the denial: reconceptualising the drugs 'problem' in prison

During the late 1980s and early 1990s, the drug problem in prison was reconceptualised and framed in new ways. The problem had progressed to the stage where it could no longer be denied nor ignored. The collusion around drugs became increasingly untenable due to a number of interlinked factors – changes in the drug problem in terms of incidence and severity, the HIV/AIDS crisis and fears of leakage into the general population, an emerging policy network around HIV and drug issues in prisons, and the growing research and evidence base. The drug problem *in* prisons was finally acknowledged reluctantly by the Prison Service. This process was referred to as the 'end of the denial' by informed members of the policy network around drug issues in prisons. As a director of a drug agency argued:

> *There was always an absolute denial that there was any drugs in prison ... Drugs are illegal therefore they don't exist. That went on right up until the early 1990s ... when there was an acknowledgement that there was a drug problem in the prison setting. Before, there was always a complete and total and utter denial, partly because no one really knew what to do about it. So if we pretend it is not there, it will just go away. But it didn't, it got bigger and bigger.* (Interview 04)

In terms of official indicators, the number of drug addicts and drug offenders in prison decreased in the latter half of the 1980s, but began to increase again by the 1990s. For example, the number of new addicts notified to the Home Office by prison medical officers fluctuated, decreasing from 1,102 in 1986 to 624 in 1989, but then increased steadily each year until 1993 when the number reached 1,941 (see Table A.1, Appendix). Similarly, the number of drug offenders sentenced to custody had decreased from 3,928 in 1986 to 3,268 in

1991, but then increased again to 4,835 in 1993 (see Table A.2, Appendix). Reflecting the greater use of cautioning for drug offenders, particularly for unlawful possession, the proportion of drug offenders sentenced to custody decreased progressively from 16 per cent in 1986 to 7 per cent in 1993 (Home Office Statistical Bulletin, 1994b). With the 'end of the denial' and the growing public acknowledgement of the drug problem, a director of a drug agency suggested that this caused the issue of drugs in prison to grow and perhaps take on its own momentum:

> *One of the consequences of public acknowledgement of things is that they increase in their incidence. Yet the objective of public acknowledgement is to try and start to control them. There's a symbiotic relationship between opening issues out and acknowledging them at a national level and the issue growing as an issue ... that's happened in prisons.* (Interview 08)

The increase in the extent of the drug problem in prisons was associated with heightened awareness of the issue and concern amongst drugs experts, civil servants and other professionals that the problem was becoming more serious with an increasing number of prisoners using drugs other than cannabis. Perceptions regarding the drugs 'problem' in prisons had shifted in terms of incidence and severity. As a civil servant commented:

> *In the late 1980s, there was an acknowledgement that drugs were in prison, but the perception was that it was all cannabis ... Although the Service didn't admit it, the general philosophy was that this contributes to a quiet jail and wasn't causing a very great problem. I remember at that time an obsessive belief that somehow as a matter of choice prisoners were not trying to smuggle anything else into the prison other than cannabis. That was the major change ... a realism with which we now view this.* (Interview 14b)

Those working within prisons suggested that heroin use had become accepted as a part of prison life. In a sense, it had become 'normalised'. The increased use of drugs, particularly class A drugs, was beginning to pose a threat to the prison environment in terms of order and control problems. Drugs were seen to be the source of more violence, bullying and intimidation within prisons (HM Chief Inspector of Prisons, 1992). A penal reformer recalled that as drug use became 'routine' in prisons, it became a problem of control and order:

> *You can't authoritatively measure it, but the use of drugs in prisons – the routine use of drugs – grew massively in the late 1980s, early 1990s. The interest in what to do about it was to a significant extent a reflection of what was happening. Drug use was becoming routine in prisons ... it offended against common sense ideas of 'law and order' and it was associated with intimidation and violence ... it presented control problems. It certainly was a control issue.* (Interview 24)

As discussed in the previous chapter, both illegal and legal drugs were viewed as functional and used as control mechanisms within the prison system during the early 1980s. During 1986–93, drugs were perceived to be more problematic as they became a major part of the informal prison economy. Sparks et al. (1996: 122) define the 'informal economy' as an endemic control problem which consists of the following activities: gambling, money lending, the trading of goods, importation of drugs, manufacture of alcohol and other 'sub rosa' trading. Staff and prisoners consider these activities to be a part of prison life, not always a matter for serious concern and may contribute to the smooth running of an institution. Major threats to prison order result from indebtedness and extortion, rather than from the activities themselves. Staff must therefore strike a delicate balance when tackling these activities as they risk destabilising the prison environment or losing legitimacy (Sparks et al., 1996: 122). However, the link between HIV/AIDS and needle sharing within prisons highlighted the problem with 'turning a blind eye', the collusion and the failure to tackle the problem of injecting drug use which was seen not only as a threat to the prison population, but also to the outside community.

HIV/AIDS crisis

Another factor, perhaps the most important, which was linked to greater awareness and the reconceptualisation of the drug problem in prison was the HIV/AIDS crisis. The first prisoners in England and Wales known to be HIV positive or to have an AIDS diagnosis were received into the prison system during the period 1984–6. The number of known reported HIV positive prisoners remained fairly stable and averaged between 40 to 70 per month from 1986–91. During 1992–3, this figure dropped to an average of 30 to 35 cases. By April 1995, a total of 449 known HIV positive prisoners had been reported since 1985, 30 prisoners with an AIDS diagnosis were notified, and 12 prisoners with an AIDS-related illness had died during their sentences (HM Prison Service, 1995c: 7).

The monotony of the prison regime produces tensions which can lead to particular forms of 'escapism' such as homosexual sex amongst heterosexual men and drug use (Thomas, 1990). There are special conditions operating within the prison environment which have implications for the risk of HIV transmission both inside prisons and on release in the community. If a syringe is smuggled into a prison, then it is likely to be widely shared amongst prisoners (Dolan et al., 1990; Stimson et al., 1988; Turnbull et al., 1991; Covell et al., 1992). Homosexual activity does occur between prisoners, some of whom lead heterosexual lives on the outside (ACMD, 1988; Harding, 1990). Tattooing, another high-risk activity in relation to HIV, also occurs in prisons. Moreover self-injury and suicide attempts carry HIV risks and are frequent occurrences in prison (Liebling and Krarup, 1993). By its nature the prison population also contains a disproportionate number of people who are likely to be at greater risk of HIV infection: young, sexually active, drug users, drug injectors, prostitutes and violent offenders (Dolan et al., 1990; Harding, 1990; HM Prison Service, 1995c). The HIV/AIDS crisis provided further disincentives for drug users to seek help because of fear that they might be coerced into taking an HIV test, segregated from the rest of the population, and subject to stricter security, searching procedures and hostile treatment from other prisoners and prison staff (Thomas, 1994).

As we saw in the earlier section on drugs policy, drug injecting prisoners were considered to be a key population in terms of HIV/AIDS prevention, education and intervention (ACMD, 1988; 1989). The main concern was the threat of transmission to the general population. Just as HIV funding allowed for a number of developments in the drugs field, such as the move away from abstinence-based approaches and the opening up of a wider range of drug treatment options, it also enabled drug agencies to expand their work in prisons and provided the thrust for the interest in the area (Exeter Drugs Project, 1990; Parole Release Scheme, 1991; Hamer, 1998). Although drug agencies had been working with prisoners for several years, the prison authorities showed little interest in the nature of the work they were doing as this would imply that they should be recognising the problems, developing effective strategies and providing resources to deal with the problem. There was still an underlying resistance by the Prison Service to fully acknowledge the problem of drugs and high-risk behaviour in prisons and implications for policy and practice. A director of a drug agency described the situation in these terms:

> *We always had this sort of 'Cinderella' existence really. We went in, people knew we did things, but people didn't want to know what we did, because if they did know what we did, then they'd have to do something about what we did. There was this whole sort of charade that was played out.* (Interview 10)

On the other hand, many groups had a vested interest in highlighting or 'talking up' the HIV issue in prisons as it provided new opportunities for funding and an expansion of their remit into the prison system:

> *There are flavours of the year. There was HIV/AIDS when it was the flavour of the year. This meant it attracted grants. We used to call it 'positively funded' ... Drugs – the war on drugs – became a hot public issue. Groups see the opportunities for funding and so it was in their interest to talk it up.* (Interview 29 with penal reformer)

The advent of HIV/AIDS eventually widened the interest around drug issues in prison. A policy network began to form around the issue which lobbied for acknowledgement of the problem and a response from the Prison Service. The key groups involved in this policy network around HIV and drugs included members of the ACMD (1988; 1989; 1991), drug treatment agencies (Trace, 1990), medical professionals (Farrell and Strang, 1991), penal reform groups (Prison Reform Trust, 1988; 1991), probation officers (Fletcher, 1990), HIV/AIDS organisations, health authorities, and social researchers who had been attempting to conduct research on the problem. The issue had also been flagged up during the Woolf Inquiry (Woolf, 1991) and by Judge Tumin in his role as Chief Inspector of Prisons (HM Chief Inspector of Prisons, 1992). There was also interest in AIDS in prison at the international level. For example, the Council of Europe sponsored a study of policy and practice in 17 European countries (Council of Europe, 1987; Harding, 1987) and the World Health Organisation also convened a consultation on the prevention and control of AIDS in prison in 1987 (WHO, 1987). It was mainly external interest, rather than internal interest in the issue which initially was driving forward policy development. As a spokesperson from a professional association argued:

> *All drug policies were driven by concern about HIV and AIDS then and prison was seen as being a major route of transmission back into the*

> *mainstream population. That's what made the medics interested. That's what made the drugs world interested. That meant that health authorities and treatment services wanted to get involved in prisons ... The drive came from that direction rather than from within prisons.* (Interview 21)

However, there is also evidence that civil servants working in the Directorate of Prison Medical Services at Prison Service Headquarters were pressuring for more systematic information on aspects of HIV/AIDS in prisons and for a more strategic approach. In particular, Len Curran, a principal psychologist, had written a number of key reports advocating change (see Curran and Morrissey, 1989; Curran 1991a; 1991b; 1991c; 1991d; 1992).

The growing research/evidence base

No official, systematic research on the extent and nature of high-risk behaviours *in* prisons, particularly on homosexuality or drug use, had been undertaken during this period. Reflecting the collusion around drugs and the reluctance to admit that drugs were being used in prison, as well as the general problems of gaining access to conduct research in prisons, researchers had been repeatedly denied access to prisons to conduct such research throughout the 1980s (Thomas, 1990; Pearson, 1990). Although there had been pressure for systematic information on HIV/AIDS issues, Ministers argued that the problem was small, under control, and research in this area would be fraught with methodological difficulties associated with sampling, ethics, self-report and the veracity of inmates' accounts (Curran, 1991a). Rumours that research on high-risk behaviours in prisons had been conducted, but suppressed were circulated within the policy network (see also Berridge, 1996a: 225). Illicit drug taking and, arguably, homosexual sex in prisons constituted disciplinary offences for which any prisoner who took part in these activities was liable to be punished. There was therefore no official recognition from the government that drugs or homosexual sex were significant 'problems' within prisons. As Thomas (1990: 2) argues, the lack of evidence and the formal, legalistic reaction allowed for an 'official' discourse to emerge which suggested that the incidence of homosexual activity, drug use and drug injecting were minimal and therefore the threat of HIV was not a major problem and did not require radical action.

By the early 1990s, another set of data and an 'unofficial' discourse were also beginning to emerge which questioned and challenged the 'official' discourse. Researchers eventually managed to gain limited access to prisons and to samples of ex-prisoners which enabled them to begin to construct a picture of the problem. Research began to show that a substantial proportion of prisoners had been dependent on drugs prior to imprisonment (Maden et al., 1990; 1991); illegal drugs were available in prisons (HM Chief Inspector of Prisons, 1992; Turnbull et al., 1994); drug use in custody was fairly widespread (Turnbull et al., 1991), injecting and sharing needles were occurring within prisons (Stimson et al., 1988; Donoghoe et al., 1989; Dolan et al., 1990; Dye and Issacs, 1991; Carvell and Hart, 1990; Kennedy et al., 1991; Turnbull et al., 1991; Bird et al., 1992; 1993; Power et al., 1992; and Covell et al., 1993); the number of needles and syringes found in prisons had increased consistently between the years 1985 and 1989 (Turnbull et al., 1991); and the first reported outbreak of HIV infection in a prison in Britain was reported at Glenochil prison in Scotland in 1993 (Christie, 1993). In terms of homosexual activity, there was still a lack of evidence. However, based on reports from prison staff and ex-prisoners, Curran and Morrissey (1989) estimated that between ten and fifty per cent of the long-term male prison population may engage in homosexual activity at some time during sentence. In relation to tattooing, Dolan et al. (1991) found that seven per cent of a total of 98 drug injectors reported sharing tattooing equipment when they were in prison.

Much of the existing research and evidence quoted above has focused on male prisoners. There has been a real lack of attention paid to needs and circumstances of female prisoners. Another limitation of the research is that much of it has been based on small sample sizes and samples of ex-prisoners. Despite its methodological flaws, this research played an important role in raising awareness of the problems in prison and placing these issues on the policy agenda. Curran (1991a: 18), a civil servant in the Directorate of Prison Medical Services, conceded:

> The department has been nervous of research into HIV seroprevalence and into risk behaviour in prison. In retrospect such an approach has merely served to attract criticism from a number of influential and vocal sources. The research has proceeded outside and has suffered from sampling problems and small sample sizes. This has not deterred wide dissemination of the results and has heightened rather than decreased speculation on risk behaviours.

The media also played a role in constructing both HIV/AIDS and drug use as problems in prisons by heightening interest and making these issues more visible. In 1989, the BBC produced a Panorama programme entitled *The Killer Inside*, which focused on drug use in prisons, needle sharing and HIV/AIDS. The reporter, Robin Denselow, interviewed prisoners and staff in Wandsworth, Saughton, and Stafford prisons. The interviews revealed that drug injectors were sharing needles in prisons. One prisoner claimed they had two sets of 'works' between 30 prisoners, while another prisoner who was HIV positive was sharing a needle with 20 other prisoners who were aware he was infected with the virus. In many ways, this programme amplified the issues of drugs and HIV/AIDS (Cohen, 1972), but it also helped to highlight the plight and treatment of HIV positive prisoners and the lack of policy response. Members of the policy network recalled that this was a particularly powerful programme at the time and had much impact in terms of raising awareness around the issues and placing them on the policy agenda.

This growing research and evidence base corresponds to the 'enlightenment' model of research utilisation (Weiss, 1986), whereby a body of evidence accumulates over time eventually sensitising policy-makers to new issues and shaping the framing and conceptualisation of problems. It also corresponds to the 'interactive' model where research, information, and data are pooled by a diverse range of actors such as civil servants, journalists, interest groups, practitioners and professionals in order to make sense of the problem. The research was used by the policy network to pressure for a different response in relation to the problems of drugs and HIV transmission in prisons (Berridge, 1996a) and to force a public acknowledgement that drugs were being used in prisons. Once this information was published and in the public sphere, it meant that the problem could no longer be denied and ignored by the Prison Service or the government. As a spokesperson from a professional association argued, it was no longer politically possible to deny the existence of a problem:

> *once the thing becomes public, once you say there are people using drugs in prison, you then get a political dynamic happening. The professionals are quite happy for people to be using drugs in prison as long as it's cannabis, as long as they're not injecting. But politically it becomes untenable for the government to allow prisoners to engage in illegal activity while they're supposedly serving a sentence. That is unacceptable to Daily Mail-driven public opinion. It then becomes unacceptable for politicians. That ratchets the awareness up that much more.* (Interview 21)

The interest around the drug problem in prison reflected the preoccupation with drugs in the outside community. Problems such as drugs and HIV/AIDS, however, appear to be subject to time lags or delays before they manifest themselves within the prison environment. This is linked to the initial denial of the problems and the speed at which the Prison Service deals with issues. Once the Prison Service acknowledged the drug problem, they were forced to 'catch up' in their response to it. A director of a drug agency recalled that this was a slow process:

> *There was sort of a 'catch-up' phase where prisons themselves hadn't recognised that they had an issue around drugs and they had a very steep learning curve to navigate ... It wasn't a problem they wanted to believe they had. How they might respond to it and what the resource implications of responding to it might be – that was a slow process.* (Interview 28)

The response to the drugs 'problem' in prisons

The period from the late 1980s to 1993 was described by one key policy actor as a time when a 'mood was developing' in terms of responding to the drug problem in prisons. More formal and explicit policy development began with the statement of policy on the throughcare of drug users in prison in 1987 which carried through some of the issues highlighted by the policy network which had formed around treatment and throughcare issues during the earlier phase. This was followed by a more comprehensive manual of policy guidelines entitled *Caring for Drug Users* in 1991. The HIV/AIDS crisis also resulted in policy development which intersected with prisons drugs policy. The next sections will explore the policy response to drugs and then examine the response to HIV/AIDS.

Treatment and throughcare policy: Policy statement on the throughcare of drug users in prisons 1987

Following the interest generated by the ACMD and the policy network around throughcare issues during the early 1980s, a statement of policy and associated guidelines on the throughcare of drug users in prison was issued by the Director of Prison Medical Services to all managing medical officers in 1987 (HM Prison Service, 1987). Although there was recognition that all prison staff could play a role in the throughcare, a more co-ordinated approach was advocated particularly between prison medical officers and seconded prison probation officers. The content of the statement did not focus on specific goals of the Prison Service in relation to throughcare, but was mainly concerned with loose guidelines regarding practice and specifying the responsibilities of the key actors involved. Prison governors were given overall responsibility for ensuring that a coherent system was established to deal with drug users. Medical officers were responsible for identifying and assessing drug users on reception to custody; arranging withdrawal programmes in accordance with their own clinical judgement; maintaining medical oversight throughout the prisoner's sentence; and advising on further drug treatment support through outside agencies or self-help groups. Prison probation officers were responsible for continuing care and support throughout prisoners' sentences, overall throughcare, and follow-up treatment and support on release. The medical officer and probation officer were to develop an effective working relationship and endeavour to communicate and liaise effectively over the care and support of drug using prisoners (HM Prison Service, 1987).

In practice, however, these throughcare guidelines were not fully implemented across the prison system. In a study conducted by National Association of Probation Officers (NAPO), probation officers indicated that the guidelines had not been acted upon and the inertia came from prison governors (Fletcher, 1990). The ACMD (1988: 63) found that the use of methadone and other drugs to alleviate withdrawal symptoms varied between prisons. Since the 1980 ACMD report, there was no evidence of any improvements in relation to drugs advice and counselling or the expansion of therapeutic programmes in prisons. Furthermore, voluntary agencies were still experiencing difficulties gaining access to undertake drug work in some prisons. Although the guidelines on throughcare placed great emphasis on the work of the probation service, there was evidence of seconded prison probation officers having very limited resources, experience and training to deal with drug users (ACMD, 1988: 63).

Policy on treatment: *Caring for Drug Users* 1991

In 1991, a manual entitled *Caring for Drug Users* was prepared by the Advisory Group for Drug Education, a multidisciplinary group of experts from the Prison Service and external drug agencies and organisations. There was growing recognition of the variations in service provision throughout the prison system and that any effective drug work was 'locally inspired and led' (HM Prison Service, 1991a: 2). The aim of policy was to build upon these efforts across the Prison Service and to make the most of 'the opportunity presented by imprisonment to help drug users break or modify their habit' (HM Prison Service, 1991a: 2). The manual included guidelines for assessment and identification of drug users, detoxification, treatment and counselling, general health care and lifestyles, harm minimisation, throughcare, and liaison with community agencies. A multidisciplinary response was advocated which involved all prison staff including prison medical officers, probation officers, prison officers, psychologists, education officers, governors as well as specialist groups and agencies in the community. The aim was to create a positive climate in which drug users would reveal their drug problems and seek help.

Under these new guidelines, it was clear however that the quality and type of care for drug using prisoners was not congruent with what they would have received in the community. The legacy of the Rolleston report and the discourse of less eligibility in relation to the treatment of drug users in the prison system endured. Ross et al. (1994) argued that the 1991 guidelines for dealing with drug users in custody breached normal standards of professional ethical care. For example, drug addicts in prison were much less likely to be receiving treatment with a notifiable drug (i.e. methadone) than their counterparts in the community. In many cases, prisoners receiving methadone treatment on the outside were not given the opportunity to continue their treatment within prisons. Where methadone was offered in prison, it was provided on an accelerated seven day regimen (HM Prison Service, 1991a, sec. 2: 4). The accelerated withdrawal programme does not replicate the physiological rate of withdrawal and can cause withdrawal symptoms and stress to patients (Ross et al., 1994). Moreover, strip cells were often used for prisoners who were addicted to opiates. Such short regimens and harsh treatment may lead prisoners to use illegal drugs in prisons. Ross et al. (1994: 1094) argued that the monopoly which the PMS had over medical provision in prisons, the non-standard treatment regimens and the abuse of the concept of clinical judgement left 'the prisoners disenfranchised to the point of suffering serious avoidable morbidity'.

At the same time as the manual was published, revised throughcare guidelines were also issued (HM Prison Service, 1991b). Re-emphasising the key roles of the probation service and prison medical officers, these were similar to those issued in 1987, but they placed much more emphasis on utilising a multidisciplinary approach involving all prison staff. As discussed in the earlier section on partnerships in drugs policy, prisons were also encouraged to become involved in wider drug partnerships in the community. Prisons were expected to be represented on DDACs where appropriate so that prisons could access local multidisciplinary staff training provision and develop contacts with the providers of services (HM Prison Service, 1991a, Appendix 2).

Despite the key roles allocated to prison probation officers and prison medical officers, the HM Inspectorate of Probation found that prison probation officers were offering very little and prison medical officers were playing only a marginal role in the provision of drug services (Home Office, 1993a). In prisons where drug work was occurring, outside drug agencies were playing the leading role in responding to the needs of prisoners. A director from a drug agency suggested that by the early 1990s, a UK model of prison drug work had emerged. This referred to the work being done by the Exeter Drugs Project in the south-west, the Parole Release Scheme in the south-east, and the York Drugs Resource Scheme in Yorkshire (see Parole Release Scheme, 1989; Tamlyn and Billings, 1995; Hamer, 1998). The model was described by a director of a drug agency as follows:

> *Each of these programmes developed independently, but when we did come together and talked about it, we realised we were doing the same thing. We were putting a large amount of emphasis on pre-release work with particular concerns regarding tolerance and overdose ... We then got caught up in the HIV/AIDS scare ... There was a fair amount of group-work. The model for counselling was very much around brief interventions ... There was an underlying consensus that prison wasn't the best place to deal with your underlying problems which may have precipitated drug use, but it may be the place where you start that journey and recognise how long the journey is and where you can go to complete that. The model used by all those agencies was about very high turnover and fairly brief work, trying to reach as many people as possible.* (Interview 26a)

This model of drug work, however, was not universally applied throughout the prison system. It existed only in a few areas in the country and depended on the innovative work of particular drug agencies, rather than any centrally driven policy. As Roger Ralli, the Deputy Chair of the Advisory Group for Drug Education, conceded, in order for the 1991 guidelines to be put into practice across the prison system, there was a need for extensive staff training and support and commitment from prison governors (Ralli, 1994). In prisons where this guidance was implemented, the quality of services to drug users improved.

However, the ACMD (1996) found that implementation was patchy and not all prison staff were aware of the existence of the manual. There was no centrally co-ordinated activity or provision. Similarly, the HM Inspectorate of Probation found that drug service provision was very ad hoc, piecemeal, and disorganised and there was a lack of an overall drugs strategy in prisons (Home Office, 1993a: 75).

It is interesting to note that at this point in time security measures to tackle drug smuggling, drug trafficking and drug use in prisons were dealt with separately under security policies. There was no overall policy or strategy which connected drug control measures with treatment and throughcare measures. The focus was solely on the treatment and 'caring' aspects of dealing with drugs. This was to change significantly in later prison drugs policy development from 1994 onwards. In effect, the response during this phase was essentially about the Prison Service reluctantly acknowledging the problem of drug use in prisons, but not initiating any action which would embarrass them or lead to public disapproval. It was an attempt to address some of the problems highlighted by the policy network around treatment and throughcare. However, it was not an integrated strategy which would address the drug 'problem' in prisons holistically.

Managing and containing the HIV/AIDS crisis in prisons

The majority of prison staff and prisoners reacted with fear, panic and antagonism towards the first group of known HIV positive prisoners (HM Prison Service, 1995c). The panic around the disease was magnified within the prison environment. The problem of HIV shifted from being primarily a medical issue to a management problem for the Prison Service. A civil servant recalled this shift:

> *It was the reaction of the staff to them that made it quite clear that this was something that had to be dealt with. Up to that point, people assumed that it could be dealt with in a reasonable way as a medical concern. It was only when staff reaction became so vivid, that in fact, it was realised that it wasn't just a medical problem, but that it was a management problem.* (Interview 31)

In 1986, the prison chaplain at Chelmsford died of an AIDS-related illness and his death sparked off industrial action by prison staff. As discussed in the previous section on penal policy, industrial relations between the Prison Officers' Association (POA) and prison management continued to be fraught with difficulty during this period due to the introduction of Fresh Start in 1987. It was within this context that at the AGM of the POA in 1987, a resolution was passed which called for the compulsory screening of all prisoners for HIV. It was argued that this would enable prison officers to protect themselves from the virus if they knew which prisoners were HIV positive. However, the then Director of the Prison Medical Service, Dr John Kilgour, decided against compulsory screening and maintained that any HIV testing should be voluntary, carried out only with the prisoner's consent, and with the provision of pre- and post-test counselling. Because many of the management decisions had been devolved to local level, there was evidence and rumour that screening was nevertheless taking place in some prisons (Berridge, 1996a). Similarly, Turnbull et al. (1991) found that some 'high-risk' groups, including drug users, were being segregated until they agreed to be tested and could prove they were negative.

Viral Infectivity Restrictions (VIR)

One of the methods of dealing with HIV positive prisoners was to subject them to Viral Infectivity Restrictions (VIR). These guidelines were originally developed in 1985 for prisoners with Hepatitis B to protect others within the institution from this highly contagious disease. The type of restrictions placed on infected prisoners was left to the discretion of the medical staff, but they could be segregated in a separate unit or isolated cells. Moreover, their regimes could also be restricted in terms of association with other prisoners and participation in work and recreation activities (HM Prison Service, 1995c: 7). In May 1986, the Prison Service produced a confidentiality code for prisoners subject to VIR. In theory, this meant that prison staff with an operational 'need to know' were informed of a prisoner's VIR status, while the actual diagnosis (i.e. HIV or Hepatitis B) remained confidential. However, the definition of 'need to know' remained vague and in practice, confidentiality was not preserved (Padel, 1990). In some cases, VIR status was stamped on prisoner's files and the code was also extended to those outside the prison including court staff, police and others involved in the criminal justice system (Prison Reform Trust, 1988). Due to the fear and panic amongst prison staff and other prisoners, VIR status became synonymous with HIV (Bright, 1995).The effect of VIR and the lack of confidentiality meant that prisoners feared revealing that they belonged to a high-risk group (i.e. drug users, prostitutes, homosexuals or haemophiliacs) due to the treatment they might receive. A drug worker recalled the difficulties in providing drug services in prisons at this time:

> *We had horrendous difficulties if we had an HIV person and it became widespread public knowledge in the late 1980s ... There was a lot of ignorance around – a lot of fear ... There was pressure at that time to disclose if someone had revealed an HIV status or even if they revealed they were [in] a high-risk group ... The way they identified HIV inmates was to put yellow and red tape around their files ... And of course, that would be in the landing office and many people got badly hurt when their status became known amongst the other inmates.* (Interview 06)

There had been several calls to end the use of VIR by various experts and organisations (WHO, 1987; ACMD, 1988; 1989; Farrell and Strang, 1991; Woolf, 1991). By 1991, the Prison Service recommended that HIV positive prisoners who were otherwise healthy should not be segregated, but kept on normal landings. However, medical officers and prison management retained the power to segregate HIV positive prisoners 'for reasons of good order, discipline, health or safety' (Home Office, 1991a, annex A, para. 18). The application of this policy was strongly localised (Berridge, 1996a). For example, on the K1 wing of Wandsworth prison, VIR and segregation still operated and prisoners were kept in a basement with little time out of their cells, whereas Bristol prison had rejected VIR, ensured full confidentiality to HIV positive prisoners and integrated them on normal landings. The practices at Wandsworth prison had been condemned in 1991 by the Woolf Inquiry as a 'travesty of justice' (Woolf, 1991: para. 360). Although there had been many calls for reform in relation to VIR, one third of prisons in England and Wales were still segregating HIV positive prisoners (ACMD, 1993). The manner in which HIV positive prisoners were dealt with in the prison system illustrates the Prison Service's preoccupation in dealing with high-risk groups rather than tackling high-risk behaviour.

By 1986, the Prison Service had established an AIDS Advisory Committee to advise the Director of Health Care on all matters relating to HIV in prison. Its membership included outside agencies, independent experts on HIV and prison staff. The Committee developed a strategy which aimed to: prevent people from becoming infected; prevent onward transmission of the virus; minimise the social stigma of HIV and provide proper medical treatment, support and care to those with HIV (HM Prison Service, 1995c: 10).

Training and education

Prisoners were excluded from the general public education effort on HIV which took place in the community, leaving them with little factual information about the virus. When the leaflets, entitled 'AIDS – Don't Die of Ignorance', were distributed to every household in the country, prisons and hospitals were not included in the initial distribution. Parliamentary questions were tabled regarding this matter and eventually the leaflets were made available (Prison Reform Trust, 1988). However, this information did not address the specific concerns of prisoners. In August 1987, a leaflet was specifically designed for prisoners, entitled 'AIDS: Information for People in Prison'. Because drug injecting and homosexual sex contravene prison rules, these issues were not addressed adequately in the leaflets and distribution to all prisons and prisoners did not occur (ACMD, 1988; Prison Reform Trust, 1988).

Prison was still being regarded as an 'opportunity' to make contact with drug users, draw them into treatment and educate them towards safer practices (ACMD, 1988). Education and training were regarded as the cornerstones of the Prison Service's response to the HIV/AIDS problem in prisons (HM Prison Service, 1995c: 21). In 1987, the AIDS Advisory Committee developed 'AIDS Inside', a training package for prison staff consisting of a video, leaflet and training manual. In 1989, a similar package, entitled 'AIDS: Inside and Out', was developed for prisoners. These training and educational efforts had limited impact, however (Turnbull et al., 1994; Berridge, 1996a); and targets for the education of operational staff and inmates had not been achieved in many institutions (Curran, 1991b). Trace (1990) argued that few staff were interested in HIV training sessions and for those who were interested, it was difficult for them to watch the videos due to other duties. The video for prisoners explored what was defined as 'risky behaviour', but failed to acknowledge that these activities actually occurred in prisons. In a section on how to protect yourself after release, the leaflet provided advice on safer sex and injecting practices (Trace, 1990). Thus, the focus was on activities on release, rather than those within prison. The ACMD (1988) recommended that private and confidential counselling should be provided on risk reduction covering activities both whilst in prison and on release. The ACMD felt it most appropriate that outside agencies undertake this work rather than prison medical officers. The educational package also failed to address the needs of women, young people, those without English as their first language and those with learning difficulties. The Prison Service, however, did not view this as a matter for concern and recommended that these particular groups could be dealt with at a local level (HM Prison Service, 1995c: 27).

In 1991, the Prison Service issued a circular instruction indicating that all prisons should set up multidisciplinary working arrangements to deal with HIV/AIDS (Home Office, 1991a). This was linked to a training manual, *HIV and AIDS: A Multidisciplinary Approach in the Prison Environment*, and three specialist training courses. These training courses included an HIV update for medical officers, an HIV counselling course for prison staff, and a multidisciplinary course for prison managers. The multidisciplinary approach was to involve medical officers, psychologists, probation officers, health care staff, prison officers, educationalists, and the prison chaplaincy. Curran (1991b: 17) suggests that there were several factors which mitigated against such an approach and the implementation of the strategy: HIV was often viewed as a medical problem by operational managers and staff; there were several competing priorities within the prison system and a large number of new initiatives (i.e. Fresh Start, Prison Service re-organisation, suicide prevention, and sex offender programmes); there was a lack of good information regarding prevalence of HIV and risk behaviour; and the numbers of prisoners known to be HIV positive was low.

Harm minimisation

As discussed earlier, the advent of HIV/AIDS in the community was eventually followed by an expansion of services for drug users, the adoption of the principles of harm minimisation, and a broad-based community approach involving doctors, pharmacists, police, social workers, and probation officers. However, prisons were excluded from these changes in practice and the liberal consensus which had been achieved (Farrell and Strang, 1991; Berridge 1996a). The incorporation of harm minimisation as a drug treatment philosophy had been met with difficulties within the prison environment resulting in inadequate choice and standards of care in relation to HIV positive prisoners compared to similar patients in the community (Young and McHale, 1992). One of the main factors in the adoption of the 'abstinence' based approach was the resistance to publicly acknowledging that either drug taking or homosexual sex is taking place in prisons. To adopt a harm minimisation and risk reduction philosophy would mean condoning two illegal activities in the prison environment. This was seen by the Conservative government, in particular, to be politically unacceptable. The Home Office's reliance on 'legal formalism' placed prisoners at greater risk from HIV/AIDS than the general public (Thomas, 1990: 90).

In the area of prison drugs policy, it is evident that the 'conflict between principle and pragmatism is most acute.' (MacGregor, 1998a: 149). Traditionally, the criminal justice system has viewed drugs as a cause of criminality and a crime in itself, not as an individual health or public health concern. This criminal justice perspective towards the control and criminalisation of drug users has constrained prison governors and others from incorporating harm minimisation into drug policies (Hayes, 1991). The definition of harm minimisation in prisons was described by a civil servant as being different to that in the community:

> *We probably still encounter a little lack of clarity by what we mean by harm minimisation. Because on the streets, [it] means needle exchanges and things like that. Now we know we're not going in the foreseeable future down the route of needle exchange.* (Interview 19)

Within the prison environment, the definition of harm minimisation could be extended to include more than just safe injecting practices, safe sex and methadone prescribing. Similar to Pearson's arguments that the principles of harm reduction should have wider application, (Pearson, 1992b), a civil servant argued that in practice the term needed to be associated with providing a safe environment for prisoners in terms of the violence and bullying around the drugs trade:

> *Harm reduction is also about going back to the violence thing [and] is linked to helping prisoners, particularly young offenders, get through their sentence safely ... Many governors [who] are aware will not say, 'don't take drugs because they'll harm you', because they realise that's not going to have impact on recreational users. What they will probably say is, 'For goodness sakes, don't borrow money to buy drugs. That's the real danger.'* (Interview 14b)

In the community, policies have vigorously promoted safe sex practices and the use of condoms in the prevention of HIV. The Prison Service, however, initially resisted the introduction of condoms mainly on legal grounds. Under the Sexual Offences Act 1956 (as amended in 1967 and 1994), homosexual sex is considered legal only if it occurs in a private place between two consenting men aged 18 or over. It is legally unclear whether a prison cell constitutes a private place as required by the Act. If a cell is not private then homosexual activity is unlawful. This issue has been the focus of much debate between the

Prison Service and its legal advisers. The Prison Service has argued that the provision of condoms would mean that illegal acts were being condoned. However, the ACMD (1988: 65) pointed out that it was difficult 'to see how allowing access to condoms in prison could be regarded as condoning unlawful acts when placed in the context of the public health considerations involved.' Other arguments were also made by the Prison Service that condoms do not provide adequate protection in anal sex; condoms would increase the incidence of homosexual activity; there was a lack of evidence that high-risk behaviour occurs; staff would object; and condoms could be used for other purposes such as drug smuggling (Curran, 1991c).

In other European prison systems, including France, Denmark, Germany and the Netherlands, condoms have been made available to prisoners (British Medical Journal, 1995). There have been various calls from outside bodies and organisations for the provision of condoms in prison (WHO, 1987; ACMD, 1988; 1989; Trace, 1990; Prison Reform Trust, 1991). Curran and Morrissey (1989) also found that the majority of prisoners and staff at Wormwood Scrubs wished to see condoms provided. Based on the House of Lords judgment in *Gillick* v. *West Norfolk*, if prison medical officers were providing the means of protection, they could not be held responsible for encouraging an illegal act. In effect, the provision of condoms in prisons was seen to be a medical matter. Therefore during the period 1986–93, the prison policy on condoms was that they could be provided subject to the clinical judgement of the prison medical officer. In practice, however, condoms were not freely available. Many prison medical officers refused to view them as a prescription and prisoners were reluctant to request them.

Similar to the issue of condoms, the provision of needle exchanges in prison has not been seen as appropriate by the Prison Service (HM Prison Service, 1995c) or by the ACMD (ACMD, 1988). Needle exchanges could be seen as encouraging drugs use and contradictory to the duties of prison staff to detect the smuggling of drugs into prisons and prevent drug use in custody. It was felt that 'the conflict between encouraging prisoners to use an exchange scheme and detecting illicit drug use would have no easy resolution' (HM Prison Service, 1995c: 30). Arguments have also been put forward that needles could be used as weapons within the prison environment (Trace, 1990; British Medical Journal, 1995). However, stopping syringes and drugs getting into prisons means that there will be more sharing of existing ones and thus, a greater threat of HIV transmission.

Because the Prison Service adopted an abstinence-based approach to drugs, this set the scene for conflict between the prison administration and the drug agencies who may be working within a harm minimisation framework. There are clear conflicts and contradictions within drugs work in the prison environment which are contained and managed by the drug agencies involved. A civil servant indicated the difficulties from their perspective:

> *It's a hard one for us in working with the agencies who quite properly would talk about harm minimisation approaches. It's hard for us to say that means that some of our prisoners are taking drugs some of the time because it's an illegal activity that we have some difficulty in countenancing. It's a rubbing point between work agencies can do and our approaches to it. Sometimes those things don't come together very neatly.* (Interview 14a)

However, drug workers have been forced to find ways of delivering realistic strategies within the prison environment:

> *We can actually work with harm reduction providing we're working towards providing an abstinence-based regime. You can get away with it ... The people on the ground are realists. They know that they need something being done.* (Interview 10)

> *Obviously we were worried about needle sharing in prisons and addressing that through harm reduction techniques ... There was a tacit condoning by the Prison Service that they intentionally would not be in the room when we were talking about harm reduction.* (Interview 26a)

These contradictions between policy and practice have allowed the Prison Service to publicly advocate a tough, abstinence-based policy towards drugs, while drug agencies are working behind the scenes in the privacy of the prison ensuring harm minimisation is taking place without the support of the institution, adequate resources or an 'official' policy framework. The Prison Service has been reviewing its policies on risk reduction and harm minimisation for many years. Issues such as the availability of sterilising tablets and condoms have been debated frequently, but some of the decisions or compromises which have been reached have not been satisfactory and have placed prisoners at greater risk of infection. The Prison Service AIDS Advisory Committee undertook a policy review of HIV/AIDS in prison which began in 1992. It was not until 1995 that the Committee published its review and its recommendations. These will be discussed in the next chapter.

It is evident that many of the ideas and discourses which were prominent in drugs policy during the 1986–93 period failed to penetrate the development of drugs and HIV/AIDS policies in prisons. The policies which did emerge, including the 1987 throughcare guidelines, 1991 treatment manual, and HIV policies on VIR and education and training, were hindered by implementation which was strongly localised. The Prison Service limits its role to setting a policy framework and standards and then local management applies these to mirror local circumstances. Although the Prison Service can highlight the importance of the policy guidelines and their recommendations for good practice, they have no power to ensure that these are implemented locally. This allows for much discretion and choice, particularly for prison governors, in implementing central policy decisions often leading to wide variation and lack of consistency across the system.

Conclusion

During the phase 1986–93, the HIV/AIDS crisis became the driving force behind the development of a more explicit prison drugs policy. By 1986, the HIV/AIDS issue had become linked to injecting drug use and fears of transmission into the heterosexual population became a reality. In the community, HIV/AIDS had become a 'national emergency' in policy terms provoking a 'wartime response' (Berridge, 1996a). Prisons were no longer immune from external scrutiny and could not deny the existence of the drug problem in prison. The 'official' discourses around drugs in prison which were evident in the early 1980s could no longer be sustained. The 'end of the denial' was linked mainly to the HIV/AIDS issue, but also to a growing evidence base which began to challenge the view that a drug problem did not exist in prisons. Furthermore, a policy network was growing around the drugs and HIV issue in prison which began to lobby the Prison Service for a humane and pragmatic response.

Although a liberal response to the issue of HIV/AIDS and drug use had eventually been achieved in the community through policies of harm minimisation and risk reduction, this was extremely difficult to extend to the prison environment (Berridge, 1996a). Such policies were constrained by the institutional context of the prison system and the unwillingness of the Prison Service to consider radical policies. The inherent conflict between care and control and concern about the public imagery of adopting anything other than a hard-line, abstinence-based approach was important during this period and became enduring features of subsequent policy development. The focus of the next chapter is the period 1993–7 in which fundamental changes occurred within drugs and penal policy and most importantly, prison drugs policy.

4
1993–7: Coming Clean and Taking Control?

Introduction

During the period 1993 to 1997, significant developments took place in prison drugs policy. This phase begins in 1993 because this year marked a dramatic U-turn in penal policy which greatly influenced the development of drugs policy in prisons. By 1995, the first prison drugs strategy was formulated involving an explicit and comprehensive plan to tackle and measure the drug 'problem' in prisons. In contrast to the earlier phases of policy development, the new strategy incorporated both supply and demand reduction measures. It introduced new powers to test prisoners for drugs, increased security measures and emphasised drug treatment and rehabilitation. For the first time, prison issues were incorporated into national drugs policy and the Prison Service was expected to play a key role in national and local drugs policies and partnerships.

In order to contextualise the changes which took place in prison drugs policy during this period, the key developments in drugs and penal policy are discussed in the first part of the chapter. These changes were occurring against the backdrop of the Major government (1990–7), which continued and intensified Thatcher's key reforms. A new 'Back to Basics' campaign was introduced which reaffirmed traditional Conservative themes such as the nuclear family, law and order, discipline, and educational standards. By the mid-1990s, the Conservative government had implemented a range of legislation which increased the state's power to intervene in the lives of those on the political and economic margins or the so-called 'problematic' groups such as single parents, young people, the homeless, drug takers, illegal immigrants, and the unemployed (Ryan and Sim, 1995). With regard to offenders, Major argued that 'we should understand less and condemn more' (quoted in Downes and Morgan, 1997: 130). During this phase, both penal and drugs policy were affected by the populist punitive rhetoric and by the new managerialism which had effectively penetrated both policy areas.

The latter part of the chapter explores the way in which the drugs 'problem' was framed by key players and the policy response. During this phase, the drug issue in prisons was officially acknowledged and politicians in a sense had 'come clean' regarding the 'problem'. Drugs were increasingly framed as a 'problem' of order and control for the institution. The response in both political and policy terms was to 'get tough' and take control of the problem by implementing a defined strategy which emphasised mandatory drug testing and security measures. As prison drugs policy became more explicit, the contradiction between treatment and punishment intensified. A number of competing objectives required balancing: safety, security, control, punishment, treatment, and care. However, the policy framework failed to address how the 'balancing act' could be achieved (Seddon, 1996). Within a framework which included a punitive political context, an increasing emphasis on managerialism and the influence of US policies and ideas, this chapter will show that the penal aims of the strategy had clearly taken precedence over those of health and treatment. In response, a policy network began to form which criticised the introduction of mandatory drug testing and the over-emphasis on control and punishment. It lobbied for increased resources and more focus for treatment and care. Although this network had some success in rebalancing the strategy, the focus on punishment, control and security continued to be predominant.

Drugs policy context: *Tackling Drugs Together*

During the period 1993 to 1997, official statistics indicated that the drugs 'problem' in the community was continuing to grow. For example, the number of new drug addicts notified to the Home Office increased steadily from 11,561 in 1993 to 18,281 in 1996, and the proportion addicted to heroin increased by 6 per cent during this period (see Table A.3, Appendix). The number of persons found guilty, cautioned or dealt with by compounding for drugs offences also increased dramatically from 68,480 in 1993 to 113,154 in 1997 (see Table A.2, Appendix). By the early 1990s, the drug problem in Britain had changed. Research began to show that poly-drug use including cannabis, amphetamines, LSD, and Ecstasy was increasing amongst young people (see Denham-Wright and Pearl, 1995; Miller and Plant, 1996; Parker et al., 1998).

In May 1995, a new drugs strategy, *Tackling Drugs Together,* was launched, outlining the government's plans for tackling drugs for the period 1995–8. This represented the first attempt to provide a national drug 'strategy' as previous frameworks tended to be more descriptive of current policy (i.e. the 1990 document *UK Action on Drug Misuse*), rather than strategic (Dorn and Seddon, 1995). The strategy focused on three main areas: crime, young people and public health. It was underpinned by the following common Statement of Purpose:

> To take effective action by vigorous law enforcement, accessible treatment and a new emphasis on education and prevention to: increase the safety of communities from drug-related crime; reduce the acceptability and availability of drugs to young people; and reduce the health risks and other damage related to drug misuse. (HM Government, 1995: 1)

As was the case in other policy areas, the strategy also introduced performance indicators to monitor and evaluate progress, indicating a more 'managerial' approach towards the problem of drugs. The new strategy represented a new conception of what constituted 'policy'. It was much more strategic, concrete and specific in relation to key aims and objectives than previous policy frameworks.

The strategy, however, focused almost exclusively on drugs and the drug problem and failed to make links between drugs and other social issues such as housing, employment and economic regeneration. The three strands of the Statement of Purpose were to be interdependent and given equal importance. Although it was stressed that the Statement was not listed in priority order, the order has been assumed by informed observers to reflect the priorities of the strategy. In response to the strategy, many groups, associations and individuals argued that a careful balancing act would have to be achieved to ensure that crime, enforcement and control objectives would not override public health, treatment and prevention objectives (see ACOP, 1995; ACPO, 1995; ADSS, 1995; All Party Drugs Misuse Group, 1995; Baroness Jay of Paddington, 1995; LDPF, 1995; LGDF, 1995; Phoenix House, 1995; Release, 1995; SCODA, 1995; Turning Point, 1995). The strategy also represented a retreat from the harm minimisation principles which had been pursued during the previous phase of drugs policy from 1986 to 1993 (Ashton, 1995). Abstinence had now become the goal of intervention with harm minimisation as a means to that end, rather than an end in itself (HM Government, 1995). During this phase of policy development, it appeared that concern around HIV/AIDS was superseded by the relationship between drugs and crime. The 'drugs-crime link' had become the driving force behind policy development. Further research on the links between drugs and crime was to be commissioned by the Home Office (HM Government, 1994). Moreover, the criminal justice system was increasingly being seen as a location or opportunity for drug treatment intervention. Findings from the National Treatment Outcome Research Study (NTORS) showed that the 1,110 drug misusers in the NTORS cohort had committed over 70,000 separate crimes in the three months before entry into treatment. In the two years prior to treatment, the cost to the criminal justice system in dealing with their offences was estimated at £4 million and the cost to their victims was estimated at £34 million (Department of Health, 1996: 11)

The emphasis on enforcement-related activities was also reflected in the amount of resources spent on each activity. The funds spent on enforcement, deterrence and controls greatly outweighed those spent on treatment, rehabilitation, prevention and education. For example, for the year 1993–4, the government spent an estimated total of £526 million on tackling drugs across the UK, with £209 million being spent on police/customs enforcement, £137 million on deterrence and controls, £104 million on prevention and education, £61 million on treatment and rehabilitation and £15 million on international action (HM Government, 1995, annex B). The new strategy did not attempt to overhaul radically or redistribute drug spending. Very few new resources were made available. Informed members of the drugs policy community suggested that the national drugs strategy was imbalanced and focused too much on enforcement issues. They thought the claim that the three strands of the Statement of Purpose (i.e. crime, young people, and public health) were to be given equal importance was meaningless rhetoric. The only way to rectify the imbalance in practice would be to radically overhaul drugs spending.

The bifurcation in drugs policy described in previous chapters continued to operate during this later phase of policy development. The emphasis was on prevention and education for young people and treatment for the 'deserving' victims of drugs, with increased enforcement and policing for the hardened user who might also be offending. Under the aim 'to increase the safety of communities from drug-related crime', one of the main objectives was 'to reduce the level of drug misuse in prisons'. This was the first time that penal drugs policy objectives had been systematically incorporated at the national level. Due to the growing interest in drug issues in prison within policy networks throughout the 1980s and early 1990s (as well as the fact that law enforcement was one of the main planks of the strategy), the drugs policy community saw the inclusion of prisons in national policy development as imperative. However, some alluded to the fact that the Prison Service was reluctant to be incorporated into the new drugs strategy. This resistance reflected the insularity of the Prison Service and their tendency to work on their own with little outside input. As a drug agency director recalled:

> *My memory basically is that the Prison Service were trying to stay out of that. They were trying to plough a single furrow on their own. They felt that they had a problem and it was a 'prison' problem and they could deal with their 'prison' problem. It was with quite considerable reluctance and a great deal of political pressure that they became part of the targets within TDT. That demonstrates things which are evident in other organisational structures as well – structures that are very self-contained which see themselves to some degree as being afflicted and criticised. They felt at the point that they could produce some sort of solution which was just their solution which didn't go beyond their own walls. My sense at that time was that the Prison Service nationally came on board reluctantly.* (Interview 08)

National and local co-ordination

The 1995 strategy stressed that in order to achieve progress towards the aims and objectives, multi-agency co-ordination needed improvement at both national and local levels. At the national level, co-ordination at Ministerial level remained with the Ministerial Sub-Committee on the Misuse of Drugs, chaired by the Lord President of the Council. At official level, the Central Drugs Co-ordination Unit (CDCU) was established in 1994 to support the Lord President in co-ordinating the implementation of the drugs strategy and to ensure the policies and practice of the lead departments involved in tackling drugs were coherent. CDCU performed a liaison role, with the various departments each retaining control of their particular policies, operations and resources (HM Government, 1995). CDCU was part of the Privy Council Office and physically located in the Cabinet Office, rather than in any particular government department with an interest in drug issues. In many ways, this new structure at the heart of government represented a new 'neutrality' in drugs policy. The location also ensured that drug issues assumed a very high-profile position within the hierarchy of government. The CDCU had the potential to resolve some of the historical tension between the Home Office and the Department of Health over drug issues.

At the local level, 105 Drug Action Teams (DATs) were established to deliver the strategy on the ground. As in other areas of social policy, there was a rediscovered emphasis on area-based policies to recognise diversity at a local level and allow for variation in response (MacGregor, 1998c). DDACs were replaced by the new DAT structures which were to be comprised of senior representatives from the police, probation and prison services, local authorities, including education and social services, and health authorities. Co-option of voluntary sector representation was also encouraged. Each Drug Action Team was expected to establish at least one Drug Reference Group (DRG) made up of individuals or groups in the community who had local knowledge, expertise, or experience in drugs. The role of the Teams was to make progress in terms of the overall aims and objectives of the national drugs strategy and adapt action to local circumstances. The starting point for the boundaries of the teams was the district health authority.

Prison representation on DATs and DRGs was considered to be very important, but as the ACMD (1996) warned, there were several practical barriers to making this a reality. First, prisons are situated in locations which do not match any neat structural map or set of boundaries. For example, some health authorities have more than one prison within their geographical boundary, while others have none. Second, the allocation of offenders to prisons is based on a number of factors with geography being only one. Therefore, health authority concern for prisoners from their district and interest in any prison within its area would often involve different populations. Third, some prisons serve an area covered by several DATs. Attendance at each might be unrealistically demanding on a particular prison and might seem of little relevance to any particular DAT if prisoners from that district were housed not only in the local prison, but in others around the country (ACMD, 1996: 34–5). In addition to these practical barriers and perhaps more fundamentally, prison involvement on DATs could be hindered by the insularity of prisons. Fitzgerald and Sim (1982) describe this as the 'crisis of visibility', a term which refers to the notorious secrecy that surrounds prisons and what takes place inside them. The 'crisis of visibility' has an impact on the relations prisons have with the outside community and agencies, and how those agencies and the community relate to prisons.

Penal policy context: the post-Woolf era

U-turn in penal policy: 'prison makes bad people worse' to 'prison works'

During the period 1993–7, the prison population increased steadily from 44,552 in 1993 to 61,114 in 1997 (see Table A.4, Appendix). Despite signs of a decreasing prison population in the early period after the implementation of the 1991 Criminal Justice Act, a speedy retreat from the principles on which that Act was founded was undertaken by Kenneth Clarke (Home Secretary 1992–3) and continued by Michael Howard (Home Secretary 1993–7). As Downes (1997: 9) argues, this sudden shift in the direction of policy was undertaken for party-political reasons. Over the period 1989–92, the crime rate had increased by over 40 per cent, the recession had deepened, and the Conservative government's standing on law and order had declined compared to the Labour party. The government refused to acknowledge the link between crime and economic factors and thus resorted to 'one golf club strategy [or] more punitive policies' (Downes, 1997: 9).

This phase of penal policy development was imbued with managerialism and what Bottoms (1995) has termed 'populist punitiveness'. A populist punitive approach appeals to politicians because they believe it will reduce the crime rate through general deterrence and incapacitation; it may help to strengthen the moral consensus against certain forms of activity such as drugs offences; and it will satisfy a particular part of the electorate (Bottoms, 1995: 39). The new politics of populism led to departures from conventional forms of policy-making. Under this framework, Rock (1995) argues government ministers act with great speed and on impulse, consulting and liaising less with policy communities of experts, professionals, practitioners, civil servants, and researchers regarding policy decisions. During this period, shifts in penal policy were more influenced and determined by forces external to the prison system such as the Home Secretary, the general public, the media, and Sir John Woodcock and General Sir John Learmont who were commissioned by the government to conduct inquiries on prison security issues (Clark, 1997).

Thus, research conducted by Roger Tarling, the then Head of the Home Office Research and Planning Unit, which showed that crime levels would not be greatly reduced through incapacitative strategies was ignored (Tarling, 1993). In October 1993, Michael Howard advocated the idea that 'prison works' on deterrent and incapacitative grounds at the Conservative party conference. He reasserted the Thatcherite 'law and order' rhetoric of the early 1980s by announcing a new 'law and order' package of 27 proposals which included the introduction of mandatory drug testing (MDT) in prisons, the building of 6 new private prisons, restrictions on bail and cautioning, and more punitive community service orders.

'Just deserts' as the sentencing rationale was thus diluted by a renewed faith in the deterrent and incapacitative qualities of the prison. These ideas came to final fruition in the 1996 White Paper, *Protecting the Public*, which outlined the government's proposals for 'honesty in sentencing', automatic life sentences for serious violent and sex offenders, mandatory minimum prison sentences for drug dealers and burglars, and a new prison building and refurbishment programme (Home Office, 1996). Any debate regarding the aims of imprisonment, improvements to the regime, or implementing Woolf's proposals were clearly absent from the policy agenda. In fact, Howard announced a package of 'new austerity measures' in 1994 which included the earning of privileges through a new incentives and privileges scheme and restrictions on home leave, temporary release and access to telephones.

During this period, the prison system was undergoing further crises of 'containment' and 'control' which fuelled and legitimised the more punitive, austere, security and control focused agenda. There were disturbances at Wymott prison in 1993 and at Everthorpe prison in 1994. In September 1994, six high security prisoners attempted to escape and Semtex was discovered at Whitemoor prison.This was followed by another escape of three prisoners at Parkhurst prison in January 1995. These escapes led to the Woodcock and Learmont inquiries into prison security. The Learmont Report represented a departure from the general consensus emanating from the Woolf Report that the requirements of security, control and justice must be met and *balanced* if the prison system is to remain stable. As Morgan (1997b) argues, Learmont effectively dispensed with the notion of 'balance' by suggesting that the primary purpose of imprisonment is 'custody' and that everything else is subordinated to this basic requirement (see Learmont, 1995: para. 3.39–3.40).Thus, Learmont did not conceptualise security and care as complementary, but as being in opposition to one another. The recommendations of the Learmont Inquiry therefore focused almost exclusively on security issues by advocating greater use of CCTVs, dedicated search teams, restrictions on visits and prisoners' property and improved physical security (see Learmont, 1995: para. 7.1–7.120).

With Michael Howard's pronouncement that 'prison works', his emphasis on austere regimes, and his adherence to law and order rhetoric, prisoners deriving pleasure from drugs use could no longer be ignored or tolerated. During a period of overcrowding, crises in security, and reduced prisons budgets, it is interesting that the drug issue assumed such a high priority within the penal system. By 1994, the Prison Service and the politicians had 'come clean' and publicly admitted that there was a drug problem in British prisons. This area became a political challenge to Michael Howard. He responded vigorously within his new plans for penal policy. As Carlen (1998: 99) argues the prison system had been opened up to the 'war on drugs'. Members of the policy networks, particularly those from penal reform groups and drug agencies, saw a clear relationship between Howard's discourses on the efficacy and austerity of prisons and the way in which prison drugs policy subsequently developed:

> *You can see certain things – MDT being the obvious one – as part of the crackdown which follows the brief period of liberalisation [after] the Woolf report ... There was a period of what you could call the 'Prague Spring' for the prison system ... It doesn't last very long. The tanks roll back in and this takes many different forms – the introduction of the incentive scheme is an example, MDT another ... so it's part of the change of mood music of the period from about 1993 onwards.* (Interview 24 with penal reformer)

Agency status

A key trend in public sector reform during the late 1980s and early 1990s was the development of 'agencies'. Under agency status, quasi-autonomous bodies are established which are responsible for the development of operational policies within a policy and resource framework set by central government (Home Office, 1988b). The agencies are responsible for delivering the services within these resource limits. On 1 April 1993, the Prison Service was detached from the Home Office, hived off from direct government control and established as an executive agency. A Director General, Derek Lewis, was recruited from the private sector to facilitate these changes. Under the new decentralised arrangements, more responsibility, control and authority for budgets, contracts, staffing and regimes was devolved from Prison Service headquarters to individual prison governors.

In 1993, six principal goals were set for the Prison Service: to keep prisoners in custody; to maintain order, control, and discipline in a safe environment; to provide decent conditions for prisoners and meet their needs; to provide positive regimes which would help prisoners to address their offending behaviour and allow them as full and responsible a life as possible; to help prisoners prepare for their return to the community; and to deliver prison services using the resources provided by parliament with maximum efficiency (HM Prison Service, 1993). Key performance indicators (KPIs) and targets were developed to measure progress towards these goals. The Corporate Plan outlined the strategies for achieving the goals over a three-year period and the Business Plan set targets for the immediate financial year.

This new approach to public sector management had a profound effect on the way in which the prison system was managed and operated. It came to be dominated by 'institutionally-defined managerial goals' (Garland, 1990: 184), prioritising measures of performance and short-term goals rather than articulating a common purpose, moral mission or set of values. There was also a shift to focusing on the 'aggregate' level, rather than the individual offender or prison. For example, data on the key performance indicators are reported as national aggregates making it difficult to ascertain what is occurring in individual prisons. The emphasis on the 'aggregate' also leads to a clash in terms of philosophy for professionals within the system who may come from social work or probation backgrounds which focus on the individual (Bottoms, 1995). Various scholars have argued that the system has become preoccupied with internal goals, rather than social goals, 'outputs' rather than 'outcomes', the aggregate level rather than the individual; and on internal system processes rather than external objectives (see Feeley and Simon, 1992; Bottoms, 1995; Garland, 1996).

The drug issue in prison was first given serious attention under these new arrangements and structures. For example, in the 1996–7 year, a new KPI was introduced which was to ensure that the rate of positive random drug testing would be lower in the fourth quarter of 1996–7 than in the first quarter of that year (HM Prison Service, 1996a). In the next sections, the ways in which the drug problem in prisons was reconceptualised and the policy response will be explored.

A threat to order, control and discipline: reconceptualising the drugs 'problem' in prisons

During the mid-1990s, the drugs 'problem' in prisons began to be framed in new ways. The concern around HIV and public health issues during the previous phase began to diminish and there was an increasing focus on drugs as a problem of order, control and discipline. This shift in emphasis was linked to the punitive political context discussed above and to a growing awareness of drugs in prison as a problem of culture and currency with links extending into the wider community. During 1993–7, official statistics indicated that the drugs 'problem' in prisons was increasing. The numbers of drug addicts notified to the Home Office by prison medical officers almost doubled from 1,941 in 1993 to 3,665 in 1996, and their proportion out of all notifications increased by 3 per cent over this period (see Table A.1, Appendix). The number of drug offenders sentenced to custody also increased dramatically from 4,835 in 1993 to 10,422 in 1997 (see Table A.2, Appendix).

During this phase, informed members of the policy network suggested that there had been not just one drug problem, but a multifaceted phenomenon. They saw a variety of different problems experienced by different people with different drugs in different contexts. They disagreed, however, as to whether drugs was primarily a problem for the 'individual' or for the 'institution'; whether it was a health problem or an enforcement problem; and whether it was an 'internal' problem within prisons or an 'external' problem extending beyond them. But on the whole, with some important exceptions, these influential groups tended to frame drugs as a problem for the institution, rather than for the individual; as an enforcement rather than a health problem; and as an internal rather than an external problem.

Drugs were particularly problematic when they became a dominant part of the prison culture. A 'culture' had built up around drugs within prisons during the mid-1990s. They had become an important currency which generated certain types of behaviours and problems for individuals and for the institution, including drug dealing, intimidation, threats, extortion, bullying, the accumulation of debts, and violence (ACMD, 1996). The fear of intimidation and violence was believed to have led to suicides, prisoners opting to be transferred to Rule 43 for protection, prostitution, bartering possessions, and failure to return from home leave due to failing to obtain drugs for others (see Leech, 1997; Turnbull et al., 1994). A civil servant described drugs as a 'penetrating problem' within the institution:

> *It is an evil that permeates every layer and area of a prison. It is a penetrating problem ... There is nothing that it doesn't touch or impact upon.* (Interview 20)

Drugs had become one of the most potent, expensive and powerful currencies within the prison system. The type of currency within prisons determines how the system will operate. Currencies, such as tobacco, telephone cards and chocolate, have always existed. The problem was not so much that drugs had become a currency, but that in some prisons they had become very expensive leading to huge debts and violence. Sparks et al. (1996) found that in prisons where cash economies operated, the price of drugs was high and a lot of money was generated through them. The illegality of drugs was also a key problem. For the first time, the currency being used not only breached prison disciplinary rules, but was also against the law. The Conservative administration was particularly concerned with the illegality issue and the public imagery of failing to take tough action on such activities. The use of alcohol is also against prison rules and creates problems around violence and control. However, alcohol was not viewed as problematic and no overall strategy existed for alcohol during this period. This suggests that the concern around drugs was set within a political rather than a practical agenda (Hewitt, 1996).

When drugs became a currency, it led to loss of control by the authorities over the prison environment. For example, the Learmont inquiry found that prior to the escapes at Parkhurst, drug use and dealing were pervasive within the prison and had led to an increase in assaults and violence between prisoners. An internal enquiry concluded that the prison 'had a serious drug problem [which was] greater than initially envisaged. The supply of drugs is spiralling out of the control' (quoted in Learmont, 1995: para. 2.247). The notion that the problem was out of control was seen to be the key to the drug problem among those most concerned with developing prison drugs policies. Drugs were no longer seen as 'functional' in keeping the system under control (as they had been in the 1980s), but as a disruptive, destabilising, threatening and dangerous factor:

> *The consequences of [drugs] affected the whole life of the prison in terms of potential violence, but also in terms of destabilising the whole system.* (Interview 18 with penal reformer)

> *It's by no means only about drug use in itself ... It is the overall sense that it leads to a more unpleasant and unmanageable environment.* (Interview 02 with civil servant)

Imprisoning more drug traffickers and offenders does not ensure that all drug-related crime will be controlled as the advocates of the 1991

Criminal Justice Act and subsequent legislation had hoped. Research indicates that many criminals continue to commit crime in the prison environment just as they had in the community (see Bottoms et al., 1990; Grapendaal, 1990; King, 1991) and drug traffickers continue to operate easily within the prison setting (see Early, 1991; Ruggiero, 1995). Drugs and drug dealing provides a source of status and 'employment' for some prisoners which continues on the outside on release (Ruggiero and South, 1995). As Ruggiero (1995: 66) observes, 'drugs cause some prisoners to become desperate and ill while others become rich and powerful'.

Although drug users in prison were seen to be difficult to engage in the regime and regular work programmes, it is important to emphasise that drugs are used as a means of coping with the pains of deprivation of prison life (Sykes, 1966; Irwin, 1980). For inmates who are locked up for 23 hours a day, drugs (particularly cannabis) provide a method of relieving the stress and boredom of being in prison, a way to pass their 'time' and an aid to sleep (Turnbull et al., 1994; Cope, 1999; Matthews, 1999). Some policy actors argued that the increase in drug use in prison could be viewed as a reaction to the decline in the quality of prison regimes due to increasing overcrowding, cuts in prison programmes, and Howard's austerity measures introduced during the mid-1990s. Drug smuggling, trafficking, dealing and use within prisons had provided a way to pass time in prisons and could be compared to a 'game' which occupied a large proportion of prisoners:

> *If the regime quality was fundamentally different, then we'd have a very different story in terms of drugs. I principally see it as a quality of regime issue which means the stultifyingly boring life is tempered by using drugs, mainly cannabis and in its wake, it becomes a control issue of bullying, violence, and trade ... Therefore what you get is the collusion of principally families [and] friends breaking through that cordon sanitaire, plus the occasional prison officer deviates. And the whole thing becomes a great game.* (Interview 05 with director of drug agency)

During this phase, there was also growing recognition amongst the policy network that the drug problem in prison extended beyond the prison walls in terms of links with crime and criminals on release, debts, trafficking, and problems for prisoners' families and friends. It was difficult for prisoners to break free of drug networks within prisons on release. The drug supply networks in prisons were inextricably linked to those operating in the community. Prisoners' families and friends were being pressurised to smuggle drugs into prisons, forced to assume responsibility for paying debts accumulated by their partners within prisons, and threatened and hassled by drug dealers operating within the community who had links with those inside prisons.

Reflecting their orientation towards treating and caring for individual drug users, it was mainly those from drug agencies who expressed the problem of drugs in prison in 'individual' and health-related terms. For them, individual problems included people beginning their drug career in prison, links between drug use and offending behaviour, unsafe practices within prisons, problems around drug addiction and other health issues. Drug using prisoners often lacked knowledge about drugs and experience of drug services and treatment in the community. This group tends to be excluded from service provision and from society in general. The OPCS survey of prisoners showed that less than one-third (31 per cent) of drug users had sought some sort of treatment prior to imprisonment. (Bridgwood and Malbon, 1995). Similarly, in Maden et al.'s study of women prisoners, one third of the women defined as dependent reported no contact with treatment services before entering prison (Maden et al., 1990), but over half of the female and male prisoner samples indicated they would accept treatment if it was offered to them (Maden et al., 1990; 1991).

In conclusion, it is clear that different drugs cause different problems for different individuals within different prisons (Turnbull et al., 1994; ACMD, 1996). In order to address the problems associated with drugs in prison effectively, this needed to be acknowledged by those involved in the formulation of policies and strategies. As a spokesperson from a professional association cogently argued:

> *The cannabis problem is a problem of gangsterism and intimidation. Problems about use of heroin are essentially around health concerns. Those two might be linked because it might be the same supplier. It might be the same user, but putting watered down bleach on landings doesn't do anything to solve the problem around the violence and intimidation associated with cannabis and vice a versa. So you've got to sort out what is 'the problem'. Is it violence and intimidation we're talking about? ... There's not one problem. There's a range of problems and you've got to be clear which one we're tackling. The odds are that as you deal with [one], you impinge on others.* (Interview 21)

The next section will explore the response to the drug problem in prison during this phase which took the form of the 1995 prison drugs strategy.

Response to the 'problem': the 1995 prison drugs strategy

In 1995, the Prison Service published a document entitled *Drug Misuse in Prison: Policy and Strategy*. This represented the first comprehensive drugs 'strategy' within the prison system with clearly defined actions, priorities, objectives and targets. Reducing the level of drug use became one of the seven strategic priorities in the Prison Service's Corporate Plan and would be monitored by a new performance indicator based on the number of positive results from random drug tests. The reduction of drug use in prisons was to be achieved through local drug strategies which focused on three areas: reducing the supply of drugs; reducing the demand for drugs and rehabilitating drug users; and measures to reduce the potential for damage to health of prisoners, staff and the wider community, arising from the use of drugs (HM Prison Service, 1995a: 2). Prison governors were responsible for developing and implementing local strategies which were to be agreed with area managers. The ACMD (1996: 32) welcomed this approach in the hope that it would help to close the wide gap that historically existed between national policy and local practice. The 1995 prison drugs strategy was presented essentially as a two-pronged approach with measures to reduce the drugs supply and measures to reduce demand for drugs (see Prison Service, 1995a: 14–15). This was the first time that supply and demand reduction activities were combined within prison drugs policy. It was therefore an attempt to manage the issues which arise from the contradiction between asserting that the Prison Service will not condone drug use and achieving public health objectives to help drug users change their behaviour (Keene, 1997a). Within the policy discourse, there was a duality as it simultaneously contained both elements of help and punishment, providing it with much political appeal (Edelman, 1984). Concern was expressed by various sources that the new strategy might over-emphasise supply reduction and concentrate resources on security measures at the expense of demand and harm reduction (see ACMD, 1996; Penal Affairs Consortium, 1996; HM Chief Inspector of Prisons, 1996). These concerns were well-founded. In practice, the elements of security, punishment and control took precedence over help and treatment. The next sections will examine the main strands of the 1995 prison drugs strategy and the balance which emerged between them.

Mandatory drug testing

The most controversial element of the 1995 prison drugs strategy was the introduction of mandatory drug testing (MDT). During a visit to the United States in Spring 1993, the Director General of the Prison Service, Derek Lewis, was impressed with American drug testing programmes and believed they could be effective in reducing drug use in British prisons (Lewis, 1997). Under the MDT protocols in 1995, ten per cent of the population of each prison was selected at random by computer. Selected prisoners were required, without warning, to provide a urine sample. The mandatory testing powers could also be used on reception; on suspicion; prior to risk-related activities such as temporary release and for persistent offenders. MDT is undertaken by specially trained prison officers, rather than health care staff who are bound by professional and ethical codes which prevent them from participating in activities without the consent of their patients. The MDT programme was resource and labour intensive and the cost for the programme was borne partly from the existing budgets of individual prisons and by diverting resources from other Prison Service areas.

Although prisoners could not be forced to provide a sample for testing, those who refused could be disciplined for refusing to obey a lawful order. Prisoners who tested positive were liable to the usual range of disciplinary action on adjudication including additional days, loss of privileges and earnings, and administrative measures such as closed visits and removal of home leave. However, it was estimated that 90 per cent of the adjudication outcomes involve awarding additional days (ACMD, 1996). The Home Office estimated that MDT would increase the prison population by 300 (Home Office Statistical Bulletin, 1996) and the annual cost for holding an extra 300 prisoners in custody would be over £7 million (Penal Affairs Consortium, 1996).

The Prison Service outlined several purposes of MDT including deterrence, identification for treatment programmes, helping prisoners to overcome peer pressure, provision of data on the scale and pattern of drugs use in prison, and information for a performance indicator of drug use (HM Prison Service, 1995b). But many key policy players argued that the link between MDT and treatment was not as sophisticated as it was presented in the strategy. MDT was primarily seen, particularly by those from penal reform groups and drug agencies, as a means of control and a method for inflicting more punishment, particularly for cannabis use:

> *MDT is essentially a solution to a perceived cannabis problem. It's all about order and control. They try and put a gloss on it saying it helps to bring people forward for treatment programmes ... That's not what it's all about.* (Interview 21 with spokesperson from professional association)

In February 1995, MDT was piloted initially in eight prisons. By Spring 1996, it was in place across the entire prison system. The great speed with which the MDT system was implemented reflected the priority that drugs had assumed on both the political and policy agendas. It was implemented in many prisons before the broader drug strategy was established. In particular, treatment provision was not in place prior to MDT. Because it was a mandatory requirement across the prison system operating within a legal framework, MDT was focused upon at the expense of other parts of the strategy. Another crucial factor was that the MDT results were the only drug-related key performance indicator (KPI) which was reported at a corporate level. As a result, MDT was often used as an indicator of the effectiveness of the overall drugs strategy. All of this was compounded by the political pressure to appear 'tough' on the drug issue in prisons. This legacy of emphasis and primacy on MDT persisted within the 1995 prison drugs strategy. This was recognised by the civil servants:

> *Undoubtedly, MDT has taken too much focus for us ... There was significant political pressure to introduce MDT and get it in quickly, which meant that we had a rather cockeyed approach in the sense that some prisons had MDT before they had a broader strategy in place. That legacy is still with us about needing to look at the balance.* (Interview 14a)

> *There's no doubt in the first roll out, because MDT was obligatory by a certain date in every prison, the emphasis has been on the control aspects.* (Interview 19)

Supply reduction

Supply reduction measures also featured prominently within the 1995 prisons drugs strategy. These included improved perimeter security (i.e. patrolling, searching near perimeter fences, use of dogs and CCTV); searching (i.e. unpredictable, random searches by specially trained staff and dog teams); supervision of visits (i.e. CCTV, use of dogs, fixed furniture, searching visitors, and using closed visits for prisoners found guilty of drugs offences); intelligence gathering and use of informants; and control of prescribed medication. These drug security measures were tied into the recommendations from the Woodcock and Learmont reports. As discussed above, the outcome of these two inquiries was a greater emphasis and more resources for security measures which Carlen (1998: 7) has aptly described as representing a 'fetishism of prison security'. The inquiries had a knock-on effect with regard to the drugs strategy which ensured that the supply reduction measures had a very high profile, were taken seriously and implemented across the prison system.

New powers were given to Dedicated Search Teams which were specially trained in searching both cells and prisoners for drugs. Media reports began to emerge that the new strip-searching powers given to these teams in Holloway Prison led to much intimidation and degradation amongst women prisoners. It was argued that this type of work attracted certain types of prison officers or the 'heavy mob', who wore a uniform of PVC leggings, Doc Marten boots and baseball caps (*The Observer*, 24 Nov. 1996, quoted in Carlen, 1998: 7–8). Similarly, the security teams undertaking the searching and testing at Stoke Heath YOI wore special SAS-style jumpsuits and heavy black boots (Howard League for Penal Reform, 1996). Such symbolic distinctions between staff carrying out security and control functions and those undertaking health and treatment activities ensured that punishment and control aspects would remain visible and paramount. In 1996, there were 8,036 drug finds in prisons and one-third of these emerged from cell searches (HM Prison Service, 1997a).

Because visits were seen to be the major route by which drugs enter the prison, the greatest impact of increased security was felt amongst visitors to prisons. Those working within prisons argued that the increased searching, use of sniffer dogs, and CCTVs have made visiting prisons an intimidating and frightening experience for many visitors. Police in the community began to work more closely with the prisons in terms of intelligence gathering, leading to raids on visitor centres connected to some prisons. These centres are supposed to be safe places where visitors can have refreshments, wait for their visiting time, use the washroom facilities, and obtain advice from centre staff. The raids were conducted insensitively. For example, some visitors were strip-searched in front of their children. This has become a gendered issue as the majority of visitors to all prisons are women (including women's prisons) who often become coerced and pressurised into bringing drugs into the prisons (ACMD, 1996: 44). Various prisons posted up photocopies of news reports giving details of people being arrested for bringing drugs into prisons in the hope that it would deter other visitors. However, it is unlikely that these measures will act as a deterrent because the pressure to smuggle drugs in is too great. Many visitors fear that their partners and friends inside prisons will be attacked, bullied or even killed if they fail to bring drugs. As a civil servant admitted:

> *We've got some victims of drugs in prisons – usually women – who are under immense pressure to bring things in. As we've said to Ministers, it's very easy to say that these measures will deter ... but, if my son was in prison and he said to me, 'Look, someone's going to knife me, if I don't get something in', you can imagine you might try to get something in.* (Interview 14b)

In 1995, 1,463 visitors were arrested for possession of drugs – an increase of over 50 per cent compared to 1994. There was a slight reduction in 1996 with 1,314 visitors arrested (HM Prison Service, 1997a). Visitor centres began to adopt a drug prevention role, for example, by putting up posters for visitors to advertise help and advice if they are pressurised into bringing in drugs. In May 1996, ADFAM National, the charity for the families and friends of drug users, developed a project which is dedicated to working with prisoners' families and visitors to prisons around drug issues.

Treatment provision

Within the 1995 prison drugs strategy document, there was very little in terms of new proposals and resources for drug treatment initiatives. With regard to treatment, counselling, and support services, it was stated that 'it is not possible to advocate a particular programme or programmes which will meet the immediate needs of the prison, the longer term needs of the criminal justice system, and the needs of the individual inmates' (HM Prison Service, 1995a: 18). It was recognised that different programmes such as short educational programmes, self-help groups, individual advice and counselling, and therapeutic communities would be needed to match varying levels and types of drug use. However, it was not specified where these programmes were to be provided, who would be delivering them, or how they would be resourced.

Drug agencies working in the prison setting have always faced the dilemma as to where they position themselves within the system (i.e. as independent professionals or as part of the penal establishment). The introduction of MDT altered the political environment of prison-based drug work and raised complex issues for agencies (Stokes, 1996). The premise that MDT would identify drug using prisoners for treatment placed tremendous pressure on drug agencies as there was insufficient treatment provision for MDT to work as a referral mechanism. Moreover, some drug agencies refused to work with MDT positives unless they were paid for working with this group. A clear separation between treatment and MDT would have ensured that the voluntary nature of treatment was maintained and that drug services were not swamped with cannabis referrals (Stokes, 1996). If agencies accepted referrals from MDT, this would change their position within the prison as they would become part of the MDT machinery, rather than independent.

There are similar debates about whether or not prison officers should be involved in drug treatment programmes. As we saw in the previous chapters, drugs tended to be an area solely for 'experts' within prisons, such as medical staff and external drug agencies. Under the 1995 strategy, there was an emphasis on a multi-professional and multidisciplinary approach. All prison staff were to undergo basic training to increase their understanding of drugs, their effects, and the problems experienced by drug users to ensure that the strategy was successful and not undermined. Cultural clashes between prison staff and service providers often occur. Prison staff tend to work within a very punitive institutional framework with their work centring around the needs of the institution, whereas service providers tend to adopt a more caring, client-centred approach with their work centring around the needs of individuals. The security and control functions of prison officers raise difficult issues around confidentiality, particularly in relation to the other parts of the drugs strategy such as MDT and supply reduction. Because prison officers' primary responsibilities and skills are around security issues, these will always take priority and often conflict with treatment programmes. There is also a perception amongst *some* prison officers and governors that security and supply reduction activities constitute high status work compared with treatment, rehabilitative and welfare-oriented work. As a spokesperson from a professional association argued:

> *Some prison service staff are more interested in sexy operations like dog searches and CCTV, than they are in things like ... working with individuals to deal with their drug use problems ... Most people would regard the second half of that as being sexier propositions than high walls, dogs and CCTVs, but the Prison Service don't, because that's where their minds are at.* (Interview 21)

Harm minimisation

Similar to the national drugs strategy, HIV and harm minimisation issues received little attention within the 1995 prison drugs strategy document. It may be that this was seen to be covered by the Prison Service AIDS Advisory Committee in their review of HIV/AIDS which was undertaken in 1992 and published in 1995 (HM Prison Service, 1995c). However, there is no mention of the work of the Committee or any link made between it and the prison drugs strategy. Local drugs strategies were expected to include education and information for all inmates on the risks and harms of drug use; options for coming off drugs; methods of reducing risk of cross infection; and the help available for HIV, other bloodborne infection diseases and drugs (HM Prison Service, 1995a). In their criticism of the strategy, the ACMD (1996: 38) suggested that in order for it to be more balanced and comprehensive, harm minimisation should be accorded a more important role and should involve three strands: reducing drug-related harm to individual prisoners, the prison regime, and the wider community.

Despite the lack of emphasis on harm minimisation within the strategy, important policy reforms were occurring quietly within the penal system. These included more liberal approaches to methadone maintenance, the provision of sterilising tablets to clean syringes and general provision of condoms. These reforms can be seen as the result of the pressure which had been building up over the previous phases of policy development from various committees and policy networks lobbying for greater congruence between community and penal provision. Guidelines on the use of methadone treatment were reviewed in 1995. Although abstinence was the overall aim of the drugs strategy, methadone treatment within prisons was to reflect more closely its use in community drug treatment programmes to ensure continuity for those prisoners receiving treatment before custody and on release (HM Prison Service, 1995a) The new guidelines for the clinical management of drug users are found in Health Care Standard 8. The ACMD (1996) warned that a gap would remain between policy and practice unless steps were taken to ensure the implementation and rigorous monitoring of the standards. These were merely 'guidelines', meaning that prisons had not been mandated to implement them. Drug agencies were sceptical about the probability of their implementation:

> *We get rainforests of paper sent out from Cleland House which are termed 'guidelines'. Why are they guidelines? Why not instructions? So for example, the Health Care Standards are guidelines ... they are a waste of paper.* (Interview 26a with director of drug agency)

The AIDS Advisory Committee made a total of 39 recommendations including the provision of sterilising tablets; easy access to condoms and lubricants; and that education concerning HIV should directly address sexual behaviour and safer sex practices. In 1993, following the outbreak of HIV infection at Glenochil prison, the Scottish Prison Service made sterilising tablets available to clean syringes. The AIDS Advisory Committee also recommended that sterilising tablets be issued to all prisoners in England and Wales as part of a health and safety pack (HM Prison Service, 1995c).

Although it appeared from the drugs strategy document that interest in harm minimisation had diminished, policy reform was slowly occurring and the lessons from the HIV experience in prisons were being applied to other communicable diseases, such as hepatitis C. Therefore, harm minimisation and risk reduction measures were seen to be still on the agenda and pressures for reform of existing policy were still occurring, but were perhaps not articulated at the political level as prominently as some of the security and control measures in the 1995 prison drugs strategy. It is clear from the 1995 prison drugs strategy document that the control and security elements were presented much more explicitly, with greater definition and detail compared to the treatment and harm minimisation elements which were much less explicit, detailed and concrete. Mandatory drug testing and the security initiatives were universal requirements across the prison system which were backed up by central funding and clear deadlines for implementation, while treatment and harm minimisation initiatives were to be established through guidelines, which would be subject to local decisions, resources and timetables. As prison drugs policy became more pronounced, defined and strategic, the contradiction between treatment and punishment grew much more acute. In an attempt to rebalance the strategy towards treatment and care, a policy network began to form and lobby for more emphasis and resources for treatment provision. The next section will examine their role in containing the increasing tensions between treatment and punishment.

The role of the policy network

In response to the new prison drugs strategy, interest in drug issues in prisons had increased and new players had been drawn into policy networks. For example, the ACMD (1996) published their report, entitled *Drug Misusers and the Prison System: An Integrated Approach*, which provided an important critique of the evolving strategy. Various groups produced discussion papers on different aspects of the strategy, such as the Penal Affairs Consortium (1996) and the Howard League for Penal Reform (1996). Drug issues in prisons were included in various official reports (see Department of Health, 1996; HM Chief Inspector of Prisons, 1996; 1997b; British Medical Association, 1997) and were the subject of various articles by practitioners and professionals attempting to influence the direction of policy (see Flynn, 1994; Tchaikovsky, 1994; Trace, 1995; Brazil, 1996; Stokes, 1996; Hewitt, 1996; Heyes and King, 1996; Rice, 1997). The new strategy also prompted research interest in this area (see Seddon, 1996; Gore et al., 1996; MacDonald, 1997; Keene, 1997a; Bird et al., 1997).

During this phase, the role of the policy network shifted from a position of setting the policy agenda, to one where they were responding to an agenda set from above. In many respects, they lost some of their power and influence, particularly during the early stages of the policy process. On the whole, there had not been open consultation with many of the key policy players over the details of the strategy, particularly those outside government. They had been sidelined. Prior to the implementation of the MDT policy, various members of the policy network attempted to lobby against its introduction. Their attempts proved futile, but they learned to adapt and deal with the new situation. In order to realign the strategy, they shifted their focus to extending treatment provision and the details of policy implementation and practice.

The battle against MDT and security measures

Before the implementation of the prison drugs strategy, there was much criticism and concern expressed by penal reform groups, drug agencies, civil liberties groups and other commentators regarding MDT and the associated security measures. The main objections were that MDT would: constitute an invasion of the right to privacy; cause switching to class A drugs which are less easily detectable compared to cannabis; lead to riots and disorder; discourage drug using prisoners from presenting for treatment; divert scare resources away from drug treatment and prevention; lead to drug-free urine becoming a currency; result in drugs, urine and injecting equipment being carried internally, thus increasing the risks of HIV; increase tension between staff and prisoners with decreased use of cannabis; lead judges and magistrates to send offenders with drug problems to prison more often; have a detrimental effect on prisoners' relationships with family members and friends; not be backed up by effective treatment provision; and finally, drugs would become more scarce and therefore more expensive leading to more violence, debts, intimidation and bullying (see Flynn, 1994; Tchaikovsky, 1994; Trace, 1995; Riley, 1996; Berger, 1995; Hewitt, 1996; Heyes and King, 1996; Brazil, 1996; Gore et al., 1996; Howard League for Penal Reform, 1996; ACMD, 1996; Wayne, 1996; Penal Affairs Consortium, 1996; Rice, 1997).

Issues of race and gender were invisible within the strategy. Local drugs strategies were to include 'an assessment of local needs and priorities which takes into account the equal opportunities implications of tackling drugs in prisons' (HM Prison Service, 1995a: 3). However, there was no specification as to what these implications might be and how prisons should deal with them. The ACMD (1996) stressed that the needs of women, minority ethnic prisoners, and young offenders needed to be more carefully considered in the development of the strategy. Concern was expressed that MDT would lead to new degradations and indignities in women's prisons (HM Chief Inspector of Prisons, 1997a; 1997b). Carlen (1998) illustrates how the construction of the MDT policy failed to consider and anticipate the differences in terms of implementation in women's prisons. There were also concerns that MDT would be applied in a discriminatory manner, in particular, there were arguments that the procedures should be ethnically monitored (Runciman, 1996; ACMD, 1996).

The overriding criticism of MDT was that it would cause prisoners to switch from using cannabis to class A drugs, such as heroin, which are less easily detectable. Data from the pilot study indicated that the proportion of prisoners testing positive for opiates or benzodiazepines rose from 4.1 to 7.4 per cent, while the proportion testing positive for cannabis decreased from 33.2 to 29.1 per cent between the first and second phases of random testing, indicating the possibility of switching from cannabis to opiates and other drugs because of lower detection rates (Gore et al., 1996). This conversion to class A drugs was also noted in the canton of Zurich, Switzerland when random mandatory drug testing was introduced. Their response was to cease testing for cannabis (Gore et al., 1996). In response to these initial findings, the Prison Service did not alter the implementation of MDT policy or procedures. Later, as part of its review of the prison drugs strategy, both quantitative and qualitative research on MDT was commissioned by the Prison Service to explore some of these issues. The fact that they were awaiting the results of this research was used by the Prison Service as a 'tactic' to deflect criticism away from the evolving strategy.

The various objections, warnings and preliminary research findings made little impact on the implementation of the policy. A spokesperson from a professional association who had been part of the lobby against the introduction of MDT recalled how he had been impressed with the planning by the Prison Service in this area:

> *We could think up 15 good reasons why MDT could never possibly work. Then we had a briefing from the people from the Prison Service who thought up 25 reasons why MDT couldn't work and sorted out 24 of them. It was a very impressive piece of work – the way they had looked at every aspect of it ... In planning terms, they did an excellent job.* (Interview 21)

Given the statutory powers surrounding the MDT procedures, there was relatively little that could be achieved through lobbying to stop implementation. As Dowding (1995: 144) argues, 'the material power and legitimacy of the elected government can ride roughshod over any policy community.' The service providers recognised this and turned this into an 'opportunity' to argue that more treatment services were needed if drug users were to be identified through MDT. In their view, MDT had to be accepted, used as an indicator of drug use and a lobbying tool for expanding treatment provision:

> *We couldn't just stand there and stamp our feet and say, 'this is a terrible thing', because you'd just be sidelined. What we did say is that the best thing it could do is give an indicative baseline of drug use in prison.* (Interview 10 with director of drug agency)

Furthermore, the Prison Service could no longer ignore or deny the problem of drug use in prisons because of the 'official' evidence base being produced through MDT procedures. For example, the key performance indicator for positive random drug testing indicated an increase from 24 per cent in the first quarter of 1996–7 to 24.2 per cent in the fourth quarter (HM Prison Service, 1997b). For the drug agencies, the MDT results helped to raise awareness of the amount of drug use taking place in prison and therefore provided a starting point for discussion about what could be done in terms of drug treatment.

Civil servants within the Prison Service also voiced their concerns around the problems of implementing a solely punitive measure. In 1994, Phillipa Drew, then the Director of Custody, and Tony Pearson, then the Director of Inmate Programmes, warned that MDT could cause disorder and staff collusion with prisoners, if it was not introduced with incentives to remain drug-free and within a broader treatment strategy (*The Guardian*, 28 Oct. 1994, quoted in King and McDermott, 1995: 195). The Chief Inspector of Prisons (1996) also argued that testing needed to be followed by either reward or treatment, and that financial provision needed to be made for these elements. Similarly, the British Medical Association recommended that MDT should only be used with the provision of a full range of treatment services (BMA, 1997). A policy network comprised of drug service providers, penal reformers, civil servants and others began to lobby for centrally funded drug treatment initiatives to back up the MDT mechanism. Given their vested interests in this area, drug service providers played key roles in this policy network.

Pilot drug treatment programmes

In a limited sense, this policy network had been successful in their lobbying for treatment provision. By 1996, the Prison Service had introduced various types of pilot drug treatment programmes within particular prisons across the country. These programmes were centrally funded by the Prison Service Directorate of Health Care and independently evaluated by PDM Consulting Ltd. In 1995–6, £3.5 million was made available for the pilots, and £5.1 million in 1996–7 (Penal Affairs Consortium, 1996). Initially, only 21 prisons were involved in the pilot programmes. Those prisons without pilot drug treatment programmes were encouraged to develop and fund their own arrangements involving external drug agencies. The pilots and evaluation were to be used as a basis to decide which facilities should be introduced across the entire prison system. The long-term aim was to provide a range of different drug treatment programmes within clusters of prisons, so that prisoners within each cluster would have access to treatment which corresponded to their assessed needs. The treatment programmes could be seen as almost an afterthought in policy development to rectify an overly punitive policy and in response to liberal sectors within the Prison Service and the Home Office, as well as criticism from lobbyists. However, there was also a growing evidence base indicating that 'treatment works' and that the criminal justice system, particularly prisons, should be regarded as an opportunity for drugs intervention, which could not be ignored (Department of Health, 1996).

In general, the type of approach adopted by the Prison Service for the pilot drug treatment programmes was abstinence-based. Politically, this was a much more expedient and clear strategy to present in the context of a 'tough' policy on drugs, than one based upon harm minimisation. There were rumours that Michael Howard had been drawn in by Phoenix House USA and attracted to the idea of a hard-line, abstinence-based approach. There was also very little evaluative research on the various types of prison-based programmes in the UK and EU to make an informed choice (Turnbull and Webster, 1998). The 12-step, abstinence-based programme at Downview prison run by Rehabilitation for Addicted Prisoners Trust (RAPt) had also been heralded as a success throughout the prison system, won the Guardian Jerwood Award for charity work, and had also been independently evaluated (see Player and Martin, 1996; Bond, 1998). Services which had an abstinence-based, rather than a harm minimisation perspective were seen to be favoured when it came to letting the contracts for the pilot drug treatment programmes and when prison governors, who were pursuing goals of drug-free prisons, decided on treatment provision for their establishments.

The Prison Service failed to undertake sufficient consultation when developing the treatment strand of the strategy. The service providers argued much could have been learnt by examining the development of services in the community:

> *Some of the commissioning decisions that they have taken look like they have not paid sufficient regard to the development of services in the community. This hell-for-leather search for abstinence – they thought that they could eradicate the drug problem within prisons by running a few programmes and detox units ... the first tranche of service development was very much based around that.* (Interview 28 with director of drug agency)

Similarly, the Prison Service could have learnt from those who had experience of delivering programmes within UK prisons. Many of the pilot programmes were very expensive, high profile, and could reach only a minority of prisoners. What was missing were the low cost, low-profile services which could reach a much broader group. As discussed in the previous chapter, such services had been developing in the UK from the late 1980s to early 1990s and had become a model for prison drug work:

> *I've always seen it as regrettable that in formulating that policy, they seemed to get very caught up in concerns about contract letting. They did their own thing rather than building upon what had evolved over a*

> *number of years in the UK. I very much saw a UK model of prisons drug work which had evolved in response to the need. All of the sudden that was run roughshod through by the Prison Service letting out some very large contracts which brought in new players who had not been previously interested in prisons work. So that we had very high profile TCS, 12 step programmes, but what we had very little of is the counselling, information and advice services. The services which are low cost, low profile, but which reach huge numbers of inmates ... The Prison Service really did not speak to the established providers about what was going on ... What they did do was to bring over people from the US – Phoenix US.* (Interview 26a with director of a drug agency)

The pressure of politics and time led to a policy response which was not 'rational' in any sense. To a certain extent, expertise within the UK was ignored. The policy and many of the programmes were not based on UK experience, but US experience and raised the issue of whether such policy.and programme transfers would be effective:

> *Michael Howard was committed to all things American ... The evolving drug strategy team ... didn't know which way to go. The simple thing would have been to go and talk to the CDCU, the ACMD and look at the various documentation and things around and take a very slow approach to it and construct a strategy which was based upon the experiences of people working in the community. The pressure of time was one thing and influence was another ... A lot of the things that we experience originate in someone having a quiet word in someone's ear somewhere.* (Interview 28 with director of drug agency)

It is not surprising that existing service providers in prisons resented the adoption of American-based programmes and practice. They had been liaising and sharing knowledge, experience and good practice between themselves and with their counterparts in other European countries. By 1994, seminars to improve the provision of drug services to prisoners had been organised by a group of British Prison Drug Services and the European Network of Drug and HIV/AIDS Services in Prison had been established by the Cranstoun Projects Prisoner's Resource Service in the UK.

The development and sustainability of treatment provision

Despite the improvements in the level of treatment provision in some prisons through the pilot programmes, there was a clear consensus amongst the policy network that treatment generally remained ad hoc, patchy and unco-ordinated. The Directorate of Health Care conducted a survey of local drug strategies and found that 90 per cent provided education and drug awareness activities; 80 per cent had counselling and support from outside agencies (although the extent of this support varied); 66 per cent were involved in throughcare and sentence planning; 30 per cent had voluntary testing units; 30 per cent had rehabilitation schemes, and the nature and extent of detoxification was variable (HM Prison Service, 1997a). In particular, there was a lack of provision for short sentence prisoners (i.e. less than 12 months), who are not subject to sentence planning and for remand prisoners. Despite the historical emphasis on throughcare and release in the previous phases of policy and service development, sentence planning, throughcare and aftercare provision for drug using prisoners were crucial areas which had not been given sufficient attention within the 1995 strategy. This was mentioned by almost all those interviewed, viewed as a key problem on DATs (Duke and MacGregor, 1997), highlighted by the ACMD (1996), and one of the key concerns of the Department of Health Task Force on drugs (Department of Health, 1996).

The treatment and throughcare strand remained underdeveloped because not all prisons received funding or central support for programmes, whereas every prison had the requirement and resources to implement MDT and supply reduction measures. In effect, security and control measures were top-down central initiatives, whereas treatment was essentially a bottom-up local initiative in the majority of prisons and depended on local enthusiasm. This was recognised by the civil servants within the policy network:

> *The Prison Service has to put its money where its mouth is in terms of treatment provision. At the moment it has been a fairly unco-ordinated approach to particular pockets of money in particular parts of the country ... There should be more on the resource planning front to make sure that there is a totality of provision across the system, rather than just on an ad hoc basis where some prisons are better off than others.* (Interview 02)

> *We've got a disparity of distribution of the contracts because it's been done as a bottom-up approach, driven by local enthusiasm and some places have different priorities and have been slower off the mark. So we've got some very well-resourced areas and we've got some which are very poorly resourced.* (Interview 19)

Existing drug treatment provision was being undermined and compromised by the real pressures of population increases, budget cuts, lack of staff, difficulties in transferring prisoners to treatment programmes, competing priorities within the prisons and other institutional demands. During this phase, the sustainability of drug treatment was a key concern. Once the pilot drug treatment programmes had been evaluated, it was unclear as to whether they would be cascaded throughout the prison system and remain centrally funded and directed, or whether responsibility for funding and developing all drug treatment provision would be devolved to governors at the local level. As discussed in the previous chapter, central policy directives and guidelines can be ignored at local level. On the other hand, if the programmes were sustained, centrally funded, and expanded throughout the prison system, there was also the question of whether the voluntary sector could expand to meet the prison system's need. As a director of a drug agency commented:

> *[The question is] whether the organisations will be able to do it. And a subsidiary of that is what will they stop doing? The voluntary sector is notably fragile in terms of expansion ... You could see a voluntary sector with three-quarters of its work in the Prison Service and one-quarter in the community – a complete warping of that sort of relationship.* (Interview 08)

The question of 'balance' in the 1995 prison drugs strategy

Despite the improvements in the level of treatment provision through the activities of the policy network, the strategy remained imbalanced and intensified the tensions between treatment and punishment. Punishment, control and security initiatives had clearly overridden treatment, health and harm reduction initiatives. This was recognised by civil servants, penal reformers, drug agencies, and other policy influencers. The development of prison drugs policy was heavily influenced by the particular context, politics and environment in which the Prison Service was operating during this phase. The policy network was constrained by these parameters in what they could achieve in their attempts to manage and contain the growing tensions between treatment and punishment. The penal policy context was a much more powerful force than the drugs policy context of *Tackling Drugs Together*. The escapes from Whitemoor and Parkhurst prisons and the subsequent Woodcock and Learmont reports emphasising increased security, as well as Michael Howard's law and order agenda meant that supply reduction and MDT, received a much higher profile, greater priority and more resources. The Chief Inspector of Prisons, Judge Stephen Tumin, also added fuel to the political fire in February 1995 when he published his inspection report on Styal prison which included the headline-catching rhetoric, 'enter a shoplifter and leave an addict!' (HM Chief Inspector of Prisons, 1995).

The political goal was therefore to eradicate the problem and to publicly articulate this goal. This was recognised by the ACMD (1996: 1) which warned that the Prison Service needed to have realistic expectations about what could be achieved in terms of reducing drug use: 'unrealistic public and political expectations put undue pressure on the Prison Service and make it more difficult to strike the necessary balance between care and control'. Members of the policy network tended to view the 1995 prison drugs strategy and its emphasis on control as an exercise in public relations and a political response to the increasing pressure to be seen to be doing something about a problem which generates great political and public concern. The strategy was therefore an attempt to introduce some order over the drug problem in prisons which appeared to be 'out of control'. As a civil servant argued, it had great appeal because it sounded 'tough' and it could be measured, particularly the MDT element of it:

> *It sounds tough – maybe more because it's tangible and measurable ... It's like the government, the authorities are taking control of the situation. All the messages from [the] drug culture in prisons are of a situation that the authorities don't have control. If you can actually test people and control them and put them into treatment, it's like you're taking control of the environment ... It's this whole feeling of things spinning out of control, so the more you can take control over that it's considered good. It's the rhetorical attraction of it.* (Interview 07)

Policy development was also affected by the new 'managerial' discourses operating in drugs and penal policy. It was much easier to develop and implement a punitive mechanism in the prison environment backed up by law and performance indicators, than it was to develop treatment programmes across the system. As a penal reformer argued, 'you couldn't pass a law to say there will be all these counselling and agencies operating'. (Interview 18). Under the 'new penology' described by Feeley and Simon (1992: 462), drug testing is used as a mechanism for classifying prisoners, for measuring the distribution of risk within the prison population, for filling the gap left by traditional interventions, and for providing penal agents with 'a means to document compliance with their internal performance requirements'. Thus, mandatory drug testing was a technological solution to a human problem which could be measured and produce quick, tangible results. In contrast, treatment and rehabilitation involves individuals working together over time with results often taking a longer period of time to achieve. As Seddon (1996) argued, the managerialism within the strategy was too simplistic in the prison context and failed to provide a long-term solution.

The growing contradiction between treatment and control was also a manifestation of the divisions within Prison Service Headquarters and the separate responsibilities of the various directorates. This structural division is evident both in terms of the work that each directorate does as well as their geographical locations. During the 1995 strategy, drug treatment and communicable diseases were the province of the Directorate of Health Care located in Cleland House, and MDT and the security functions were the province of the Security group – Order and Control – located in Abell House. Due to these distinctions and separations, personalities and willingness to work together cross-directorally became of paramount importance. Underlying these structural divisions, there was also the notion that health and control issues should not be integrated or mixed. These divisions and differences within Prison Service Headquarters also filtered down into the prison system. Health care staff were not initially encouraged to get involved in the new drugs strategies as they were mainly seen to be about control and security. This had an impact on the balance between treatment and enforcement and it also led to much confusion within government, the prison system and the treatment agencies. As one civil servant argued:

> *There was a view held by previous senior people in the Service that health and control didn't mix and shouldn't mix and therefore health staff were discouraged from having anything to do with the establishment drugs strategy. They were told to keep very well clear of anything to do with MDT ... You had therefore people who were quite expert who were discouraged from becoming [involved] because it had to deal with the disciplinary side as well. That was sort of a fundamental philosophy that treatment and mandatory testing and discipline didn't go together, so they stayed very separate.* (Interview 19)

It became clear during the 1995 strategy that there will always be some sort of 'balance' between treatment and punishment. The difficulty for policy-makers was to determine the 'correct' balance between the two activities and to accept that the balance might shift. Within the policy network, there were key differences in how the two activities were perceived (i.e. as a continuum or two separate activities). Some described care and control as two separate continuums or dimensions which are not necessarily connected:

> *Because the two initiatives came from different ends of the political spectrum – treatment and punishment. It would be very difficult linking them from the start ... It wasn't really a proper strategy. MDT was introduced quite quickly.* (Interview 09 with civil servant)

In contrast, others argued that care and control should not be viewed as separate and independent, but integrated and working together:

> *At worst one should hope for an uneasy alliance where there will be tensions, but you can rub alongside each other. At best, I'm sure what we can achieve is an understanding that the two things work hand in glove. They are two sides of essentially the same coin and they are moving towards helping individuals make decisions about changing their lives ... But they are also doing that on a macro level ... They are doing it for the prison. They are doing it for the wider community ... Although there will be times where they diverge, they fall out – a prisons blows up and there's a great big security issue and everything gets shut down, the balance can be restored. It just requires an understanding of what these things really are.* (Interview 28 with director of a drug agency)

At the end of this phase, some members of the policy network, particularly the civil servants, were optimistic that in theory a balance could be achieved between care and control, while others, mainly representatives of drug agencies and penal reform groups, felt that security concerns would always work to the detriment of any type of treatment and rehabilitation activities. Their scepticism may be a reflection of their experience on the ground of working with prisoners and within prisons. It was not only the drugs strategy which was subject to this tension between care and control, but it was an enduring conflict within all prison activities. The balance between treatment and punishment within the prison drugs policy was affected by the Prison Service Statement of Purpose which places security as the number one priority. Working within this context, drug treatment and counselling are destined to have a lower priority than enforcement and security. Another consideration is whether 'care' or treatment can be facilitated in a coercive environment such as the prison. This raises a number of complex issues and questions:

> *Can you facilitate cure in a coerced environment? Is a prisoner ever free to make a decision? ... Can we then say that he's a volunteer? I think that sort of balance faces the Prison Service in virtually everything that it does and drug treatment is no exception to this.* (Interview 18 with penal reformer)

At the end of this phase, the continuing dilemmas for the policy network were to grapple with the contradiction between treatment and punishment, to attempt to shift the focus of policy away from security and punishment and to make the treatment strand of the strategy more explicit and defined. Their ideas and activities informed the review of the 1995 strategy and the next phase of policy development which will be explored in the next chapter.

Conclusion

During the period 1993 to 1997, important shifts and changes occurred in the development of prison drugs policy. The first comprehensive drugs strategy was developed, the Prison Service had been formally incorporated into drugs policy at the national level, and prisons were expected to become involved in drug issues outside the prison walls through local partnerships. The drug issue in prison had finally been acknowledged at a political level and had become a highly politicised issue. It was increasingly framed as a problem of order, control and discipline which threatened the stability of the prison system. The response was to impose order on a problem which was perceived to be spiralling out of control. A more explicit prison drugs policy began to develop and interface with the overall frameworks of both penal and drugs policy. As policy became more explicit and defined, the contradiction between treatment and punishment became more intense.

The political context and the emphasis on managerialism during this period ensured that the new prison drugs strategy was dominated by punitive, but measurable, mechanisms such as MDT and increased security. Drug treatment initiatives emerged as an afterthought in policy development and in response to pressure from a policy network which began to lobby for greater emphasis on treatment. This policy network was led by drug service providers who saw the opportunity for expanding their work in prisons and securing funding for it. During this phase, it appears that policy-makers and politicians were less confident with existing approaches to dealing with the drug problem in British prisons, failed to consult many of those who had experience in this area, and looked instead to the United States for policies and programmes which could be transferred. Despite the attempts of the policy network to rebalance the 1995 prison drugs strategy, there was a clear consensus that enforcement, punishment and control aspects remained the key focus and priority. In May 1997, the Labour government was elected to power, presenting new opportunities for the policy network to express their concerns and views, influence the development of policy, and reformulate the existing strategy.

5

1997– : Eradication to Realism?

Introduction

This chapter focuses on the period from mid-1997 and outlines the main developments in prison drugs policy which are planned for the next decade. On 1 May 1997, Labour won the general election. Their victory heralded the opportunity for new ideas, discourses and issues to infiltrate policy agendas. However, during the lead up to the election, the party had successfully reinvented and repositioned itself as New Labour, signalling 'the end of Old Labour, old policies and old welfarism' (MacGregor, 1998d: 251). 'Soft' policies on crime, drugs, welfare dependency, and the family were replaced by 'tough' new policies. Although there have been significant changes and reforms within public policy since the election of New Labour, the remnants of Tory populism remain, and some of the new policies possess a striking continuity to the old. During this period, 'policy feedbacks' or the ways in which the legacy of established policies and inherited policy structures shape and constrain what is possible within policy development, have been significant for the new government (Skocpol, 1992). Policy development in all areas, including prisons and drugs, has also been heavily influenced by transferring the ideas and discourses from the United States.

This chapter begins by highlighting the main developments in drugs and penal policy since the 1997 election, which provide the backdrop for the changes within prison drugs policy. Borrowing ideas from American drugs policy, an anti-drugs co-ordinator or 'drugs tsar' was appointed who was to guide, co-ordinate and implement the new national drugs strategy. The new strategy did not, however, mark a significant departure from the previous one, *Tackling Drugs Together*.

The 'managerial' discourses around assessment, targets, performance, partnership and co-ordination intensified. Despite the increased focus on prevention and treatment, it will be argued that the punitive discourses of 'enforcement', 'control' and 'punishment' have endured. Policy-makers and politicians have become increasingly preoccupied with the relationship between drugs and crime and the role of the criminal justice system in dealing with drugs was further enhanced. Similarly, developments in penal policy under Labour have not indicated a fundamental overhaul of previous Conservative policies. Labour's 'tough on crime' policies have not been successfully integrated with their 'tough on the causes of crime' policies and the populist punitive rhetoric of earlier phases of policy development has continued.

In the latter part of the chapter, the nature and extent of the drug 'problem' in prison is explored by examining three key pieces of research commissioned by the Prison Service and their review of the 1995 prison drugs strategy. As Spector and Kitsuse (1977) argue, an official response or implementation of policy is not the final stage of a social problem. The process continues whereby 'second generation' problems arise through existing policies and form the basis for new responses or policy reforms. In the construction of second generation social problems, 'assertions about the inadequacy, inefficacy, or injustice of the procedures may themselves become the conditions around which new social problem activities are organized'(Spector and Kitsuse, 1977: 151). Thus, during this phase of policy development, the concern was not so much around the drug problem itself, but with the policies and procedures which had been designed to eradicate it and the growing contradiction between treatment and punishment.

The evaluation of the 1995 prison drugs strategy highlighted problems around mandatory drug testing (MDT) procedures and inadequacies in treatment provision. The revised 1998 strategy represents an attempt to ameliorate some of the problems raised by the policy network during the previous phases of policy development. In many ways, these reforms denote a new 'realism' or pragmatism in relation to tackling the drug 'problem' in prison compared to the previous strategy and an attempt to rebalance the strategy towards treatment and care for drug using prisoners. However, the basic punitive framework for delivering the strategy remains intact and the emphasis on the discourses of 'security', 'control' and 'punishment' has continued. It remains to be seen whether the balance between treatment and punishment will be dramatically altered. In the process of attempting to rebalance the new strategy towards treatment, the policy network around prison drug issues has been reshaped with drug agencies entering into more formalised partnerships with the Prison Service. The final section of the chapter explores the impact of prison drugs policy on wider policy development and suggests that some of the initiatives which began in the prison, such as testing and coerced treatment, have now gained greater acceptance and have been extended outside to the community.

Drugs policy context: 'breaking the vicious circle'

The attention given to the relationship between drugs and crime and the role of the criminal justice system in dealing drugs during 1993–7 was continued and reinforced by the new Labour government. In opposition, Labour portrayed the drugs and crime problems as inextricably linked and produced a document entitled *Breaking the Vicious Circle*, which outlined its proposals to tackle drug-related crime (Labour Party, 1996). Drawing upon selected pieces of research, Labour policy on drugs was to be underpinned by the following key principles: drug treatment works and is cost-effective; coerced treatment is just as effective as voluntary treatment; drug testing helps to identify drug users and ensure they conform to treatment regimes; and offenders should be kept in treatment for a minimum of three months. Within Labour's election manifesto, three main commitments in relation to drugs were outlined which they pursued once in office: the appointment of an American-style 'drugs tsar'; the introduction of a new treatment and testing order based on the US drug court models in Dade County, Miami; and the extension of access to voluntary testing for all prisoners.

Appointment of the UK Anti-Drugs Co-ordinator

The concept of a 'drugs tsar' was put forward initially by the Bush administration in 1989 in response to the growing public concern regarding drugs in the United States. However, successive drug tsars, including William Bennett and Barry McCaffrey, have been criticised for failing to meet expectations (Jenkins, 1997). In the UK there were over 200 applications for the position of 'drugs tsar' or anti-drugs co-ordinator, including doctors, drugs specialists and academics (*The Guardian*, 6 Oct. 1997). Many of those working within the drugs field expressed concerns regarding the disproportionate emphasis on enforcement and the shift towards combative language in the government rhetoric around the appointment and the American label of 'drugs tsar' (see also Jenkins, 1997; Eaton, 1997; Strang et al., 1997). However, civil servants argued that the appointment was not intended to signal a fundamental shift in drugs policy and the person's role was to co-ordinate action on drugs and build upon the existing strategy, *Tackling Drugs Together*. It was important that the person appointed could demonstrate that s/he had the confidence of all the principal professions and interest groups. However, it would be difficult to fulfil the expectations of all the actors involved in drugs policy networks.

In the end, however, two appointments were made. In October 1997, Keith Hellawell, the Chief Constable of West Yorkshire police, was appointed to the position of UK Anti-Drugs Co-ordinator, and Mike Trace, the director of the prison-based treatment agency, RAPt (Rehabilitation for Addicted Prisoners Trust), was appointed as Deputy Co-ordinator. The appointments were billed as a 'dream ticket' in the media in that both enforcement and treatment aspects were covered (*The Guardian*, 15 Oct. 1997). This appeared to signal a commitment to ensuring that action and policy on drugs would be balanced between the treatment and punishment dimensions. There was also the potential to highlight prison issues more prominently in future drugs policy debates as the Deputy had an established reputation in prison-based work. The Co-ordinators embarked on an intense period of familiarising themselves with the existing approach to drugs, reviewing research and consulting with key groups and individuals in the drugs field. After six months, they developed a new national drugs strategy.

The 1998 national drugs strategy: Tackling Drugs to Build a Better Britain

In April 1998, the government introduced a new drugs strategy entitled *Tackling Drugs to Build a Better Britain*. It represents continuity with the previous phase of policy development, but also signals important changes. The 1998 strategy was to run over a longer term of ten years. For the first time, drug problems were seen to be linked to other social and environmental problems such as unemployment, homelessness, and social exclusion. Drugs policies were therefore expected to interface with other social policies including welfare-to-work, social exclusion, youth justice, education, public health, and community safety and with other policy structures such as the Social Exclusion Unit. The new anti-drugs effort was to be targeted on the geographical areas of greatest need and risk and upon drugs which cause the most damage, such as heroin and cocaine. The 'managerial' approach to the drug problem intensified with the various anti-drugs activities being subjected to a programme of rigorous and objective measurement, monitoring, evaluation and research. In order to reduce competition between agencies, performance indicators at the corporate level were to be developed. Under the new strategy, there was an explicit commitment to base future policy and practice on real 'evidence', rather than rhetoric. This shift was welcomed by professionals and practitioners working in the drugs field (see Farrell and Strang, 1998).

For the first time, there was also a commitment to re-distribute drugs spending and transfer resources towards treatment, rehabilitation, prevention and education. The strategy proposed a shift away from reactive expenditure and dealing with the consequences of drug use towards investment in prevention. New funds were to be generated from seizing the assets from drugs traffickers and channelling these into anti-drug programmes. The government's Comprehensive Spending Review (CSR) also allocated an additional £217 million to departments to fund additional proactive anti-drugs work over the years commencing 1999/2000 (DPAS, 1999).

The strategy is organised around four elements: young people, communities, treatment, and availability. The main aims are to help young people resist drug use in order to achieve their full potential in society; to protect communities from drugs-related anti-social and criminal behaviour; to enable people with drug problems to overcome them and live healthy and crime free lives; and to stifle the availability of illegal drugs on the streets (HM Government, 1998a). By 2000, targets were established for each aim. Similar to the 1995 strategy, emphasis on enforcement, punishment and the drugs-crime link continued. Under the aim 'to protect our communities from drug-related anti-social and criminal behaviour', a key objective was to 'reduce the levels of repeat offending amongst drug misusing offenders'. In order to achieve this reduction, one of the main activities was to implement drug treatment and testing orders and promote 'caution plus' schemes in the community. Prison-related aims and objectives also figured prominently in the new strategy. A key treatment objective was to increase the participation of problem drug users, including prisoners, in drug treatment programmes. In particular, throughcare and aftercare arrangements for drugs using prisoners were to be coherent, focused and linked to provision in the community. The reduction of the supply of drugs within prisons continued to be emphasised as a key availability objective (HM Government, 1998a).

The main structures developed under the previous strategy, *Tackling Drugs Together*, were to remain intact. The Central Drugs Co-ordination Unit was renamed the UK Anti-Drugs Co-ordination Unit and continued to support the monitoring and implementation of the strategy. Drug Action Teams (DATs) and their associated Drug Reference Groups (DRGs) continued to be the main mechanism to ensure that the strategy was translated into action at the local level. An interim evaluation of DATs in 1997 concluded that they had been successfully established across the country; improved relations and communication between the various agencies; and many initiatives had been implemented or co-ordinated by the new structures (Duke and MacGregor, 1997). However, community safety and criminal justice were viewed as one of the most difficult areas to impact upon. In particular, prisons were seen as difficult to engage in DAT and DRG structures.

As highlighted in the previous chapter, structural problems around coterminosity of boundaries were viewed as real impediments to partnership work with prisons. A key difficulty with prisons is that they are neither national nor local structures and therefore do not have the same commitment as other DAT agencies to the local area. Prisons were considered to be different 'culturally' from the other agencies represented on DATs as they have no history of joint working, work within a punitive rather than rehabilitative culture and are often located geographically away from the community and other agencies. Other agencies represented on DATs often lacked understanding of prisons and the constraints within which they work (Duke and MacGregor, 1997). Under the 1998 strategy, the Prison Service was encouraged to direct resources from within their budgets to drugs-specific partnership and give this work priority in their business plan (HM Government, 1998a).

After the 2001 general election, significant changes occurred in the co-ordination and delivery of the drugs strategy. The strategy targets were criticised by professionals in the drugs field as 'unrealistic', 'unworkable', 'unmeasurable' and 'insufficicently grounded within evidence' (Home Affairs Select Committee, 2002). Similar to the fate of their US counterparts, the British drugs tsars were given little power to make changes within drugs policy and then blamed for failing to meet the expectations of the government. They stepped down from their coordinating roles in June 2001. The responsibility for the strategy was then transferred from the Cabinet Office to the Home Office. The Home Office Drugs Strategy Directorate replaced the old structure of the UK Anti-drugs Co-ordination Unit (UKADCU), the Action Against

Drugs Unit (AADU), and the HQ of the Drugs Prevention Advisory Service (DPAS). A new director, Sue Killen, was appointed to the Directorate. Another important development was the National Treatment Agency which was set up in June 2001 to raise standards and ensure consistency in drug treatment.

Various demands for a major reform of Britain's drugs law have been made by the Police Foundation (1999) and the Home Affairs Select Committee (2002). Most of their recommendations regarding changes to the law have been deemed too radical by the Labour government. However, after the Conservatives announced they would be reconsidering drugs legislation following their defeat in the 2001 Election, the new Home Secretary, David Blunkett, proposed that cannabis be reclassified from a class B to a class C drug. This means that cannabis would remain a controlled drug and using it would remain a criminal offence, but possession of the drug would be no longer an 'arrestable' offence. Although this is a far cry from legalisation or decriminalisation, it does signal a small but significant shift in terms of liberalising drugs law. It also prompts the question as to how cannabis possession will be dealt with in prisons.

Penal policy context: 'tough on crime, tough on the causes of crime'?

During the early 1990s, the Labour party had begun to challenge the Conservative government on criminal justice issues. New Labour altered its traditional image of being 'soft on crime' to presenting itself as the 'party of law and order' by promising it would be 'tough on crime, and tough on the causes of crime' if elected (Blair, 1993). By 1997, the opinion polls indicated that the public had gradually become more confident in Labour's new populist rhetoric and image (Downes and Morgan, 1997). The New Labour government introduced and implemented many of its own law and order ideas, but it also continued to develop some of the policies which were proposed by the Conservative government. It is clear that the populist punitiveness of the Tories has endured.

Although New Labour claimed it was committed to reducing the prison population, there is no evidence thus far that the 'prison works' discourse has been successfully overturned (Morgan, 1999). The prison ship docked in Portland, Dorset, which had been commissioned from the New York prison authorities by the Conservative administration in 1997, was put into operation by the Home Secretary, Jack Straw, shortly after he took office to provide more prison accommodation. By 1998, the average prison population had reached an all-time high of 65,299 with a small decrease to 64,400 in 2000 (see Table A.4, Appendix). Although various commitments have been made to improve the provision offered to prisoners such as basic skills, drug treatment and offending behaviour programmes, there have been no serious attempts to reduce the prison population. In fact, an extra 2,660 prison places are to be made available (Home Office, 2001). The Labour government has failed to engage with the more fundamental question of 'what are prisons for'. Any debate or proposals which would involve a radical overhaul or transformation of the prison system, particularly in terms of its overall aims or purposes, appear to be absent from the policy agenda.

The government's ideas for criminal justice are located in the Crime and Disorder Act 1998 which focuses on three key themes: youth justice reform, community safety and local partnerships, and improving the performance of the criminal justice system by reducing delay. As in other areas of the public sector, the managerialist discourse with its emphasis on targets, measurement, performance and partnership has also intensified under the Labour government (McLaughlin et al., 2001). One key example is the establishment of new local partnerships to reduce crime and disorder consisting of representatives from local authorities, police and other statutory agencies. Their role is to conduct audits of the levels and patterns of crime in their local areas, consult their local communities, develop strategies and targets for tackling crime and disorder, and measure and report their performance against these indicators (see Home Office, 1998a: 5). The Crime and Disorder Act contains 121 sections introducing wide-ranging provisions such as anti-social behaviour orders, parenting orders, detention and training orders, extended supervision for sexual and violent offenders, local child curfews, the abolition of the *doli incapax* rule, child safety orders, a new Sentencing Advisory Panel and an extensive range of measures to reform the youth justice system (see Home Office, 1998a). The treatment of youth within the Act allows for intervention at an earlier stage of an offender's history and signals a fundamental shift in Labour's thinking on dealing with crime. For example, there is an increasing movement away from non-punitive, non-stigmatising and reintegrative strategies which they advocated in the past towards an approach of deterrence through punishment (Brownlee, 1998).

Although the adoption of the discourse 'tough on crime, tough on the causes of crime' suggests that Labour recognises that offending behaviour has its roots in social structures rather than individual pathologies, ministers and spokespersons have chosen publicly to articulate individual factors at the political level (Brownlee, 1998). In effect, the discourse has become divided into two separate discourses which have not been effectively linked either in rhetoric or, as yet, in practice. Soft and hard approaches are being pursued simultaneously. Policies are therefore being developed which are 'tough on crime' such as providing more intense punishment for persistent offenders (see Home Office, 2001) which have not been linked explicitly to its wider policy agendas such as welfare-to-work, social exclusion, homelessness, unemployment, and lack of services for young people (Heidensohn, 1998). Since the 2001 General Election, the punitiveness of the rhetoric and policies has accelerated and deepened. It is clear that those who do not respond to the new inclusive strategies, such as Welfare-to-Work, the New Deal and Sure Start, will be dealt with harshly through the criminal justice system.

Drug treatment and testing orders

Another example of the Labour government's continuing punitiveness is the introduction of drug treatment and testing orders (DTTOs), which run concurrently with regular probation supervision. Their purpose is 'to break the links between drug misuse and other types of offending' (Home Office, 1998b: 3). The orders are directed at offenders aged 16 or over 'who are convicted of crime (s) to fund their drug habit and who show a willingness to co-operate with treatment' (Home Office, 1998a: 16), who are users of opiates, cocaine and amphetamines, and who are considered to have a disproportionately disruptive effect on their communities or who persistently offend (Home Office, 1998b). They are imposed only with the 'consent' of offenders. However, if they choose not to comply, one option available is to impose a custodial sentence. The probation service is responsible for the supervision of the orders and treatment providers undertake the testing and treatment components.

The new order is supposedly based upon the Miami Drug Court model which was developed in 1989 in the USA and has been shown to be successful in reducing drug use and reconviction (Labour Party, 1996). However, as Philip Bean (1996; 1998) illustrates, this policy has not been transferred as a whole and there are important differences between the features of the drug court model and the proposed treatment and testing orders. In the USA, drug courts are a slow-track treatment system developed and led by the judiciary, rather than the criminal justice system or drug treatment agencies. Bean (1998: 103) argues that the most important criteria of the US model is the court's direct control over treatment provision. The probation and treatment services cannot produce the necessary control. He suggests that in order to replicate drug courts in Britain, there would need to be more resources; legislative and structural change; a loss of independence and restructuring for treatment agencies; an increase in the number of court administrative staff; and the development of rapid response urine testing and analysis facilities (Bean, 1998).

DTTOs have not received unanimous support within the drugs field (Barton and Quinn, 2002). Prior to implementation, drug treatment providers were sceptical about the proposed orders for a number of reasons. Coerced treatment raises fundamental ethical dilemmas and places strains on the therapeutic relationship between treatment providers and 'clients'. Concern was also expressed about the lack of resources for treatment provision. Drug agencies have always had difficulties in coping with the demand for their services and waiting lists are common (Chadwick, 1997). The orders would generate a new demand for treatment and there was a danger that existing drug agencies may not be able to expand quickly enough to meet it. Although those working within drug treatment and the penal reform lobby welcomed the diversion of drug offenders from custody, there was the danger of net-widening with the treatment and testing orders failing to be utilised as a true diversionary measure, but as an opportunity to make non-custodial sentences more punitive and tough. They may concentrate on the small-time offenders or 'minnows', rather than the 'big fish' who cause the most problems for communities. Moreover, those who test positive are also at risk of being re-sentenced to custody, thus increasing the prison population.

The drug testing and treatment orders were piloted and evaluated in three areas. Although the evaluations indicate that drug use and acquisitive crime were reduced substantially for offenders who completed their orders, the research also revealed fundamental problems, particularly around interagency working and standardisation in relation to referrals, testing procedures and supervision (see Turnbull, 1999; Turnbull et al., 2000). There were clashes of ideologies, organisational priorities, working styles, traditions and values between health care professionals and the criminal justice agencies. In order for DTTOs to be successful, an effective partnership between health and criminal justice systems is mandatory. DTTOs were introduced across the country in October 2000. It is clear that further longer-term research is required to evaluate their effectiveness and to assess whether these interagency tensions have been overcome.

These themes of continuity and change in drugs and penal policy provide the context for the review of the 1995 prison drugs strategy and the formulation of the new strategy. These developments will be explored in the next sections.

Review of the 1995 prison drugs strategy

In September 1997, a review of the 1995 prison drugs strategy was undertaken by the Prison Service with a view to formulating a new revised strategy (HM Prison Service, 1998a). The reasons for the review were associated with the appointment of the UK Anti-Drugs Coordinator, the development of the new national drugs strategy, as well as the criticisms and questions raised by the policy network in the previous phase of policy development around the balance between treatment and control within the existing strategy. The review was informed by three pieces of research commissioned by the Prison Service. These included two projects assessing the impact of mandatory drug testing (Edgar and O'Donnell, 1998; Farrell et al., 1998) and an evaluation of the pilot drug treatment programmes (PDM Consulting Ltd, 1998). During the previous phase, the existence of this ongoing research had enabled the Prison Service to adopt a 'wait and see' stance and to deflect criticism away from the evolving strategy, particularly in relation to the question of possible switching from cannabis to heroin. By 1997, interest in drugs and other related issues in prison had expanded. In addition to the internal review by the Prison Service, there were also other committees, groups and researchers which had published reports (see Home Office, 1997b; All Party Parliamentary Drugs Misuse Group, 1998; Home Affairs Select Committee, 1999; Health Advisory Committee for the Prison Service, 1997; London Drug Policy Forum, 1997; MacDonald, 1997; Keene 1997a; 1997b).

Nature and extent of the problem: the impact of the 1995 strategy

A judgement on the efficacy of the 1995 prison drugs strategy depends on the criteria used to measure effectiveness. Such criteria could include the proportion of positive mandatory drugs tests, the proportion of prisoners successfully completing drug treatment programmes, the number of treatment referrals, the number of drug finds in prisons, rates of recidivism and/or rates of drug use on release. However, the only systematic objective indicators produced through the monitoring and research commissioned by the Prison Service related to MDT results and supply reduction measures.

As we saw in the previous chapter, one of the key objectives of mandatory drug testing (MDT) was to provide systematic data on the extent and nature of drug use within the prison system. Evidence from the research shows that MDT had the greatest impact on recreational cannabis use. For example, the study conducted by the National Addiction Centre, King's College London, showed a clear downward trend in detected cannabis use across the entire prison system since the implementation of MDT, with a fall in positive tests for cannabis from 30 to under 20 per cent during the first 18 months of the programme. However, opiate positivity did not decrease, but remained fairly constant at a level of 5 per cent (Farrell et al., 1998). Qualitative research conducted by the Centre for Criminological Research at Oxford also indicated that MDT had an impact on the prevalence of drug use with over half (52 per cent) of their sample claiming that they had either desisted (27 per cent), reduced (15 per cent) or altered (10 per cent) their drug use as a result of MDT (Edgar and O'Donnell, 1998: 14). Despite anecdotal evidence from prisoners, staff, the media and various reports and articles, there was no concrete evidence of prisoners switching from cannabis to heroin in the commissioned research. However, there was evidence of persistent use in relation to opiates. Thus, the researchers from the National Addiction Centre concluded that despite the amount of effort and resources which had been directed towards MDT, it had greatest impact on recreational cannabis use and little success in deterring those who may have more serious addiction problems to hard drugs, such as heroin (Farrell et al., 1998: 6).

Research also underlined other problems around the MDT procedures (Edgar and O'Donnell, 1998). Prisoners perceived the MDT process as unfair and a means of restricting cannabis use, which they regarded as a legitimate activity. Similarly, prison staff did not see cannabis use as problematic for good order and discipline and evidence was uncovered by researchers that staff continued to 'turn a blind eye' when they found prisoners using cannabis. Prisoners also believed that MDT had increased tension within the prison, increased their resentment of staff, led to switching to hard drugs, and made inmates more wary. Their perception of MDT was that it was used as a method of discipline and punishment, rather than a means of identifying prisoners who needed treatment. In 1996 and 1997, the Prison Ombudsman received a number of complaints from prisoners over adjudications relating to the MDT process and procedures (see Prison Ombudsman, 1997; 1998). The research revealed that prisoners were more concerned about the effect of MDT on privileges such as temporary release, parole, loss of in-cell television, and risk of being placed on closed visits than they were about the threat of additional days on their sentence. This highlighted a fundamental flaw with the MDT disciplinary system of awarding additional days which ultimately led to increases in the prison population and overcrowding. For example, the researchers estimated that for the year 1997, 159,000 days were added to prisoner's sentences due to MDT, which is equivalent to 360 prisoner years. Thus, the extra prisoner days in custody can be estimated at approximately £7 million in additional running costs to the prison system (Edgar and O'Donnell, 1998: ix).

Given the great emphasis placed on security in the 1995 prison drugs strategy, the impact of the Learmont and Woodcock recommendations, and the increased resources for security measures, it is not surprising that efforts to reduce the supply of drugs, such as improved perimeter security, searching, closed visits, CCTVs, targeting visitors, use of sniffer dogs, and intelligence gathering had been deemed as generally successful by the Prison Service in deterring the use of drugs (HM Prison Service, 1998a). For example, the number of 'finds' of drugs or drug implements fell from 9,503 in 1995–6 to 7,587 in 1996–7 (HM Prison Service, 1998a: 12). Targeting, arresting and punishing visitors to prisons was also perceived to have a deterrent effect. The number of visitors arrested for drugs-related offences fell from 1,463 in 1995 to 1,176 in 1997 (HM Prison Service, 1998a: 14).

Although MDT and supply reduction measures were seen as generally successful in meeting their objectives, the review by the Prison Service and the evaluation by PDM Consulting Ltd of the pilot drug treatment programmes indicated that treatment provision required more fundamental improvements and changes before some of the programmes and ideas were extended more widely across the prison system (HM Prison Service, 1998a; PDM Consulting Ltd, 1998). Although there had been some expansion in drug treatment through the pilot programmes, provision remained patchy. As argued by treatment providers during the previous phase of policy development, low cost and low intensity interventions on a large-scale basis were missing within existing provision. Resources and effort had been primarily concentrated on high intensity and high cost programmes. The need to match drug treatment programmes with the needs of individual drug users was also highlighted. More specifically, the lack of specialist provision for certain groups in the prison system, such as women, vulnerable groups, young offenders, and those in the dispersal system was underlined. Aftercare and follow-up work was viewed as wholly inadequate and requiring immediate attention. In particular, prisons needed to initiate joint working arrangements with external agencies at the local level in order for the throughcare of drug using prisoners to be improved. The PDM evaluation and research in three Leicestershire prisons indicated that prison staff, both those involved in running treatment programmes and those providing support to prisoners, still lacked sufficient general knowledge about drugs and treatment and counselling issues (PDM Consulting Ltd, 1998; Hucklesby et al., 1999).

Response to the 'problem': the 1998 prison drugs strategy

Upon completing the review of the 1995 strategy and considering the research findings, the Prison Service concluded that its basic structure – tackling supply, demand and the health consequences of drug use – should remain intact (HM Prison Service, 1998a: 23). The existing strategy would therefore not be subjected to a radical overhaul. In many ways, the research was used to justify the existing policy framework. However, there is evidence that some of the lessons from the research and concerns expressed by the policy network around the 1995 strategy had been taken on board. Their activities and lobbying during the previous phase had informed and influenced the reformulation of policy. The new 1998 strategy would place greater emphasis on voluntary testing; effective treatment provision; education for young offenders; throughcare; discrimination between dealers and users and between less harmful and more damaging drugs; and identifying strategies for short-term and remand prisoners (HM Prison Service, 1998b). The particular needs of women prisoners would be examined separately. However, issues relating to race remained invisible within the reformulated strategy and the particular problems of minority ethnic prisoners in accessing drug services had not been considered (see Awiah et al., 1992). Under the new strategy, there was also a commitment to develop the research base around the strategy with an emphasis on exploring recidivism rates for those participating in drug treatment programmes. Plans to develop future policy in relation to other substance use, particularly alcohol, were also indicated. In a report on alcohol and prisons, the Health Advisory Committee for the Prison Service (1997) argued that there was an overlap between the groups using alcohol and those using other substances and advocated an integrated approach for future policy development.

Within the 1998 drugs strategy, even more emphasis was placed on partnership, liaison and co-ordination. As discussed in the previous chapter, the structural division within Prison Service Headquarters between the Directorate of Health Care, responsible for health and treatment concerns, and the Security group, responsible for security and control matters, was to be overcome by establishing a new single Drugs Strategy Unit within the Directorate of Regimes. The new unit would deal with all drugs-related issues and bring together the various threads of prison drugs policy. Co-ordination and partnership would also be improved by the appointment of area drugs strategy co-ordinators who would be responsible for a group of prisons within a geographical area. Their task was to develop the strategy at the regional and local levels by ensuring consistent application of effective practice and promoting links between prisons and communities. The Prison Service was also expected to improve its representation on Drug Action Teams under the new strategy.

For the period 1999–2002, the Prison Service received an additional £76 million from Comprehensive Spending Review (CSR) allocations to fund the new drug initiatives (DPAS, 1999). At the time of the policy review, members of the policy network were generally optimistic about the potential for change under the new strategy. Civil servants suggested that under the Labour administration there was now a possibility of altering the balance between care and control. This balance would depend on their perception of the 'problem' over time:

> *The current review [has been] approached with particular enthusiasm because we've got a new government and Ministers are particularly interested. It's very much interested that we've got that 'balance', as we see it at the moment, right. My guess is that it will change from time to time. We might have a new drugs strategy in a few years and we might change that balance quite considerably as our perception of the problem changes.* (Interview (14b) with civil servant)

They argued that the Labour government has focused more closely on the connection between MDT and treatment:

> *What is particularly important and what Ministers in this administration are focusing on is that there is actually a connection between the two. In that testing is not just a punitive or record keeping initiative, but that it*

> *genuinely results in determining appropriate referrals on individuals for treatment.* (Interview 02 with civil servant)

Although the revised strategy was more realistic and pragmatic in its approach, by targeting problematic drug use and focusing more on treatment and throughcare, the basic punitive framework for delivering the strategy, whereby drug users are punished, remains in place. Moreover, there is some cause for concern around the proliferation of voluntary testing which has also been incorporated into this framework of punishment. The following sections will briefly examine the main developments within the new strategy.

Mandatory and voluntary drug testing

Overall, the new policies around mandatory drug testing (MDT) indicate a more flexible, practical and cost-effective approach. Rather than every prison testing ten per cent of its population per month, governors are allowed to set their own levels of random mandatory testing between five and fifteen per cent (HM Prison Service, 1998a). The new strategy places more emphasis on promoting greater flexibility in the use of disciplinary and administrative penalties for positive tests. Where appropriate, both administrative sanctions and the incentives and earned privileges scheme can be used as responses to positive testing, rather than relying solely on awards of additional days. Greater differentiation was to be made between sanctions for cannabis and class A drugs. Whilst these developments indicate a much more pragmatic response in terms of MDT, prisoners testing positive for class A drugs are subjected to more frequent mandatory testing under the new strategy. This highlights the continuation of the punitive response to drug use. Unless prisons utilise MDT solely as a means of identifying those requiring treatment, this group will remain targeted and punished for their addiction problems.

The election manifesto commitment to extend access to voluntary drug testing to all prisoners by 2001 was given much prominence in the new strategy. Since the implementation of the 1995 prison drugs strategy, voluntary testing units (VTUs) proliferated across the prison system. This can be attributed partly to the success of the VTU and treatment programme run by RAPt at Downview prison (Kinchin, 1998). The new VTUs have taken many different forms in terms of structure and operation, but they are based on the premise of providing specially designated areas for 'prisoners who agree to avoid drugs and to prove it by undergoing regular, but random urine testing' (HM

Prison Service, 1998a: 17). Many of the existing units were established with very little central guidance and range from enhanced regimes and compacts to remain drug-free to relapse prevention units. The 1998 strategy issued detailed guidance to governors identifying the key issues they should consider when drawing up their own programmes for voluntary testing (see HM Prison Service, 2000). A single model for VTUs was not recommended as governors need the flexibility to adapt VTUs to the physical space of their prison and the needs of their population.

The key difference between mandatory and voluntary testing is that positive tests under MDT result in disciplinary action and positive voluntary tests result in administrative action. Although VTUs are popular with prisoners (Kinchin, 1998) and broadly supported by key policy players, there are a number of important issues raised by their extension across the prison system. Voluntary testing can be used as a method of assessing prisoners for greater privileges and for retaining them. Hence, differential regimes have developed on the basis of drugs use alone. If prisoners consent to voluntary tests and prove negative, then they may become eligible for privileges such as temporary release, in-cell television, desirable jobs or moving to an enhanced regime. This raises the question of 'voluntary' consent because there are penalties for those who do not consent in that they cannot receive such benefits. The units have been established mainly for those who have never taken drugs and those who have given up the habit. As Hewitt (1996) argues, this has the potential to create scenarios where a recidivist armed robber who has never used drugs is better treated than a ex-heroin addict who is rehabilitated and occasionally uses cannabis. Furthermore, those who have real problems with addiction are further punished by not having access to such privileges. There are also issues relating to the evidential standards for voluntary testing. Mandatory drug testing is subject to national standardisation and rigorous evidential standards (HM Prison Service, 1995b), whereas less stringent procedures are often followed for voluntary testing which take place on-site and are generally cheaper, such as dip and read tests and urinalysis machines.

Voluntary testing essentially means more testing and more resources for the increased volume of testing, staff time and training, structural alterations to the prison to create VTUs, and additional counselling provision. Over the period 1999–2002, £17 million was spent on the voluntary testing programme (HM Prison Service, 1999). Because voluntary testing is inextricably linked to rewards and punishments, it cannot be considered truly 'voluntary' and it could become difficult in the future to distinguish between mandatory and voluntary testing as they appear to be merging. Furthermore, what appears to be occurring with the increased use of voluntary testing is the division of the physical space and populations within the prison on purely 'drug' lines. A director of a drug agency described this emerging demarcation and classification between users and non-users within the prison:

> *There is a move now to create voluntary testing for enhanced regimes and congregate on basic regimes all the drug users and suppliers, so they'll be isolated – all the ones who want to stay on drugs and all the ones who are caught dealing. It's up to them if they want this very basic, very austere regime and almost segregated from the rest of the population. The rest of the population is going to be on enhanced regimes with voluntary testing which even though it sounds like the people who need the most help are getting the least ... But it does offer a tiered response.* (Interview (15) with director of drug agency)

There is therefore a growing trend towards a bifurcated prison drugs policy with voluntary testing units and new rewards for prisoners who conform, while for those who fail to conform or are unable to regulate themselves, there is mandatory drug testing, greater surveillance and punishment.

Supply reduction

The measures to reduce the supply of drugs in prisons outlined in the 1995 prison drugs strategy were further enhanced under the revised strategy. Such initiatives were supported by the Home Affairs Committee exploring the management of the Prison Service. They recommended that security measures such as fixed furniture in visits rooms, CCTV, sniffer dogs, random strip searching of prisoners after visits, closed visits for prisoners who have received drugs, and rigorous searching of visitors should be extended across the prison system (Home Office, 1997b). The review of the 1995 strategy highlighted various examples of good practice in relation to supply reduction and deterrence including imposing closed visits on those found guilty of drugs offences; use of CCTV recordings to provide evidence of passing drugs for subsequent adjudications; drawing up protocols between prisons and police for arrest procedures and intelligence gathering; displaying posters and newspaper articles detailing the risk of arrest and prosecution in visitors centres; and the provision of support to visitors who feel pressurised to bring drugs into prisons (HM Prison Service, 1998a). Under the 1998 strategy, the Prison Service promised 'to continue to target those who seek to profit from the misuse of drugs ... we will not let up on the battle to reduce the flow of illegal drugs into prisons' (HM Prison Service, 1998b: 6–7). Three new supply reduction objectives were introduced: to develop a performance indicator on action taken against suppliers and dealers; to establish anti-social drugs-related activity as a key criterion within incentives and earned privileges schemes; and to disrupt the distribution networks for illegal drugs (HM Prison Service, 1998b).

In January 1999, supply reduction measures were further enhanced when Jack Straw announced that visitors who were caught or suspected of smuggling drugs into prisons would be banned for a three-month period from further visits (Home Office, 1999). This illustrates that the government has failed to grasp the dynamics and complexities of drug smuggling and victimisation in prison and ignored the gender dimension to the problem as outlined in the previous chapter.

Harm minimisation

As with the previous drugs strategy, harm minimisation measures did not receive a high profile in the policy review or the 1998 strategy. The review revealed that Health Care Standard 8 dealing with detoxification had been implemented in the pilot residential drug detoxification units, but these were found to be expensive, resource intensive, and only had the potential to deal with a minority of prisoners (HM Prison Service, 1998a). As the ACMD (1996) had warned, compliance with the implementation of Health Care Standard 8 was found to be variable across the prison system. This further highlights the enduring problem of the autonomy of prison medical officers in implementing national standards with regard to detoxification and also the continuing tension between central policy directives and local decisions about implementation. The evaluation of pilot drug treatment programmes recommended that specialist NHS services should be used to meet the need for safe and adequate detoxification and to provide specialist supervision when required (PDM Consulting Ltd, 1998). Within the 1998 strategy, a key harm minimisation objective was to provide appropriate interventions within the framework of a revised Health Care Standard 8, concurrent with Department of Health guidelines, to minimise drugs-related harm (HM Prison Service, 1998b). Subsequent inquiries have further highlighted the continuing inconsistency regarding detoxification and methadone maintenance practices across the prison system and between prisons and the community (Home Affairs Select Committee, 1999; 2002).

After a long delay, research commissioned by the Prison Service which had been conducted in 1994 on HIV/AIDS risk behaviour was finally published late in 1998 (Strang et al., 1998). This involved interviews with a random sample of 1,009 prisoners in 13 prisons about their knowledge, attitudes and behaviour concerning HIV/AIDS. In relation to drug risk behaviour, the main finding was that the majority of drugs injectors ceased to inject on entry to prison and the rest tended to inject less frequently. However, those who continued to inject whilst in prison were more likely to share needles (Strang et al., 1998). These findings provide the 'official' evidence, which was missing during early phases of policy development, that there is a group of prisoners who continue to engage in high-risk drug behaviour and are therefore at greater risk of transmission of HIV and other blood-borne viruses such as Hepatitis C. As we saw in the previous chapter, the Prison Service recognised this threat and was developing a scheme to provide sterilising tablets for cleaning syringes to prisoners who continue to inject. The pilot scheme for sterilising tablets was introduced in July 1998 in eleven prisons for a three month period. Prisoners were to have easy access to the tablets without having to identify themselves as drug users. However, it is questionable given the punitive, security-focused culture surrounding drugs within the prison system whether prisoners would risk the possibility of being seen accessing the tablets.

It is interesting that no reference was made to the introduction of sterilising tablets in either the new drugs strategy or the policy review documents. It may be that the Prison Service was concerned that incorporating such an initiative into their drugs strategy document would appear as an admission of policy failure, that they were condoning drug use and as a contradiction to their 'tough' stance on drugs in prison. Despite the low profile of harm minimisation in the Prison Service's public discourse on drugs, key policy players felt that the new government was more willing to engage in harm minimisation debates and implement such measures. As a civil servant commented:

> *Politically, there's [been] a shift ... in that harm minimisation was almost a banned phrase in the previous administration ... Whereas I think there's much more ability to talk in terms of harmful drug misuse against a backdrop of drug misuse per se and try to make sense of what is it we're trying to tackle and where do the problems lie from a rather more informed sort of base now.* (Interview 14a with civil servant)

However, the 'official' discourse around harm minimisation is likely to continue to be articulated 'privately', rather than 'publicly' for political reasons. The public face of the new drugs strategy continues to project the hard-line abstinence approach of the previous phase. Despite the greater willingness to adopt harm minimisation principles within the prison system during this recent phase, overall progress in this area remains slow and incongruent to policy and practice in the community. Reflecting on developments in harm reduction since 1988, Strang (1998: 301) argues that the 'continued failure to use health opportunities in prisons stands as one of the resistant black spots' in the development of policy and practice.

Treatment

As argued by the policy network which emerged around the 1995 strategy and documented in the policy review and the evaluation of treatment programmes, existing treatment provision required much improvement and change to meet the Prison Service's goal of every prison having access to 'a comprehensive range of prevention, treatment and rehabilitation programmes which meet the needs of all prisoners' (PDM Consulting Ltd, 1998: 1). In order for this to become a reality, prisons would need to liaise and make treatment referrals to other prisons in their area. Under the new strategy, treatment provision was to be developed on an area basis. It was based on the success of the area-wide model in Kent which established inter-prison and inter-agency co-operation through a referral system and area co-ordinator (see Appleyard, 1998).

The goal of the new strategy was to develop a drug treatment service framework which provides 'an equitable provision of basic and enhanced specialist services to meet low level, moderate and severe drug problems' (HM Prison Service, 1998a: 4). Drug services were configured to provide low cost and low intensity interventions across the prison system, with fewer higher cost and higher intensity programmes offered on an area and national basis. An integrated Counselling, Assessment, Referral, Advice and Throughcare service (CARATS) was developed within and across Prison Service areas which was tailored towards the specific needs of the populations in each prison (DPAS, 1999). From October 1999, CARATS were to provide a range of easily accessible interventions and act as the link between courts and prisons, different departments within an individual prison, different prisons when prisoners are transferred, and prisons and community agencies. Prisoners requiring more intensive treatment could be referred to enhanced drug treatment services, such as residential programmes and detoxification services. Multidisciplinary teams consisting of drug agency staff, prison officers, probation officers, and health care staff would deliver the CARATS. The effectiveness of treatment provision was to be subject to independent research and evaluation and performance indicators on increasing treatment referrals, programme completions and reducing recidivism amongst drugs using offenders were to be developed (HM Prison Service, 1998b). Programmes must achieve central accreditation to ensure they meet the required standards by the Prison/Probation Service Panel.

Preliminary research conducted by Burrows et al. (2000) has shown that in order for CARATS to be successful in preventing relapse and recidivism, effective interagency working and throughcare arrangements are vital. There are fundamental problems which must be overcome both structurally and philosophically (see Home Affairs Select Committee, 1999; Kothari et al., 2002; Hucklesby and Wilkinson, 2001). Arrangements to share information and deal with confidentiality issues need to be established between health professionals and prison staff. The conflict between the harm reduction ethos of some drug agencies and the abstinence-based nature of the drug strategy needs to be addressed. Both prison staff and community agencies need to develop an understanding and appreciation of each other's working practices. Finally, the expansion of treatment provision needs to be fostered through long-term funding and training.

Although it remains to be seen how CARATS will progress, the development of a universal treatment framework with its emphasis on integrating treatment between prisons and between prisons and the community had been long awaited by the policy network which had lobbied for many years for a more explicit and defined drug treatment policy. The new framework was particularly welcomed by many of the drug service providers (see Hamer, 1998). Under this structure, they have assumed more prominent roles within prison drugs policy and have entered into more formalised contractual relationships with the Prison Service. A mutually dependent exchange relationship has emerged whereby the Prison Service has become dependent on outside drug agencies to develop and implement the treatment strand of the strategy, while the treatment providers have become dependent on the Prison Service for large and often lucrative contracts. This has altered and reshaped the traditional policy networks around prison drug issues. Drug treatment agencies have moved towards the core of these network structures, rather than operating on the periphery in more independent roles. Under the new framework, it is unclear as to which group will lead drug treatment in prisons.

The key question is whether treatment will be led by prison management or by service providers? Although the previous arrangements were often ad-hoc and informal, drug agencies working in prisons did have a certain degree of autonomy to determine their own styles and methods of working. The danger involved with these new formalised partnerships between drug agencies and the Prison Service is that they could lead to some agencies becoming 'incorporated', losing their independence and critical stance, and compromising their underlying ethos, values and philosophies. A director of a penal reform group offered an alternative view of partnerships arguing that they are often dangerous, particularly where prisons are concerned, and that the Home Office had successfully incorporated parts of the voluntary sector into the punitive framework of the prison environment.

> *the Home Office has successfully incorporated the voluntary sector. I wish the voluntary sector could be renamed the independent sector because the independence is crucial ... So you call it partnership. I call it incorporation. It's a scary thing ... the emulation of one group by the other.* (Interview 29 with penal reformer)

Impact and influence of prisons drugs policy

The development of prison drugs policy has been affected by shifts in the wider social, political and policy context. However, by the late 1990s, there was also evidence that the reverse process was occurring with many of the ideas, initiatives and practices within prison drugs policy influencing the way in which subsequent drugs policy has been shaped. These include greater acceptance of coerced treatment by policy-makers and practitioners; increased emphasis on the criminal justice system as an arena for drug treatment; and the proliferation of testing across other areas. The developments within prison drugs policy have laid the foundation for a much more punitive and coercive system around drugs and drug control.

Coerced treatment has become accepted almost universally within policy debates. Similarly, there appears to be a sea change in terms of the willingness of treatment providers to work within the criminal justice system. As we saw in previous chapters, drug agencies had been reluctant to accept referrals from the criminal justice system in the past due to the coercion involved. Because of the new resources being made available for drug treatment, opportunities are now available for drug agencies and many have an interest in pursuing contracts within the criminal justice system. Concern was expressed that treatment providers had compromised their principles by working with prisoners who were not entering treatment on a voluntary basis. Key policy actors maintained that in order for treatment to be effective, it had to be entered into on a voluntary basis. As a penal reformer argued:

> *You've got the voluntary sector with their vested interests and all their jobs, and their monies and their fundraising. They shouldn't work in prisons where prisoners are punished ... They've swallowed a lot of the principles. Drug groups used to argue that they wouldn't take anybody in a rehab unless it was voluntary and they were committed to the programme. Now they're working with people in prisons who are so-called committed to the programmes, but if they have a relapse or found with drugs in their urine, they're sent down the plonk or they lose their remission.* (Interview 29 with penal reformer)

On the other hand, the view emerging from the service providers was that they no longer had the luxury of dealing with voluntary clients:

> *Most drug treatment services are being impacted to a greater or lesser extent by coercive drug treatment. You've got the Crime and Disorder Bill with the testing and treatment orders ... So we're sort of coming in from the cold ... We used to have the luxury of being entirely voluntary. People arrived here if they wanted to and we talked to them. That luxury doesn't exist anymore.* (Interview 26a with director of drug agency)

Increasingly, the criminal justice system as a whole is seen as having significant potential as a location and opportunity for drug treatment (Kothari et al., 2002). At each stage of the criminal justice process – arrest, court, sentencing, probation, prison, and parole – drug treatment has been developed and provided. In many ways, British drug treatment appears to be moving towards an American model of service provision where providers are diverted from their work in the community and the criminal justice system becomes the 'front end' of treatment. A director of a drug agency described this shift in the following terms:

> *A lot of the treatment services are now linked to the criminal justice system, so in a sense the criminal justice system has become the 'front*

> *end' of treatment services ... Now, services are actively engaging with prisons and the criminal justice system ... So those groups are now more closely aligned with one another. A lot of it has to do with the flow of the money, but it actually reflects what is happening in the American approach ... There [are] dangers in having the criminal justice system at the front end of treatment ... Drug agencies need to be quite cautious about their relationships with the criminal justice system. There are benefits. There is the potential to meet the needs of individuals. We also need to think about global consequences of that and what it says about their role in relation to users. Basically I still believe that it is better if people who have got drug problems make decisions on their own to seek help and treatment.* (Interview 03)

With the new emphasis on treatment within the criminal justice system, there is also the potential danger that offenders will be sentenced to prison and community penalties with drug treatment options in the hope that they will receive help for their drug problem, rather than as punishment for their offence which may not warrant such a severe sentence.

In Britain, mandatory drug testing has its antecedent within the prison system. The new DTTOs are the most obvious examples of transferring prison policies to community penalties. Similarly, the Criminal Justice and Court Services Act 2000 includes provision to drug test for specified class A drugs those charged with property crime, robbery or class A drugs offences and those under probation service supervision (see Mallender et al., 2002 for a preliminary evaluation). By the late 1990s, drug testing had generally become accepted by policy-makers and practitioners as a key mechanism within drugs control policy. There was a clear consensus amongst those most involved in drugs policy development that testing would continue and spread into other spheres of social life, including education and employment.

The development of drugs policy in prisons has also affected penal policy and regimes. Drugs had assumed a high priority within the prison system at a time when other programmes were being cut back. This impacted upon the treatment programmes in prison in that drug workers were often having to deal with a range of other problems presented by those undergoing treatment. However, the priority given to drugs was subject to change and was contingent upon how much of a security problem it remained within the prison system. Because drugs were seen to be connected to issues of order and control, they had been given more attention. As a director of a drug agency commented:

> *They're still juggling and there's a number of plates spinning at the moment and drugs is becoming a bigger plate and it spins faster and it looks like it's going to fall more frequently so they have to keep giving it attention. Whether it becomes a greater priority depends on how much of a major security problem it is. That will be the driving force. They risk losing control of the prison environment through drugs and they certainly have come close to that. That's not about health care, it's about maintaining control of the prison.* (Interview 28)

Similarly, drugs in prison has remained an important political issue under the Labour government which appears committed to continuing Michael Howard's punitive zero tolerance campaign. This political commitment may also change, but in the current phase of policy development, drugs policy in prison has remained high profile and impacted upon wider policy development and agendas.

Conclusion

This phase of policy development continues to evolve and it remains to be seen how the new strategy will develop in practice, but it is possible to reflect on the significance of the proposed changes. Although some of the recent policy developments represent a new 'realism' in responding to the drugs 'problem' in prisons, the underlying punitive framework remains within the new strategy. This 'realism' is characterised by the increasing recognition that the drug problem cannot be fully eradicated, the commitment to evidence-based policy and practice, and by new government interest in attempting to rectify the balance within the strategy towards the treatment end of the continuum. It is clear that some of the criticisms raised by the policy networks around drug issues in prisons have been considered and taken on board in the new strategy.

There has been some attempt to contain and manage the increasing contradictions between treatment and punishment which emerged during the previous phase. This is illustrated by the emphasis on improving treatment and throughcare provision, the issuing of sterilising tablets to prisoners who continue to inject, the differentiation between hard and soft drugs, the partial relaxation of MDT procedures and the increasing recognition of alcohol in policy development. However, at the same time, responses which emphasise 'punishment' and 'control' have also been further improved and enhanced and run parallel to the more liberal response. The focus on testing, whether it be mandatory or voluntary, has continued. Similarly, supply reduction and security measures have been strengthened. The official discourse remains focused on 'control', 'order' and 'punishment' and these are the discourses which are often articulated publicly. Moreover, the policy network around drug issues in prisons has been reshaped during this phase. Drug agencies have entered into more formalised partnerships with the Prison Service and moved from the periphery toward the core of the policy networks. The key danger for future policy development is the 'incorporation' of this important sector of the policy network and the silencing of a critical voice in prison drugs policy.

One of the most significant developments is the influence that prison drugs policy has had on overall policy development. The proliferation of drug testing in community penalties and other initiatives, the almost universal acceptance of coerced treatment and the criminal justice system moving to the 'front end' of treatment provision are all indications of the impact, influence and power of the developments in prison drugs policy and practice. In many ways, as Cohen (1985) has argued, this represents the dispersal of control and the blurring of the boundaries between the prison and the community, setting the stage for future policy developments.

6

Conclusions: Shifting Agendas and Policy Networks

The aim of this final chapter is to reflect on the pervasive themes which have emerged from this history of drugs policy development in prisons and to consider these in relation to the activities of policy networks and future policy agendas. The 'problem' of drugs in prisons has shifted from being a relatively obscure policy issue to a mainstream one. Over the four phases of policy development, drug issues within the penal system have become fully institutionalised in government policies and bureaucracies. The preceding chapters have illustrated a growing contradiction between treatment on the one hand and punishment on the other. This contradiction has become more intense, acute and difficult to contain and manage over time. In response, a significant shift has occurred from a situation of 'no policy' to a more explicit and defined prison drugs policy. The first phase of policy development was characterised by policy which was implicit, unstated, informal, private and internal. During the second phase, there was a move towards more formal, documented policy, taking the form of loose guidelines which were subject to local variations in implementation. The last two phases were characterised by policy which was much more explicit, formal, public and overt compared with the previous phases.

Activating and resisting agendas

Over the four phases of policy development, policy networks have activated, shaped and reshaped the development of drugs policy in prisons. In the analysis, policy networks were characterised as primarily issue-based. They played key roles in the processes of identifying, defining and framing drugs issues in prisons. The framing process was not only influenced by the reactions, perceptions and experiences of those involved, but also by real pressures such as increases in drug addict notifications by prison medical officers and the number of drug offenders sentenced to custody, the threat of HIV, and the results of mandatory drug testing. Different policy issues, problems or functions at various times provided the occasion for the formation of policy networks. In the first phase, throughcare and release was the key policy issue; this was followed by HIV/AIDS; then by mandatory drug testing and treatment provision; and finally by the review and reformulation of the 1995 prison drugs strategy (see Table 6.1).

Some of the policy issues were generated exogenously or by external pressures such as HIV/AIDS, while others were generated endogenously or by internal factors such as the review of the 1995 strategy. Policy issues shaped the formation of policy networks. In turn, these networks further shaped and defined the issues through their activities. In some instances, the policy network was aided in the framing process by research and evidence. For example, during the second phase of policy development from 1986 to 1993, research, evidence and knowledge began to accumulate which assisted the policy network around HIV and drug use in exposing the drug 'problem' in prison, challenging the view that it was insignificant and pressuring the Prison Service for a more liberal and humane response. In effect, this growing evidence base helped to sensitise policy-makers to the drug issue in prisons and turn what was perceived as a 'non-problem' into a

Table 6.1: Policy issues and policy outcomes in prison drugs policy

	Key policy issues	*Policy outcomes*
1980–6	Throughcare & release	Service development (Parole Release Scheme)
1986–93	HIV/AIDS & drug use	1987 Statement on throughcare of drug using prisoners 1991 Caring for drug users manual Policies on HIV/AIDS
1993–7	MDT (mandatory drug testing) & treatment provision	1995 prison drugs strategy (MDT, increased security measures, & pilot drug treatment programmes)
1997–	Review & reformulation of the 1995 prison drugs strategy	1998 prison drugs strategy (move towards voluntary testing & more comprehensive treatment provision i.e. CARATS)

'problem'. However, in the earlier phase from 1980 to 1986, the framing of the drug problem in prison was hindered by the lack of research and evidence. The collusion around drugs in prison during this phase meant that research access was virtually impossible to negotiate (Pearson, 1990).This lack of research had an impact on policy development in that in the absence of any evidence of a drugs 'problem', it justified a policy of 'no policy' or one which was internal and hidden from outside scrutiny. Although the models put forward by Weiss (1986) do not allow for such circumstances, it is evident that just as research may have an impact upon policy, so too does the *absence* or *lack* of research.

As we saw in Chapter 1, one of the key criticisms of the policy network approach is that it cannot explain policy change. Although it addresses *how* policy changes, it does not address *why* policy changes. In order to understand the changes within prison drugs policy over the last twenty years, policy networks need to be integrated with micro and macro level analyses. The work of the policy network in the process of framing drug issues in prisons and advocating their solutions was influenced by and occurred within a wider context. The Wilks and Wright model of policy networks stresses the need to disaggregate to the subsectoral level of policy, enabling researchers to explore how developments within wider policy sectors affect subsectors (Wilks and Wright, 1987). As outlined in Chapter 1, Rein and Schon (1993) put forward the idea of 'nested contexts' which can be broken down into internal, proximate, macro, and global contexts. This framework illustrates the complex process by which policy issues overlap and interact with wider issues, contexts and policy solutions. In the case of prison drugs policy, the framing and reframing of the drug issue in prison and the development of policy occurred as the four nested contexts shifted and impacted upon one another.

The *global context* of prison drugs policy refers to changes at the broadest level affecting policy development. At this level, the rise of New Right ideology with its emphasis on neo-conservative politics and neo-liberal economics influenced all sectors of public policy. The contraction of the welfare state was accompanied by an expansion of the penal complex (Hudson, 1993). Through a systematic comparative analysis, Weiss (1998) argues that the world recession of the 1970s represented the turning point in post-war penality towards an increasing punitiveness with world-wide increases in imprisonment, sentence lengths, and severity of penal regimes. During the 1960s and early 1970s, there was a clear consensus amongst penal practitioners and commentators regarding the correctionalist framework which was based on notions of reform, treatment and rehabilitation. As David Garland (1999: 8) argues, such a consensus no longer exists as the old penological frameworks have disappeared and new ones have not yet emerged to replace them. Penal policy and institutions are therefore in a state of transition between different policy regimes. Within this uncertainty, Garland identifies a number of converging penal trends in the western world: the erosion of correctionalist ideologies; the shift to expressive justice and punitive measures; the return of the victim; the emphasis on public protection; the management of risk; the changing objectives of community penalties and custodial institutions; the politicisation of penal policy discourse; the commercialisation of penality and the drift towards mass imprisonment. As we have seen in the preceding chapters, most of these penal dimensions influenced and shaped the development of prison drugs policy in the British context.

A related development has been the increasingly common practice of importing or transferring policy ideas and procedures, particularly from the United States. In the UK, this has become a trend in many areas of public policy, occurring under both the Conservative and Labour governments. For example, private prisons, boot camps, electronic monitoring, 'prison works', and 'three strikes and you're out' sentencing policies have their antecedents in US penal policy. This trend is not just evident within the UK, but in other countries such as Canada (see Roberts, 1998). Garland (1999: 7) observes the growing 'internationalization in penal matters [which] ensures that purportedly successful (or merely popular) policy measures emerging in one context will quickly be emulated elsewhere'. Similarly, various commentators argue that the US 'war on drugs' has been exported to other nations (see Ryan, 1998; South, 1998; Stares, 1996). This has resulted in the development of a punitive and prohibitionist global discourse around drugs as opposed to a treatment, public health oriented one. In the UK, the 1995 prison drugs strategy was heavily influenced by the US drug testing and abstinence-based treatment programmes. The appointment of an American-style drugs tsar and the introduction of the new treatment and testing orders based on the US drug court models are also key examples of policy emulations or transfers. Given the failure of the American 'war on drugs' and the drift towards mass imprisonment, it seems absurd to look to the US for policy ideas. As Elliot Currie (1993: 3) argues, 'The failure of American drug policy is depressingly apparent. Twenty years of the 'war' on drugs have jammed our jails and prisons, immobilized the criminal justice system in many cities, swollen the ranks of the criminalized and unemployable minority poor, and diverted desperately needed resources from other social needs.'

The *macro context* of prison drugs policy refers to changes in the overall direction of policy and the influence of wider social, political, economic and institutional change. The managerial reforms and restructuring implemented by the Conservative governments from 1979–97 have transformed the public sector beyond recognition. Moreover, the managerialist trend has continued, even intensified under the new Labour government. The 'new public management' with its emphasis on performance, value for money, privatisation, partnership and community has successfully penetrated all areas of public policy. Although the shift towards managerialism within the criminal justice system occurred later compared to other policy areas, it was not immune from these pressures. One of the ways to manage the emerging uncertainty and contradiction within the penal system has been to apply managerial techniques, rather than to engage in debates around penal values and ideology. The three E's – economy, effectiveness, and efficiency – began to manifest themselves in prisons during the late 1980s. As we saw in Chapter 3, particular examples include the overhaul of working arrangements for prison officers and management structures under the Fresh Start initiative in 1987 and the introduction of two private prisons in 1989. By 1993, managerialism within the prison system culminated in the Prison Service becoming a Next Steps agency. This involved a greater distinction between operational and policy matters, greater emphasis on 'strategic' planning with the formulation of corporate and business plans, the development of performance indicators and greater emphasis on co-ordination and partnership within the criminal justice system. Drugs policy was also influenced by the managerial discourses of performance and partnership. This can be seen most clearly in the 1995 and 1998 drugs strategies with their emphasis on action plans, performance indicators, audits and evaluations, and partnership and co-ordination structures.

Managerialism forced the development of a prison drugs policy which is much more explicit and can be measured. This shift corresponds with the growing patterns of conflict, contradiction and convergence between treatment and punishment and can be seen as part of the attempt to manage these tensions. Managerialism and its associated techniques create a myth of rationality, planning and control within policy-making. However, key players within the policy process argued that the development of prison drugs policy should not be viewed as 'rational' in any sense. In particular, the 1995 drugs strategy was perceived to be the result of a number of issues which coalesced into a policy, rather than the result of a systematic process:

> *Though it is now presented as the Prison Service drugs strategy, I'm not sure it was actually conceived as a 'strategy'. There were different strands that coalesced into something ... It's never as clean and as neat and as rational as sometimes in hindsight you like to present it.* (Interview (24) with penal reformer)

Similarly, policy development was compared to a process of 'osmosis' and as a reactive, rather than a proactive process:

> *If one is looking at policy development, it's a process of osmosis, rather than anything else sometimes. There aren't too many think tanks going on in the [department] ... There are bits of research, reports which come out of incidents or catastrophes – a prison breakout, a death, or several deaths close together. Then we develop a policy on security or how to treat prisoners who are at risk of suicide. That's the way it happens ... Although we call ourselves policy-makers, really we're very much resourced to deal with incidents ... We have annual planning exercises where we think about what we're supposed to be doing and what we will be doing. We set objectives ... That all goes on, but the process at the end of day is that we spend so much of our time firefighting. The sort of blue skies type approach, you know, what shall we do to improve the position of drugs next? It doesn't develop like that. We need a few deaths or [something] to go completely haywire before anything gets done or someone to jump in there and say, 'this is a disgrace'.*
> (Interview (12) with civil servant)

It is within this context that the 1995 prison drugs strategy revolved around the results of MDT as an indicator of its success or failure. The managerialist trend was paralleled by the growing punitive rhetoric in penal policy. Within the managerialist dominated framework, MDT produced tangible, 'objective' results very quickly, providing it with much appeal to policy-makers and politicians. Furthermore, MDT was attractive because it gave the impression of 'taking control' of the drug problem in prisons by punishing drug users. Sanctions could be applied immediately to those who tested positive. Drug testing became a mechanism for managing and classifying prisoners into a risk group (Feeley and Simon, 1992). In comparison, it is much more difficult to assess the individual effects of treatment and rehabilitation. In theory, this would involve greater subjectivity and longer time periods to produce results. Although the delivery of the new CARATS (counselling, assessment, referral, advice and throughcare service) programme is being assessed, this work has been similarly preoccupied with monitoring and performance measurement activity which can have a detrimental effect on the quality of service provision. Following her experience of managing CARATS, Lowthian (2002: 171) argues, 'Work is target driven and it is sheer throughput of numbers that governs the "success" or otherwise of the delivery ... this can impact negatively on the extent to which meaningful interventions can be offered to prisoners.'

The *proximate context* of prison drugs policy includes developments in both drugs and penal policy. However, in the first two phases of policy development, these two policy areas developed separately with very little overlap. Prisons generally remained on the periphery of drugs policy debates, while drugs remained on the periphery of penal policy debates. During the first phases, prison drugs policy was relatively insulated from developments in wider penal and drugs policy. By the early 1990s, however, the interface between these two policy areas became much more explicit and visible.

Penal policy and the prison environment have generally acted as constraints on the development of liberal, pragmatic and progressive drugs policies. For example, the enduring penal 'crisis' characterised by an increasing population, overcrowding, riots, industrial disputes, lack of resources, and inadequate conditions has limited what can be proposed and achieved within policy development. Particularly in the early phases of policy, drugs were kept hidden as they were functional as mechanisms of control within this penal context. The collapse of the rehabilitative ideal and the move towards a just deserts, punishment and law and order framework also helped to curtail the development of drug treatment provision. Early attempts at drugs and HIV policy development were further hindered by implementation which was strongly localised. By 1993, penal policy started to influence the direction of drugs policy in prisons with Michael Howard's pronouncement that 'prison works', his commitment to tackling the drug problem, and the influence of the Learmont recommendations. Prison drugs policy began to focus more closely on security, control and punishment, taking on the attributes of the austere and punitive penal policies which were emerging during this period. In contrast to developments in treatment provision, the MDT procedures and Learmont recommendations were universal requirements and this ensured that they were implemented across the entire penal system.

During the first two phases, prisons were generally excluded from developments and innovations in drugs policy. There were different discourses operating outside and inside the prison walls. During the first phase from 1980 to 1986, the re-definition of drug addiction and the expansion of service provision in the community were not paralleled within the prison environment. The new partnership structures (i.e. District Drug Advisory Committees) and the 1985 national drugs strategy omitted prisons from their remits. This began to change with the HIV/AIDS crisis when drug issues in the prison system moved into mainstream drugs policy debates. However, the new harm reduction principles and techniques which were operating successfully in the community failed to fully penetrate the development of HIV and drugs policies in prison. The constraints of the institutional context and the concern around the public imagery of such 'soft' policies meant that these principles were greatly modified and adapted within the prison environment. Under the 1995 national drugs strategy, there was a clear interface between penal and drugs policy. For the first time, prison-related aims and objectives were incorporated into policy at the national level and the Prison Service was expected to become involved in local and national partnership structures. The national strategy placed greater emphasis on enforcement, control and punishment and this was mirrored in the new punitiveness which was being advocated within penal policy. These two policy discourses had a profound effect on how the 1995 prison drugs strategy developed. Under the 1998 drugs strategy, the increasing focus on the link between drugs and crime will ensure that the interface between these two policy areas strengthens.

The *internal context* of prison drugs policy has been affected by changes in the membership and organisation of policy networks and structures. Depending on the issue at the centre of policy development, membership within the policy networks has changed and adapted over the phases. As drug issues in prison gained more prominent positions on the policy agenda, interest in this area expanded and more players became involved in the policy process. Some members, however, had long histories of involvement and were consistently represented over the various phases, including civil servants within the Prison Service and some drug agencies such as the Parole Release Scheme. In particular, the Prison Service played important gatekeeping roles within all the policy networks which emerged. Various committees such as the ACMD, the House of Commons Social Services Committee, and Home Affairs Select Committee also played key roles in shaping policy and often their membership overlaps with the networks.

In the first phase of policy development, the work of the ACMD (1980) and Social Services Committees (1985; 1986) served to initiate a small policy network around throughcare and release issues for drug misusing prisoners. Although the Home Office and the Prison Medical Service occupied central positions at the core of this network, the negotiation and planning by SCODA, NACRO, the probation service and various drug agencies was instrumental in ensuring that a service was developed for drug using prisoners on release during the early 1980s. In the second phase from 1986 to 1993, the advent of HIV/AIDS widened interest in prison drug issues, bringing new players into policy networks including more drug treatment agencies, medical professionals, penal reform groups (e.g. Prison Reform Trust), professional associations (e.g. ACPO, NAPO, POA), social researchers, HIV/AIDS organisations, and health authorities. During this period, the ACMD also sought to influence the policy process by producing three influential reports on drugs and AIDS which covered the penal system (ACMD, 1988; 1989; 1993). Although civil servants in the Directorate of Prison Medical Services were the key state actors involved at the core of this network, the power of the Prison Medical Service was diluted over time as more agencies gained access to policy networks and to prisons to work with drug users.

By 1993, interest in prison drugs policy further increased and the shift towards partnership and multidisciplinary approaches brought more players into the process. The increasing contradiction between treatment and punishment within policy development led to an increase in the number of representatives within the fields of drug treatment, penal reform, civil liberties and research. These groups were involved in lobbying against the introduction of MDT and for more comprehensive treatment provision. Interest in this area also expanded within the state. As drug issues in prisons became increasingly politicised, the Home Secretary and Director General of the Prison Service began to occupy powerful positions within policy development. Civil servants in the Security Group and Health Care Directorate of the Prison Service and the Central Drugs Co-ordination Unit were also involved at the core of the network. However, this is not to suggest that the Prison Service was unified in their interests around policy. There were structural and philosophical divisions between the Health

Care Directorate and Security Group which led to the control and treatment elements of the 1995 strategy developing separately. By 1998, the Prison Service Drugs Strategy Unit was established as an attempt to overcome these divisions and unite policy interest. This unit is likely to remain at the core of any future policy networks around drug issues in prisons. With the greater emphasis on treatment and the growing interdependence between the Prison Service and service providers, drug agencies are also likely to move from the periphery towards the core of future networks.

In order to understand policy change, analysis at the micro level dealing with the role of human agency is necessary. As Rhodes (2000: 86) argues, analyses of governing structures need to be connected with the beliefs and narratives of individuals. This was recognised by members of the policy network. In the interviews, respondents discussed the characteristics of particular individuals such as their backgrounds, knowledge bases, training, allegiances, preferences, management styles and their impact on the policy process. As a director of a drugs agency argued:

> *I don't think you can get away from individuals. You've got to look at the people ... There might be some good sound policy reasons, but there are other sociodynamic, psychodynamic forces at work – you've got the right person in the right job at the right time ... For me, structures only do so much ... What you're dealing with at the end of the day is personalities.* (Interview 05)

The 'institutional embedding' of the different policy players influenced the processes of identifying, defining and framing drugs issues in prisons. There are important differences related to the different structural locations and ideological foundations of the various groups involved. For example, those within the traditional 'caring' roles, including drug workers and probation officers, tended to express the drugs problem in individual, health-related terms, rather than institutional, enforcement-related terms. In order to gain access to the policy process, some groups neutralised their discourses and tended to present themselves in a conservative, rather than radical light. For example, many of the drug agencies involved advocate abstinence publicly, but privately promote harm reduction practices within the prison environment. Similarly, most penal reform groups would not present themselves as overtly 'abolitionist'. As Ryan (1978) argues, such groups need to be seen as 'acceptable' to government.

The framing of drugs policy issues in prison and the activities of policy networks occurred within these nested contexts. When features within these contexts shifted, it produced a ripple effect, often leading to the reframing of issues and renaming of the policy terrain. The policy networks adapted and changed in response to these shifting contexts and terrains. The shifts provided opportunities for policy networks to influence the policy process, but also set the limits to their activities. The reverse process also occurred whereby the reframing of prison drug issues shaped the contexts. This can be seen in the policies and structures developed by the Conservatives which were then inherited by the Labour government. This policy feedback mechanism set the parameters for subsequent policy development, often limiting and constraining what can be achieved. Moreover, the emerging context and experience of prison drugs policy is influencing wider policy frameworks. This can be seen in the expansion of drug testing into other spheres of policy, such as community penalties and policing, and the greater acceptance by practitioners of coerced treatment.

The role, influence and power of policy networks within the policy process varied over the different phases. Over time, they demonstrated an ability to identify opportunities at key moments, articulate their ideas and respond to agendas within the constraints, pressures and limitations of the wider policy, political, social and institutional contexts. They were successful in challenging and changing perceptions, policy and practice. Through this process however, parts of the policy network were drawn in and incorporated by the state, losing their independence and capacity for criticism. In the first two phases of development, policy networks played central roles in drawing attention to drug issues in prison and placing these on the policy agenda. In particular, their main concern was the way in which drug using prisoners were treated and the lack of congruence and continuity between the provision in prisons and that in the community. These networks were instrumental in helping to expose the drug problem in prison and pressing the Prison Service both to acknowledge the problem and to develop more explicit and humane policies. During the early stages, policy development was therefore driven by external interest, emanating from below or from the fringes of policy networks with drug agencies, professional associations, and penal reform groups playing key roles. Their success is illustrated by the development of specific services for prisoners in the first phase of policy and by the formulation of guidelines for their treatment and throughcare and the cautious HIV policies which emerged during the second phase (see Table 6.1).

In the last two phases of policy development however, policy networks were not as powerful in terms of activating the agenda and contributing to the initial stages of the policy process. Instead, they responded to and resisted an agenda determined by politicians. As in other policy areas, the increasing shift towards the populist punitive and managerial discourses led to less consultation between government and experts during the 1990s. Outside groups did not have the same opportunities to influence policy development (Rock, 1995; Downes and Morgan, 1997). Although they lost control over the agenda, the networks around drug issues in prisons adapted to these new circumstances. Under the punitive drugs policy framework which emerged from 1995 with its focus on mandatory drug testing and security measures, the contradiction between treatment and punishment became much more acute and pronounced. In response, the policy network attempted to lobby against the introduction of MDT.However, given the statutory powers surrounding the testing procedures, these attempts proved futile. The service providers recognised this and turned this into an opportunity to argue for an expansion of treatment within prisons to rebalance the strategy. Their success can be seen in the pilot drug treatment programmes which emerged during the course of the 1995 strategy and in the greater prominence given to treatment under the revised 1998 strategy. There is evidence that some of their criticisms around the 1995 strategy were taken on board and infiltrated the new policy agenda which emerged in 1998.

Since 1980, drug treatment agencies have remained important players in policy networks. In the latter phases of policy development, the Prison Service increasingly recognised that it needed these agencies to develop and provide drug treatment programmes in prison and therefore allowed them greater access to the policy process. Similarly, the Prison Service provides the drug agencies (many of which previously had insecure contracts or no contracts at all), with security, stability and a source of longer-term funding. Under the new CARATS framework, this mutually dependent exchange relationship was reinforced further. In the most recent phase, the policy network therefore changed shape. Over time, it evolved from a structure which was diffuse and informal to one which is more identifiable, formal, concrete and institutionalised. In a sense, some drug agencies moved from operating in independent roles on the periphery of policy networks towards being fully 'incorporated' into the core of these networks. They now have a stake in the continuation and expansion of the current policy framework. Given their vested interests and dependence on the Prison Service in relation to contracts, it remains to be seen whether these agencies will continue to play such central roles in lobbying for change and reform in prison drugs policy in the future. As their relationship with the state becomes more formalised and concrete, the danger is that a prominent voice in prison drugs policy will be silenced.

Future agendas and policy networks

This policy analysis has illustrated the movement towards a more refined and explicit prison drugs policy. This increasing clarity has been accompanied by a growing contradiction between treatment and punishment. Within prison drugs policy development, contradictory discourses and strategies have co-existed. There are overlapping systems of regulation including treatment and care and punishment and control. Particularly in the early phases of policy development, many prisoners were serving time for drug offences or offences relating to problematic drug use, but were denied access to appropriate care and treatment. In the most recent phases, new techniques have been devised to punish individuals for their drugs use within the prison environment, while at the same time, they are offered opportunities to address their problems through new modes of treatment and rehabilitation. Similar to other areas of social policy (see MacGregor, 1999b), the bifurcation within prison drugs policy has become increasingly polarised. The practice of putting forward 'soft' and 'hard' approaches simultaneously within drugs and penal policy has become a potent theme. For prisoners who conform to the new regulations, tests and mechanisms of control, there is prevention, treatment and rehabilitation, as well as new incentives and privileges. For those who do not conform, there is increased surveillance, punishment and harsh treatment. At the same time, these contradictions are converging and becoming blurred. This can be seen in the greater acceptance of coerced treatment and so-called 'voluntary' drug testing.

The current phase of policy continues to develop and evolve. A key priority for the Prison Service is to get the CARATS system of drug treatment established, accredited, and evaluated. Interest in this area continues to increase and expand. For example, the Home Affairs Select Committee recently undertook an inquiry specifically to explore drug issues within prisons under the new 1998 strategy (Home Affairs Committee, 1999).They concluded that the contradictions between disciplinary and therapeutic responses within the strategy have not been resolved:

> Devising a policy for tackling drugs in prison is important. As well as reducing tensions and criminal behaviour within prison, it has a major contribution to make to reducing offending outside prison. The prize at stake for success is high. But there are very real difficulties which have to be addressed; these include the need to strike a balance between cracking down on the supply of drugs and providing humane treatment of prisoners, and a balance between a disciplinary and therapeutic response to drug use in prison. (Home Affairs Committee, 1999: para. 173)

However, can such a balance ever be achieved within penal policy? Although policy networks were influential in their attempts to contain and manage these contradictory pressures between treatment and punishment, they had little success in actually resolving them. There are clear limitations as to what can be achieved within policy in terms of reconciling such competing objectives within the penal arena. Fundamental clashes remain between the ideologies, values and philosophies of some of the community drug agencies which advocate harm minimisation and the Prison Service drug strategy which is abstinence-based. As policy develops and the treatment programmes are established, it is clear that there is a degree of incorporation and what Carlen refers to as 'carceral clawback' occurring. The limits to prison reform or 'carceral clawback' relates to the involuntary nature of imprisonment, the priority of keeping prisoners in prisons and the fact that prisons are for punishment. Carlen (2002: 116) argues that the possibilities of a benign prison persist and multiply for a number of reasons including the constant need to legitimate the continued use of imprisonment, the prison has a key role in the development of new therapeutic initiatives, and penal reformers have accepted invitations to shape regimes to reduce the pains and damage of imprisonment. In the case of prison drugs policy, there was the persistent belief amongst some members of the policy network that balance or a compromise could be achieved between the treatment and punishment strands of the strategy. However, once non-state agencies become involved in prison administrative discourse, their reforming ideologies are often neutralised and forgotten. Once they begin to influence within policy networks, their discourse and critique around prisons becomes less radical as they concentrate on establishing and accrediting programmes, monitoring their effectiveness, and delivering value for money. As Carlen (2002: 120) argues, '[the prison] is becoming a lucrative and staple source of financing for many newcomers to the prison industry who appear not at all unwilling to legitimate the use of imprisonment by reference to the 'effectiveness' of their 'programmes' in reducing crime.'

The key dilemma for non-state organisations and particularly for drug agencies in the case of prison drugs policy is whether to refuse invitations to participate and thus lose their power to influence at all or accept invitations to participate and become incorporated into the penal apparatus. Policy networks are structures which both constrain and enable agents. The activities of the policy network will always be limited by the very nature of the prison environment. Similarly, those engaged with developing policy need to recognise the limits of drug programmes within the prison environment where security and control issues will always assume a higher priority. However, as long as drug users are sent to prison, there needs to be treatment and rehabilitation on offer for those who *wish* to participate. Such programmes need to be developed with the recognition of the structural obstacles to providing treatment in prisons and of the ways in which the prison environment amplifies the problems experienced by drug users (Malloch, 2000). For those prisoners who enter treatment programmes voluntarily, prison might be the place where their recovery from problematic drug use begins. The goal of policy and programme development should be to minimise the detrimental effects of imprisonment, rather than exacerbate them.

So, what should policy networks around drug issues in prisons concentrate their efforts on in the future? Instead of defining drug use as a 'prison problem', it must be framed or defined as a problem located outside the prison walls and linked to wider social issues including poverty, deprivation, unemployment, racism, and sexism. Various commentators argue that the real challenge to drugs and prisons must come at the sentencing stage, rather than tinkering with regimes and programmes. The emphasis must shift away from developing, accrediting and auditing more and more drug programmes within the prison system and towards developing and implementing strategies to divert drug users from custody. The development of 'real' alternatives to imprisonment, rather than another layer of punitive sanctions are needed. Although the development of the Drug Treatment and Testing Orders (DTTOs) hold promise in terms of diverting drug users from custody, their coercive nature, the emphasis placed on testing and the problems around inter-agency working need to be resolved if they are to be true 'alternatives'. The drug programmes which are developed need to be holistic and address the structural constraints and practical difficulties which prisoners face such as homelessness, poverty, debt, unemployment, and childcare, rather than locating the causes of drug use and offending within the individual. There is also a need to recognise the diversity within drug using population and different approaches to dealing with drugs. Moreover, as has been long recognised by drug agencies and increasingly acknowledged by policy makers, the throughcare of prisoners receiving drug treatment needs to be properly co-ordinated and resourced. Prevention and treatment need to be viewed along a continuum from the community to the prison and back to the community.

The increasing interest in drug issues in prisons and subsequent policy development have influenced the research agenda. The new policies have generated both commissioned and independent research on drug issues within the penal system. Compared with the first phase of policy development in the early 1980s, there has been a proliferation of studies on drugs issues in prisons and the criminal justice system. This interaction between research and policy illustrates the complexity and reflexivity of the relationship between the two areas. The political, economic and social context of research utilisation has been important during this period of policy development. The dominance of managerialism has influenced the types of research and researchers which are favoured, commissioned and used by government. The type of research which fits into this context focuses on the 'management' of the criminal justice system. It is generally quantitative in the form of evaluations, audits and surveys, emphasises inputs, outputs, throughputs, monitoring and efficiency, and produces statistics or measures of performance and clear recommendations for action and intervention (Pollitt et al., 1992). In the case of prison drugs policy, the concern of much of the research has been on the rates of positive MDTs and the incidence of switching to class A drugs. The focus of future research is likely to extend to completion rates for treatment programmes and recidivism rates. The emphasis has therefore been on *what* happens rather than on the meanings, choices or behaviours associated with drug use or *why* prisoners begin or continue to use drugs both within and outside custody. Moreover, research which explores and probes the causes of drug use and crime and their wider social, political and economic contexts would assist the policy network in defining and framing the drugs problem and how it relates to the prison system.

Policy analysis itself could also play an important role in the future development of policy. By studying policy networks, we can better understand the dynamics and contradictions within policy-making. As Edwards (1990: 30) argues, 'what needs to be more firmly acknowledged is that policy analysis focused on drug dependency issues is becoming a necessary tool for further policy development, rather than being seen as mere academic diversion'. In the areas of drugs and criminal justice, there is a need for research at the micro level, which examines the beliefs, values and ideologies of policy actors and how these become influenced and altered when they become engaged in policy networks. The focus could be on the biographies of key actors and how their backgrounds, knowledge bases, beliefs and values interface and/or conflict with the work and activities of policy networks. Connecting this level of analysis with an examination of the ways in which the global, institutional and internal contexts of policy-making shift and impact upon one another would further illuminate the processes of incorporation and issues around power, influence and dependence.

Appendix

Table A.1: All drug addicts[1] notified to the Home Office by prison medical officers by addict status 1981–96

	New drug addicts	*% of all notifications[2]*	*Renotified drug addicts[3]*	*% of all notifications*	*All drug addicts notified*	*% of all notifications*
1981[4]	320	14	—	—	—	—
1982	322	12	—	—	—	—
1983	472	11	—	—	—	—
1984	819	15	—	—	—	—
1985	1 138	18	—	—	—	—
1986	1 102	21	—	—	—	—
1987	685	15	653	11	1 338	12
1988	689	13	622	9	1 311	10
1989	624	11	535	6	1 159	8
1990	730	11	690	6	1 420	8
1991	955	12	792	6	1 747	8
1992	1 268	13	1 318	9	2 586	10
1993	1 941	17	1 823	11	3 764	13
1994	2 080	15	1 843	9	3 923	12
1995	2 602	18	2 464	11	5 066	14
1996	3 665	20	3 269	13	6 934	16

Sources: Home Office Statistical Bulletins, Issues 6/92, 15/93, 10/94,17/95, 15/96, 22/97, 'Statistics of Drug Addicts Notified to the Home Office, United Kingdom', Tables 8a and 8b.
Notes: (1) The statistics relate to notifications under the Misuse of Drugs Regulations 1973, which required doctors up until 30 April 1997 to send the details of people they considered to have been addicted to any of the following 14 controlled drugs to the Chief Medical Officer at the Home Office: cocaine, dextromoramide, diamorphine (heroin), dipipanone (Diconal), hydrocodone, hydromorphone, levorphanol, methadone (Physeptone), morphine, opium, oxycodone, pethidine, phenazoncine, and piritramide. (2) The other sources of notifications include general medical practitioners, police surgeons, and hospitals/treatment centres. (3) Full data on renotified addicts are available for the years 1987 onwards. (4) Data on notifications by prison medical officers is only available for the years 1981 onwards.

Table A.2: Drug offenders and custodial sentences 1980–2000

Year	*Number of persons found guilty, cautioned or dealt with by compounding for drugs offences*[1]	*Number sentenced to immediate custody*	*Average sentence length (months)*
1980	17 158	1 676	15.8
1981	17 921	1 931	17.0
1982	20 356	2 248	15.4
1983	23 442	2 819	17.9
1984	25 240	3 694	18.8
1985	26 958	4 535	19.2
1986	23 905	3 928	19.8
1987	26 278	3 939	20.9
1988	30 515	3 523	21.3
1989	38 415	3 855	23.6
1990	44 922	3 402	23.9
1991	47 616	3 268	21.6
1992	48 927	3 366	24.0
1993	68 480	4 835	23.3
1994	85 691	5 596	20.8
1995	93 631	7 086	21.1
1996	95 198	8 788	21.2
1997	114 627	10 580	22.8
1998	130 503	11 052	17.7
1999	120 777	11 428	20.2
2000	103 540	9 386	19.6

Source: Home Office Statistical Bulletins, Issues 18/84, 25/88, 10/98, 4/02, 'Statistics of Drugs Seizures and Offenders Dealt With. United Kingdom'.
Notes: (1) Drug offences include unlawful possession and trafficking (unlawful production of drugs other than cannabis, unlawful supply, possession with intent to supply unlawfully and unlawful import and export).

Table A.3: Number of new and renotified drug addicts[1] notified to the Home Office and percentages addicted to heroin 1980–96

	New drug Addicts	*% addicted to heroin*[2]	*Renotified Drug addicts*[3]	*% addicted to heroin*	*All drug addicts notified*	*% addicted to heroin*
1980	1 600	72	—	—	—	—
1981	2 248	74	—	—	—	—
1982	2 793	76	—	—	—	—
1983	4 186	66	—	—	—	—
1984	5 415	91	—	—	—	—
1985	6 409	93	—	—	—	—
1986	5 325	91	—	—	—	—
1987	4 593	89	6 123	83	10 716	86
1988	5 212	89	7 432	83	12 644	85
1989	5 639	87	9 146	83	14 785	84
1990	6 923	84	10 832	80	17 755	82
1991	8 007	79	12 813	68	20 820	72
1992	9 663	79	15 040	62	24 703	69
1993	11 561	78	16 415	60	27 976	68
1994	13 469	78	20 483	57	33 952	66
1995	14 735	79	22 429	58	37 164	66
1996	18 281	84	25 091	61	43 372	70

Sources: Home Office Statistical Bulletins, Issues 18/83, 25/88, 6/92, 10/94, 17/95, 15/96, 22/97, 'Statistics of Drug Addicts Notified to the Home Office, United Kingdom'.
Notes: (1) The statistics relate to notifications under the Misuse of Drugs Regulations 1973, which required doctors up until 30 April 1997 to send the details of people they considered to have been addicted to any of the following 14 controlled drugs to the Chief Medical Officer at the Home Office: cocaine, dextromoramide, diamorphine (heroin), dipipanone (Diconal), hydrocodone, hydromorphone, levorphanol, methadone (Physeptone), morphine, opium, oxycodone, pethidine, phenazoncine, and piritramide. (2) Heroin addicts can be addicted to other drugs. (3) Full data on renotified addicts are available for the years 1987 onwards.

Table A.4: Annual average[1] population in Prison Service establishments in England and Wales by sex 1975–2000

Year	*Males*	*Females*	*Total*
1975	36 601	1 219	37 820
1976	40 161	1 282	41 443
1977	40 212	1 358	41 570
1978	40 409	1 387	41 796
1979	40 762	1 458	42 220
1980	40 748	1 516	42 264
1981	41 904	1 407	43 311
1982	42 381	1 326	43 707
1983	42 072	1 390	43 462
1984	41 822	1 473	43 295
1985	44 701	1 532	46 233
1986	45 163	1 607	46 770
1987	46 722	1 704	48 426
1988	47 113	1 759	48 872
1989	46 736	1 764	48 500
1990	43 378	1 597	44 975
1991	43 250	1 559	44 809
1992	43 157	1 562	44 719
1993	42 991	1 561	44 552
1994	46 810	1 811	48 621
1995	48 983	1 979	50 962
1996	53 019	2 262	55 281
1997	58 439	2 675	61 114
1998	62 194	3 105	65 298
1999	61 523	3 247	64 771
2000	61 252	3 350	64 602

Sources: Home Office, Prison Statistics, England and Wales 1985, 1989, 1994, 2000.
Notes: (1) Figures on the prison population are based on counts of prisoners at Prison Service establishments. These counts are usually made on the last day of the month. The annual average population is an average for the monthly returns.

References

Primary sources

Government documents and official publications

Prison drugs policy and related documents

HM Prison Service (1987) *Policy Statement on Throughcare of Drug Misusers in the Prison System*. London: HM Prison Service.

HM Prison Service (1991a) *Caring for Drug Users: a multi-disciplinary resource for people working with prisoners*. London: HM Prison Service.

HM Prison Service (1991b) *Circular Instruction 12/1991: throughcare of drug misusers*. London: HM Prison Service.

HM Prison Service (1995a) *Drug Misuse in Prison: policy and strategy*. London: HM Prison Service.

HM Prison Service (1995b) *The Introduction of a Mandatory Drug Testing Programme for Prisoners in England and Wales: a guide to the main issues*. London: HM Prison Service.

HM Prison Service (1995c) *The Review of HIV and AIDS in Prison by the AIDS Advisory Committee*. London: HM Prison Service.

HM Prison Service (1996b) *Pilot Drug Treatment Programmes – leaflet*. London: HM Prison Service.

HM Prison Service (1997a) *Briefing: Drugs Strategy: progress report – No. 107, 1 August 1997*. London: HM Prison Service.

HM Prison Service (1998a) *The Review of the Prison Service Drug Strategy: 'Drug Misuse in Prison'*. London: HM Prison Service.

HM Prison Service (1998b) *Tackling Drugs in Prison: the prison service drug strategy*. London: HM Prison Service.

HM Prison Service (1999) *Press Release: Home Secretary announces big expansion in drug treatment services for prisoners*. London: HM Prison Service.

HM Prison Service (2000) *Voluntary Drug Testing Units and the Framework for Voluntary Drug Testing Units. Prison Service Order 3620*. London: HM Prison Service.

Home Office (1980) *The Government's Response to the ACMD Report on Drug Dependants within the Prison System in England and Wales*. London: Home Office.

Home Office (1993a) *Offenders who Misuse Drugs: the Probation Service response*. London: HMSO.

Home Office (1999) *Press Release: Bans for Visitors Smuggling Drugs Into Prison: Home Secretary Announces Tough New Anti-Drug Measures*. London: Home Office.

National drugs policy and related documents

Drug Prevention and Advisory Service (DPAS) (1999) *Drug Interventions in the Criminal Justice System: guidance manual*. London: Home Office.

HM Government (1994) *Tackling Drugs Together: a consultation document on a strategy for England 1995–1998. Cm 2678*. London: HMSO.

HM Government (1995) *Tackling Drugs Together: a strategy for England 1995–1998. Cm 2846*. London: HMSO.

HM Government (1998a) *Tackling Drugs to Build a Better Britain: the government's ten year strategy for tackling drugs misuse. Cm 3945*. London: HMSO.

HM Government (1998b) *Comprehensive Spending Review – Chapter 13: Cross-Departmental Review of Illegal Drugs*. London: HMSO.

Home Office (1985) *Tacking Drug Misuse: a summary of the government's strategy*. London: HMSO.

Home Office (1990b) *UK Action on Drugs Misuse: the government strategy*. London: HMSO.

Home Office Central Drugs Prevention Unit (1993) *Annual Progress Report 1992/93*. London: Home Office.

Penal and criminal justice policy and related documents

Health Advisory Committee for the Prison Service (1997) *Alcohol Misuse and the Prison Community*. London: HM Prison Service.

HM Prison Service (1992) *Briefing, Number 49, 8 May 1992*. London: HM Prison Service.

HM Prison Service (1993) *Framework Document*. London: HM Prison Service.

HM Prison Service (1996a) *Corporate Plan 1996–1998*. London: HMSO.

HM Prison Service (1997b) *Annual Report April 1996–March 1997*. London: HM Prison Service.

Home Office (1964) *The Organisation of the Prison Medical Service*. London: HMSO.

Home Office (1975) *Report on the Work of the Prison Department 1974*. London: HMSO.

Home Office (1977) *Report on the Work of the Prison Department 1976*. London: HMSO.

Home Office (1978) *Report on the Work of the Prison Department 1977*. London: HMSO.

Home Office (1983) *Report of the Work of the Prison Department 1982*. London: HMSO.

Home Office (1985b) *Report of the Work of the Prison Department 1984/85*. London: HMSO.

Home Office (1988a) *Punishment, Custody and the Community*. London: HMSO.

Home Office (1988b) *Improving Management in Government: the Next Steps. Government Efficiency Unit*. London: HMSO.

Home Office (1990a) *Crime, Justice and Protecting the Public*. London: HMSO.

Home Office (1990c) *Report on a efficiency scrutiny of the Prison Medical Service*. London: Home Office.

Home Office (1990d) *The Prison Medical Service in England and Wales – recruitment and training of doctors: a report of a working party of the Royal College of Physicians to the Chief Medical Officer March 1989*. London: HMSO.

Home Office (1991a) *HIV/AIDS: Organisation and Procedures at Establishment Level. Circular 30/1991*. London: HMSO.

Home Office (1991b) *Organising Supervision and Punishment in the Community: a decision document*. London: HMSO.

Home Office (1991c) *Custody, Care and Justice: the way ahead for the Prison Service in England and Wales. Cmnd. 965*. London: HMSO.

Home Office (1996) *Protecting the Public: the government's strategy on crime in England and Wales*. London: HMSO.
Home Office (1997a) *Drug Treatment and Testing Order: background and issues for consultation*. (http://www. homeoffice. gov. uk/dtto. htm).
Home Office (1997b) *The Management of the Prison Service (Public and Private): the Government reply to the second report from the Home Affairs Committee session 1996–97, HC57*. London: HMSO.
Home Office (1998a) *Crime and Disorder Act 1998: introductory guide*. London: Home Office.
Home Office (1998b) *The Crime and Disorder Act: guidance for practitioners involved in drug treatment and testing order*. (www. homeoffice. gov. uk/cdact/dttguid. htm).
Home Office (2001) *Criminal Justice: the way ahead. Cm. 5074*. London: HMSO.

Official Statistics

Federal Bureau of Prisons (2002) *Quick Facts May 2002*. Washington, DC: US Department of Justice.
Home Office. *Prison Statistics, England and Wales* (for the years 1975–2000). London: HMSO.
Home Office (1993b) *Criminal Statistics England and Wales 1992. Cm 2410*. London: HMSO.
Home Office Statistical Bulletin (1984) *Statistics of the Misuse of Drugs in the United Kingdom, 1983. Issue 18/84*. London: Home Office.
Home Office Statistical Bulletin (1987) *Statistics of the Misuse of Drugs, United Kingdom, 1986. Issue 28/87*. London: Home Office.
Home Office Statistical Bulletin (1988) *Statistics of the Misuse of Drugs, United Kingdom, 1987. Issue 25/88*. London: Home Office.
Home Office Statistical Bulletin (1989) *Statistics of Drug Addicts Notified to the Home Office, United Kingdom, 1988. Issue 13/89*. London: Home Office.
Home Office Statistical Bulletin (1990) *Statistics of Drug Addicts Notified to the Home Office, United Kingdom, 1989. Issue 7/90*. London: Home Office.
Home Office Statistical Bulletin (1991) *Statistics of Drug Addicts Notified to the Home Office, United Kingdom, 1990. Issue 8/91*. London: Home Office.
Home Office Statistical Bulletin (1992) *Statistics of Drug Addicts Notified to the Home Office, United Kingdom, 1991. Issue 6/92*. London: Home Office.
Home Office Statistical Bulletin (1993) *Statistics of Drug Addicts Notified to the Home Office, United Kingdom, 1992. Issue 15/93*. London: Home Office.
Home Office Statistical Bulletin (1994a) *Statistics of Drug Addicts Notified to the Home Office, United Kingdom, 1993. Issue 10/94*. London: Home Office.
Home Office Statistical Bulletin (1994b) *Statistics of Drug Seizures and Offenders Dealt With, United Kingdom, 1993. Issue 28/94*. London: Home Office.
Home Office Statistical Bulletin (1996) *Projections of long term trends in the prison population to 2004. Issue 4/96*. London: Home Office.
Home Office Statistical Bulletin (1997) *Statistics of drug addicts notified to the Home Office, United Kingdom, 1996. Issue 22/97*. London: Home Office.

Other government documents

Department of Health (1988) *Preventing the spread of HIV infection among and from injecting drug misusers. HC (88) 53/LAC (88) 18*. London: Department of Health.

Department of Health (1996) *The Task Force to Review Services for Drug Misusers: a report of an independent review of drug treatment services in England.* Wetherby: Department of Health.

Parliamentary papers

Hansard
Select Committee Reports:
House of Commons Home Affairs Committee (1999) *Drugs and Prisons, Fifth Report, Session 1998–99, HC 363-I.* London: HMSO.
House of Commons Home Affairs Committee (2002) *The Government's Drug Policy: is it working? HC 318.* London: HMSO.
House of Commons Social Services Committee (1985) *Fourth Report from the Social Services Committee, Misuse of drugs with special reference to the treatment and rehabilitation of misusers of hard drugs, session 1984/85.* London: HMSO.
House of Commons Social Services Committee (1986) *Prison Medical Service, Third Report from the Social Services Committee, session 1985/86.* London: HMSO.

Non-government official publications[1]

ACMD (1980) *Report on Drug Dependants within the Prison System in England and Wales.* London: Home Office.
ACMD (1982) *Treatment and Rehabilitation.* London: HMSO.
ACMD (1984) *Prevention.* London: HMSO.
ACMD (1988) *AIDS and Drug Misuse, Part One.* London: HMSO.
ACMD (1989) *AIDS and Drug Misuse, Part Two.* London: HMSO.
ACMD (1991) *Drug Misuse and the Criminal Justice System, Part One: Community Resources and the Probation Service.* London: HMSO.
ACMD (1993) *AIDS and Drug Misuse – update.* London: HMSO.
ACMD (1994) *Drug Misusers and the Criminal Justice System, Part Two: Police, Drug Misusers and the Community.* London: HMSO.
ACMD (1996) *Drug Misusers and the Criminal Justice System, Part Three: Drug Misusers and the Prison System – an integrated approach.* London: HMSO.
All Party Parliamentary Drugs Misuse Group (1995) *Comments from the All-Party Parliamentary Drugs Misuse Group on the Government's Consultation Document, 'Tackling Drugs Together'.* London: House of Lords.
All Party Parliamentary Drugs Misuse Group (1998) *Prisons and Drugs Misuse: a report of the All Party Parliamentary Drugs Misuse Group.* London: House of Lords.
HM Chief Inspector of Prisons (1992) *Report of Her Majesty's Chief Inspector of Prisons. April 1991–March 1992.* London: HMSO.
HM Chief Inspector of Prisons (1995) *Report on HMP/YOI Styal.* London: HMSO
HM Chief Inspector of Prisons (1996) *Annual Report of HM Chief Inspector of Prisons for England and Wales. April 1995–March 1996.* London: HMSO.

1 These documents refer to those authored by individuals or organisations who act in an official advisory capacity to the government such as the ACMD, Her Majesty's Chief Inspector of Prisons, the Prisons Ombudsman, and other individuals who are appointed to investigate specific issues or events such as Lord Mountbatten, Lord Justice May, Lord JusticeWoolf, and General Sir John Learmont.

HM Chief Inspector of Prisons (1997a) *HM Prison Holloway: report of an unannounced inspection*. London: Home Office.
HM Chief Inspector of Prisons (1997b) *Women in Prison: a thematic review*. London: Home Office.
Home Office (1979) *Report of the Committee of the Inquiry into the United Kingdom Prison Service. Cm 7673*. ('The May Report') London: HMSO.
Home Office (1990e) *Report of Her Majesty's Chief Inspector of Prisons, 1989*. London: HMSO.
Labour Party (1996*) Breaking the Vicious Circle: Labour's proposals to tackle drug related crime*. London: Labour Party.
Learmont, General Sir John (1995) *Review of Prison Service Security in England and Wales and the Escape from Parkhurst Prison on Tuesday, 3rd January 1995. Cm 3020* ('The Learmont Inquiry'). London: HMSO.
Prisons Ombudsman (1997) *Annual Report 1996. Cm 3687*. London: Home Office.
Prisons Ombudsman (1998) *Annual Report 1997. Cm 3984*. London: Home Office.
Woolf, Lord Justice (1991) *Prison Disturbances April 1990: Report of an Inquiry by the Rt. Hon Lord Justice Woolf (Parts I and II) and His Honour Judge Stephen Tumin (Part II), Cmnd 1456*. London: HMSO.

Non-government/non-official publications[2]

ADFAM National (1997) 'The Road to Release: supporting the families of imprisoned drug users', *ADFAM National News*, 19, Spring/Summer 1997.
ACPO (1995) *Government Green Paper 'Tackling Drugs Together': the response of the Police Service in England*. Wakefield: ACPO.
ACOP (1995) *ACOP Response to Tackling Drugs Together*. Wakefield: ACOP.
ADSS (1995) *Tackling Drugs Together: Response of the Association of Directors of Social Services*. Salford: ADSS.
Cranstoun Drugs Services (1997) *Proposed standards for UK prison drug services* – unpublished document.
Exeter Drugs Project (1990) *Third Annual Report 1989–1990*. Exeter: Exeter Drugs Project.
Howard League for Penal Reform (1996) *Teenage prisoners and MDT*. London: Howard League for Penal Reform.
LGDF (1995*) Response to the Green Paper 'Tackling Drugs Together'*. London: Local Government Drug Forum.
LDPF (1995) *'Tackling Drugs Together': joint response from the London Drugs Policy Forum, Association of London Authorities and the London Boroughs Association and the London Borough's Grants Committee*. London: London Drug Policy Forum.
Parole Release Scheme (1983) *Parole Release Scheme: a brief guide for non-statutory agencies*. London: PRS.
Parole Release Scheme (1984) *A Guide to the Parole Release Scheme*. London: PRS.
Parole Release Scheme (1985) *Monitoring Report Year One 1983/84*. London: PRS.
Parole Release Scheme (1986) *Parole Release Scheme and Sisters Avenue Monitoring Report September 198 –March 1986*. London: PRS.

[2] These documents refer to those authored by non-governmental organisations which do not act in an 'official' advisory capacity to government.

Parole Release Scheme (1989) *Project Report 1988/89*. London: Cranstoun Projects.

Parole Release Scheme (1991) *Annual Report 1990/91*. London: Cranstoun Projects.

Penal Affairs Consortium (1996) *Drugs on the Inside*. London: Penal Affairs Consortium.

Phoenix House (1995) *A response to the consultation paper from Phoenix House*. London: Phoenix House.

The Police Foundation (1999) *Drugs and the Law: report of the independent inquiry into the Misuse of Drugs Act 1971*. London: The Police Foundation.

Prison Reform Trust (1988) *HIV, AIDS, and Prisons*. London: Prison Reform Trust.

Prison Reform Trust (1991) *AIDS Update*. London: Prison Reform Trust.

Release (1995) *'Tackling Drugs Together': response to the Government Green Paper*. London: Release: the National Drugs and Legal Advice Service.

SCODA (1995) *Tackling Drugs Together: a response from drug service providers*. London: SCODA.

Turning Point (1995) *A response to the Green Paper 'Tackling Drugs Together'*. London: Turning Point.

Secondary sources: books, articles, pamphlets, etc.

Adler, M. and Longhurst, B. (1994) *Discourse, Power and Justice: towards a new sociology of imprisonment*. London: Routledge.

Allen, F. (1981) *The Decline of the Rehabilitative Ideal*. New Haven: Yale University Press.

Andrew Irving Associates (1986) *Anti-Heroin Campaign: qualitative evaluation research report* London: Andrew Irving Associates.

Appleyard, L (1998) 'Targeting drugs', *Prison Service News*, 16 (167): 8–9.

Ashton, M (1995) 'Meeting of minds over Green Paper plans', *Druglink*, 10 (2): 5–7.

Atkinson, M. and Coleman, W. (1992) 'Policy networks, policy communities, and the problems of governance', *Governance*, 5 (2): 154–80.

Atkinson, P. and Coffey, A. (1997) 'Analysing documentary realities', in: D. Silverman (ed.), *Qualitative Research: Theory, Method, And Practice*. London: Sage.

Atkinson, R. and Savage, S. P. (1994) 'The Conservatives and public policy', in: S. P. Savage, R. Atkinson and L. Robins (eds), *Public Policy in Britain*. London: Macmillan.

Auld, J., Dorn, N., and South, N. (1986) 'Irregular work, irregular pleasures: heroin in the 1980s', in: R. Matthews and J. Young (eds), *Confronting Crime*. London: Sage.

Awiah, J., Butt, S., Dorn, N., Pearson, G., and Patel, K. (1992) *Race, Gender and Drug Services*. London: ISDD.

Baker, R. and Runicles, D. (1991) *Co-ordinating Drugs Services: the role of regional and district drugs advisory committees*. London: London Research Centre and National Local Authority Forum on Drugs Misuse.

Baroness Jay of Paddington (1995) 'Wishes for a White Paper', *Druglink*, 10 (2): 11.

Bartley, M (1996) 'Probably Minister ... the strong programme approach to the relationship between research and policy' in: C. Samson and N. South (eds), *The Social Construction of Social Policy: methodologies, racism, citizenship and the environment.* London: Macmillan.

Barton, A. and Quinn, C. (2002) ' Risk management of groups or respect for the individual?: issues for information sharing and confidentiality in Drug Testing and Treatment Orders', *Drugs: education, prevention and policy,* 9 (1): 35–43.

Bean, P. (1993) 'Cocaine and crack: the promotion of an epidemic', in: P. Bean (ed.), *Cocaine and Crack: Supply and Use.* London: Macmillan.

Bean, P. (ed.) (1993) *Cocaine and Crack: supply and use.* London: Macmillan.

Bean, P. (1996) 'Viewpoint: new developments in the US drug courts', *Drugs: education, prevention and policy,* 3 (2): 211–13.

Bean, P. (1998) 'Transplanting the USA's drug courts to Britain', *Drugs: education, prevention and policy,* 5 (1): 101–4.

Becker, H. (1963) *Outsiders: studies in the sociology of deviance.* Glencoe: Free Press.

Becker, H. (ed.) (1966) *Social Problems: a modern approach.* London: John Wiley and Sons.

Berger, A. (1995) 'Welcome to Cell Block Heroin', *New Scientist,* 21 Oct. 1995, 14–15.

Berridge, V. (1978) 'War conditions and narcotics control: the passing of Defence of the Realm Act Regulation 40B', *Journal of Social Policy,* 7 (3): 285–304.

Berridge, V. (1989) 'Historical issues' in: S. MacGregor (ed.), *Drugs and British Society: responses to a social problem in the 1980s.* London: Routledge.

Berridge, V. (1990) 'Drug research in Britain: the relation between research and policy', in: V. Berridge(ed.), *Drug Research and Policy in Britain.* Aldershot: Avebury.

Berridge, V. (1991) 'AIDS and British drugs policy: history repeats itself ... ?', in: D. K. Whynes and P. T. Bean (eds), *Policing and Prescribing: the British System of Drug Control.* London: Macmillan.

Berridge, V. (1994) 'Researching contemporary history: AIDS', *History Workshop Journal,* 38: 228–34.

Berridge, V. (1996a) *AIDS in the UK: the making of policy 1981–1994.* Oxford: Oxford University Press.

Berridge, V. (1996b) 'Drug policy: should the law take a back seat?' *The Lancet,* 347: 301–5.

Berridge, V. (1997) 'Doctors and the state: the changing role of medical expertise in policy-making', *Contemporary British History,* 11 (4): 66–85.

Berridge, V. (1999) *Opium and the People: opiate use and drug control in nineteenth and early twentieth century England.* London: Free Association Books Ltd.

Berridge, V. and Thom, B. (1996) 'Research and policy: what determines the relationship?', *Policy Studies,* 17 (1): 23–34.

Bird, A. G., Gore, S. M., Jollife, D. W., and Burns, S. M. (1992) 'Anonymous HIV surveillance in Saughton prison, Edinburgh', *AIDS,* 6: 725–33.

Bird, A. G., Gore, S. M., Burns, S. M., and Duggie, J. G. (1993) 'Study of infection with HIV and related risk factors in young offenders' institutions', *British Medical Journal,* 307: 228–231

Bird, A. G., Gore, S. M., Hutchinson, S. J., Lewis, S. C., Camerson, S. and Burns, S. (1997) 'Harm reduction measures and injecting inside prison versus mandatory drugs testing: results of a cross sectional anonymous questionnaire survey', *British Medical Journal*, 315: 21–4.

Blair, T (1993) 'Why crime is a socialist issue', *New Statesman and Society*, 29 Jan. 1993, 27–28.

Blom-Hansen, J. (1997) 'A 'new institutional' perspective on policy networks', *Public Administration*, 75: 669–693.

Bond, P. (1998) 'The development of good practice and treatment in the rehabilitation of alcoholic and drug-addicted inmates in Her Majesty's Prisons', *Alcohol and Alcoholism*, 33 (1): 83–8.

Booth, T. (1988) *Developing Policy Research*. Aldershot: Avebury.

Bottoms, A. E. (1980). 'An introduction to the "Coming Penal Crisis"', in: A. E. Bottoms and R. Preston (eds), *The Coming Penal Crisis*. Edinburgh: Scottish Academic Press.

Bottoms, A. E. (1995) 'The philosophy and politics of punishment and sentencing', in: C. M. V. Clarkson and R. Morgan (eds), *The Politics of Sentencing Reform*. Oxford: Clarendon Press.

Bottoms, A. E., Hay, W., Sparks, R. (1990) 'Situational and social approaches to the prevention of disorder in long term prisons', *The Prison Journal*, 86 (1): 83–95.

Brake, M., and Hale, C. (1989) 'Law and order', in P. Brown and R. Sparks (eds), *Beyond Thatcherism: social policy, politics and society*. Milton Keynes: Open University Press.

Brake, M. and Hale, C. (1992) *Public Order and Private Lives: the politics of law and order*. London: Routledge.

Brazil, C. (1996) 'Drug users in the prison system in the UK', in: A. Rainford and S. Woods (eds), *Drug policy in the 1990s: the changing scene – a series of papers presented in response to the Government White Paper, 'Tackling Drugs Together'*. Liverpool: Centre for Drugs Studies.

Bridgwood, A. and Malbon, G. (1995) *Survey of the Physical Health of Prisoners*. London: HMSO.

Bright, S. (1995) *HIV and AIDS in Prisons: probation responses. Social Work Monograph 138*. Norwich: University of East Anglia.

British Medical Association (1997) *The Misuse of Drugs*. London: Harwood Academic Publishers.

British Medical Journal (1995) 'Editorial: prison policies put inmates at risk', 310 (4): 278–83.

Brown, P. and Sparks, R. (eds) (1989) *Beyond Thatcherism: social policy, politics, and society*. Milton Keynes: Open University Press.

Brownlee, I. (1998) 'New Labour – new penology? Punitive rhetoric and the limits of managerialism in criminal justice policy', *Journal of Law and Society*, 25 (3): 313–35.

Bulmer, M. (1978) 'Social science research and policy-making in Britain', in: M. Bulmer (ed.), *Social Policy Research*. London: Macmillan.

Bulmer, M. (1982) *The Uses of Social Research: social investigation in public policy-making*. London: George Allen and Unwin.

Burrows, J., Clarke, A., Davison, T., Tarling, R. and Webb, S. (2000) *The Nature and Effectiveness of Drug Throughcare for Released Prisoners*. Home Office Research Study 109. London: Home Office.

Butcher, T. (1995) *Delivering Welfare: the governance of the social services in the 1990s*. Buckingham: Open University Press.

Butcher, T. (1998) 'Managing the Welfare State', in: H. Jones and S. MacGregor (eds), *Social Issues and Party Politics*. London: Routledge.

Carlen, P. (1998) *Sledgehammer: women's imprisonment at the millennium*. London: Macmillan.

Carlen, P. (2002) 'Carceral clawback: the case of women's imprisonment in Canada', *Punishment and Society*, 4 (1): 115–21.

Carlen, P. and Tchaikovsky, C. (1996) 'Women's imprisonment in England at the end of the twentieth century: legitimacy, realities and utopias', in: R. Matthews and P. Francis (eds), *Prisons 2000: an international perspective on the current state and future of imprisonment*. London: Macmillan.

Carvell, A. L. M. and Hart, G. J. (1990) 'Risk behaviours for HIV infection among drug users in prison', *British Medical Journal*, 300: 1383–4.

Cavadino, M. and Dignan, J. (1992) *The Penal System: an introduction*. London: Sage.

Cavadino, M. and Dignan, J. (1997). *The Penal System: an introduction* (2nd edition). London: Sage.

Cavanagh, M., Marsh, D. and Smith, M. (1995) 'The relationship between policy networks at the sectoral level and sub-sectoral levels: a response to Jordan, Maloney and McLaughlin', *Public Administration*, 73: 627–33.

Chadwick, T. (1997) 'Drug crime: an election priority', *Drugs Forum Focus – the newsletter of the Local Government Drugs Forum*, 12: 1&5.

Christie, B. (1993) 'HIV outbreak investigated in Scottish jail', *British Medical Journal*, 307: 151–2.

Clark, R. B. (1997) 'Are custody, control and justice compatible? The aims of imprisonment revisited', in: A. Liebling (ed.), *Security, Justice and Order in Prison: developing perspectives*. Cambridge: Institute of Criminology.

Cohen, S. (1972) *Folk Devils and Moral Panics: the creation of mods and rockers*. London: MacGibbon and Kee.

Cohen, S. (1985) *Visions of Social Control*. Cambridge: Polity.

Coleman, W. D. and Skogstad, G. (1990) 'Policy communities and policy networks: a structural approach' in: W. D. Coleman and G. Skogstad (eds), *Policy communities and public policy in Canada*. Toronto: Copp Clark Pitman.

Collison, M (1993) 'Punishing drugs: criminal justice and drug use', *British Journal of Criminology*, 33 (3): 382–99.

Collison, M. (1994) 'Drug crime, drug problems and criminal justice: sentencing trends and enforcement targets', *The Howard Journal*, 33 (1): 25–40.

Collison, M. (1995) *Police, Drugs and Community*. London: Free Association Books.

Cope, N. (1999) *Drugs, crime and imprisonment: the experience of young offenders*, Paper presented to the British Criminology Conference, Adelphi Hotel, Liverpool, 13–16 July 1999.

Council of Europe (1987) *Health Problems Facing Prison Administrations with Special Reference to Transmissible Diseases*. Strasbourg: Council of Europe.

Covell, R. G., Frischer, M., Taylor, A., Goldberg, D. et al (1993) 'Prison experience of injecting drug users in Glasgow', *Drug and Alcohol Dependence*, 32: 9–14.

Cranfield, S., Feinmann, C., Ferlie, E., and Walter, C. (1994) 'HIV and drug services – the challenge of change', in: J. Strang and M. Gossop (eds), *Heroin Addiction and Drug Policy: the British system*. Oxford: Oxford University Press.

Curran, L (1991a) *The Need for Systematic Information into Aspects of HIV/AIDS in Prison*. London: HM Prison Service.

Curran, L. (1991b) *The Need for a Strategic Approach to HIV in Prison*. London: HM Prison Service.

Curran, L. (1991c) *Arguments For and Against the Issue of Condoms in Prison as a Preventive Measure in the Fight against HIV and AIDS*. London: HM Prison Service.

Curran, L. (1991d) *Sampling the Prison Population for HIV infection*. London: HM Prison Service.

Curran, L. (1992) *Drugs, HIV infection, the Prison Service and the Police*. London: HM Prison Service.

Curran, L and Morrissey, C. (1989) *AIDS/HIV High Risk Behaviour in Prison: an exploratory study at HMP Wormwood Scrubs: summary report*. London: HM Prison Service.

Currie, E. (1993) *Reckoning: Drugs, the Cities and the American Future*. New York: Hill and Wang.

Cutler, T. and Waine, B. (1997) *Managing the Welfare State: text and sourcebook* (2nd edition). Oxford: Berg.

Denham-Wright, J. and Pearl, L. (1995) 'Knowledge and experience of young people regarding drug misuse 1969–1994', *British Medical Journal*, 310: 20–24.

Ditton, J., and Speirits, K. (1981) *The Rapid Increase of Heroin Addiction in Glasgow during 1981*. Glasgow: University of Glasgow.

Dolan, K. A., Donoghoe, M. C., Stimson, G. V. (1990) 'Drug injecting and syringe sharing in custody and in the community: an exploratory survey of HIV risk behaviour', *The Howard Journal*, 29 (3): 177–86.

Dolan, K. A., Donoghoe, M. C., Jones, S., Stimson, G. V. (1991) *A Cohort Study of Syringe Exchange Clients and Other Drug Injectors in England, 1989 to 1990*. London: Centre for Research on Drugs and Health Behaviour, Charing Cross and Westminster Medical School.

Donnison, D. (1978) 'Research for policy', in: M. Bulmer (ed.), *Social Policy Research*. London: Macmillan.

Donoghoe, M. C., Stimson, G. V., Dolan, K., and Alldritt, L. (1989) 'Changes in HIV risk behaviour in clients of syringe-exchange schemes in England and Scotland', *AIDS*, 5 (3): 267–72.

Dorn, N, (1986) 'Media campaigns', *Druglink*, 1(2): 8–9.

Dorn, N. (1990) 'British policy on prevention', in: H. Ghodse, C. D. Kaplan and R. D. Mann (eds), *Drug Misuse and Dependence*. Carnforth, Lancs: Parthenon Publishing Group.

Dorn, N. and Murji, K. (1992) 'Low level drug enforcement', *International Journal of the Sociology of Law*, 20: 159–71.

Dorn, N. and Seddon, T. (1995) 'Oh to be in England: Tackling Drugs Together in the prison system' in: C. Martin (ed.), *Dealing with Drugs: a new philosophy? Report of a conference organised by the Institute for the Study and Treatment of Delinquency*. London: ISTD.

Dorn, N. and South, N. (1985) *Helping Drug Users*. Aldershot: Gower.

Dorn, N. and South, N. (1987) 'Reconciling policy and practice', in: N. Dorn and N. South (eds), *A Land Fit for Heroin: drug policies, prevention and practice*. London: Macmillan.
Dorn, N. and South, N. (1994) 'The power behind practice: drug control and harm minimisation in inter-agency and criminal law contexts', in: J. Strang and M. Gossop (eds), *Heroin Addiction and Drug Policy: the British system*. Oxford: Oxford University Press.
Dorn, N., Murji, K. and South, N. (1992) *Traffickers: drug markets and law enforcement*. London: Routledge.
Dowding, K. (1995) 'Model or metaphor? A critical review of the policy network approach', *Political Studies*, 43: 136–58.
Downes, D. (1997) 'What the next government should do about crime', *Howard Journal*, 36 (1): 1–13.
Downes, D. and Morgan, R. (1997) 'Dumping the 'hostages to fortune'? The politics of law and order in post-war Britain', in: M. Maguire, R. Morgan and R. Reiner (eds), *Oxford Handbook of Criminology*. Oxford: Oxford University Press.
Duke, K. (2000) 'Prison drugs policy since 1980: shifting agendas and policy networks', *Drugs: education, prevention and policy*, 7 (4): 393–408.
Duke, K. (2001) 'Evidence-based policy-making? The interplay between research and the development of prison drugs policy', *Criminal Justice*, 1 (3): 277–300.
Duke, K. (2002) 'Getting beyond the "official line": reflections on dilemmas of access, knowledge and power in researching policy networks', *Journal of Social Policy*, 31(1): 39–59.
Duke, K. and MacGregor, S. (1997) *Tackling Drugs Locally: the implementation of Drug Action Teams in England*. London: HMSO.
Dye, S. and Issacs, C. (1991) 'Intravenous drug misuse among prison inmates: implications for the spread of HIV, *British Medical Journal*, 302: 1506.
Early, P. (1991) *The Hot House*. New York: Basic Books.
Eaton, L. (1997) 'Wish upon a tsar', *Community Care*, 26 June–2 July 1997: 27.
Edelman, M. (1964) *The Symbolic Use of Politics*. Chicago: University of Illinois Press.
Edelman, M. (1971) *Politics as Symbolic Action*. New York: Academic Press.
Edelman, M (1984) 'The political language of the helping professions', M. Shapiro (ed.), *Language and Politics*. Oxford: Blackwell.
Edelman, M. (1988) *Constructing the Political Spectacle*. Chicago: University of Chicago Press.
Edgar, K. and O'Donnell, I. (1998) *Mandatory Drug Testing in Prisons: the relationship between MDT and the level and nature of drug misuse. Home Office Research Study 189*. London: Home Office.
Edwards, G. (1990) 'What drives British drug policies', in: H. Ghodse, C. D. Kaplan, and R. D. Mann (eds), *Drug Misuse and Dependence*. Carnforth, Lancs: The Parthenon Publishing Group.
Ericson, R., Baranek, P., and Chan, J. (1991) *Representing Order: Crime, Law and Justice in the News Media*. Milton Keynes: Open University Press.
European Monitoring Centre for Drugs and Drug Addiction (2001) *An Overview Study: Assistance to drug users in European Union prisons*. Lisbon: EMCDDA.
Evans, P. (1980). *Prison Crisis*. London: George Allen and Unwin.
Farrell, M., and Strang, J. (1991) 'Drugs, HIV, and prisons: time to rethink current policy', *British Medical Journal*, 302: 1477–8.

Farrell, M. and Strang, J. (1998) 'Britain's new strategy for tackling drugs misuse: shows a welcome emphasis on evidence', *British Medical Journal*, 316: 1399–1400.

Farrell, M., Macauley, R., Taylor, C. (1998) *An Analysis of the MDT Programme: key findings*. London: National Addiction Centre.

Faulkner, D. (1996) 'Policy-making in the Home Office', in: P. Barberis (ed.), *The Whitehall Reader: the UK's administrative machine in action*. Buckingham: Open University Press.

Feeley, M. M. and Simon, J. (1992) 'The new penology': notes on the emerging strategy of corrections and its implications', *Criminology*, 30: 449–74.

Feeley, M. M., and Simon, J. (1994) 'Actuarial justice: the emerging new criminal law', in: D. Nelken (ed.), *The Futures of Criminology*. London: Sage.

Finch, J. (1986) *Research and Policy: the uses of qualitative methods in social and educational research*. Lewes: Falmer Press.

Fitzgerald, M. and J. Sim (1982). *British Prisons* (2nd edition). Oxford: Blackwell.

Fletcher, H. (1990) *Drug Users and Custody*. London: National Association of Probation Officers.

Flynn, N. (1994) 'Drugs in prison – another quick fix?', *Release Drugs Edition: prisons special*, 4: 1–3.

Garland, D. (1985) *Punishment and Welfare*. Aldershot: Gower.

Garland, D. (1990) *Punishment and Modern Society: a study in social theory*. Oxford: Clarendon Press.

Garland, D. (1996) 'The limits of the sovereign state: strategies of crime control in contemporary society', *British Journal of Criminology*, 36 (4): 445–71.

Garland, D (1999) 'Editorial: punishment and society today', *Punishment and Society*, 1(1): 5–10.

Garland, D. (2001) *The Culture of Control: crime and social order in contemporary society*. Oxford. Oxford University Press.

Gordon, I., Lewis, J., Young, K. (1993) 'Perspectives on policy analysis', in: M. Hill (ed.), *The Policy Process*. London: Harvester Wheatsheaf.

Gore, S., Bird, A. G., and Ross, A. J. (1996) 'Prison rights: mandatory drug tests and performance indicators for prisons', *British Medical Journal*, 312: 1411–13.

Grapenndaal, M. (1990) 'The inmate subculture in Dutch prisons', *British Journal of Criminology*, 30: 341–56.

Green, P. (1991) *Drug Couriers*. London: Prison Reform Trust.

Green, P. (1996) *Drug Couriers: a new perspective*. London: Quartet Books.

Greenberg, D. (1975) 'Problems in community corrections', *Issues in Criminology*, 19: 1–34.

Griffiths, P., Gossop, M., and Strang, J. (1994) 'Chasing the dragon: the development of heroin smoking in the United Kingdom', in: J. Strang and M. Gossop (eds), *Heroin Addiction and Drug Policy: the British System*. Oxford: Oxford University Press.

Hajer, M. A. (1993) 'Discourse coalitions and the institutionalization of practice: the case of acid rain in Great Britain', in: F. Fischer and F. Forester (eds), *The Argumentative Turn in Policy Analysis and Planning*. London: UCL Press.

Hall, S., Critcher, C., Jefferson, T., Clarke, J., and Roberts, B. (1978) *Policing the Crisis*. London: Macmillan.

Hall, S. (1980) *Drifting into a Law and Order Society*. London: Cobden Trust.

Ham, C. and Hill, M. (1993) *The Policy Process in the Modern Capitalist State* (2nd edition). London: Harvester Wheatsheaf.
Hamer, S. (1998) 'Fear and loathing in reducing doses', *AMBoV Quarterly*, Summer 1998: 3–5.
Harding, G. (1988) *Opiate Addiction, Morality and Medicine: from moral illness to pathological disease*. London: Macmillan.
Harding, T. W. (1987) 'AIDS in Prison', *Lancet*, ii: 1260–63.
Harding. T. W. (1990) 'HIV infection and AIDS in the prison environment: a test case for the respect of human rights', in: J. Strang and G. Stimson (eds), *AIDS and Drugs Misuse: the challenge for policy and practice in the 1990s*. London: Routledge.
Hayes, P. (1991) 'Changing goals: the criminal justice system and drug misuse', *Justice of the Peace*, 155: 598–600.
Heclo, H. (1972) 'Policy analysis', *British Journal of Political Science*, 2: 83–108.
Heidensohn, F. (1998) 'Criminal justice: security, social control and the hidden agenda', in: H. Jones and S. MacGregor (eds), *Social Issues and Party Politics*. London: Routledge.
Henham, R. (1994) 'Criminal justice and sentencing policy for drug offenders', *International Journal of the Sociology of Law*, 22: 223–38.
Hewitt, A. (1996) 'Drug testing in prisons', *Druglink*, May/June 1996: 16–18.
Heyes, J. and King, G. (1996) 'Implementing a drug strategy in a British prison', *Prison Service Journal*, 108: 15–19.
Hill, M. and Bramley, G. (1986) *Analysing Social Policy*. Oxford: Blackwell.
Hogwood, B. W. and Gunn, L. A. (1984) *Policy Analysis for the Real World*. Oxford University Press.
Howard, R., Beadle, P., and Maitland, J. (1994) *Across the Divide: building community partnerships to tackle drug misuse*. London: Department of Health.
Hucklesby, A., Wilkinson, C., Pearson, Y., Butler, L., Hill, A., and Hodgkinson, S. (1999) *Drug Misuse in Prison: a staff perspective*, Paper given at the British Criminology Conference, Britannia Adelphi Hotel, Liverpool, 13–16 July 1999.
Hucklesby, A. and Wilkinson, C. (2001) 'Drug misuse in prisons: some comments on the Prison Service drugs strategy', The Howard Journal, 40 (4): 347–63.
Hudson, B. (1993) *Penal Policy and Social Justice*. London: Macmillan.
Hudson, B. (1994) 'Punishing the poor: a critique of the dominance of legal reasoning in penal policy and practice', in: A. Duff, S. Marshall, R. E. Dobash and R. P. Dobash (eds), *Penal Theory And Practice: Tradition And Innovation In Criminal Justice*. Manchester: Manchester University Press.
Hughes, R. (2000) 'Drug injectors and prison mandatory drug testing', *The Howard Journal*, 59 (1): 1–13.
Irwin, J. (1980) *Prisons in Turmoil*. Boston: Little Brown and Co.
James, A. and Raine, J. (1998) *The New Politics of Criminal Justice*. London: Longman.
Jamieson, A., Glanz, A., and MacGregor, S. (1984) *Dealing with Drug Misuse: crisis intervention in the city*. London: Tavistock.
Jenkins, C. (1997) 'War on drugs: how effective will a "drugs czar" prove in the fight against narcotics', *Police Review*, 22 Aug. 1997.

Jenkins, W. I. (1978) *Policy Analysis: a political and organisational perspective*. Oxford: Martin Robertson.

Jones, T. and Newburn, T. (2002) 'Policy convergence and crime control in the USA and the UK: streams of influence and levels of impact', *Criminal Justice*, 2 (2): 173–203.

Kassim, H. (1994) 'Policy networks, networks and European Union policy-making: a sceptical view', *Western European Politics*, 17: 15–27.

Keene, J. (1997a) 'Drug misuse in prison: views from inside – a qualitative study of prison staff and inmates', *The Howard Journal*, 36, (1): 28–41.

Keene, J. (1997b) 'Drug use among prisoners before, during and after custody', *Addiction Research*, 4 (4): 343–53.

Kennedy, D. H., Nair, G., Elliot, L., and Ditton, J. (1991) 'Drug misuse and sharing of needles in Scottish prisons', *British Medical Journal*, 302: 1507.

Kinchin, D. (1998) 'Inside our prisons: HM Prison Downview – almost a drug free prison', *Justice of the Peace*, 163: 623–4.

King, R. (1991) 'Maximum security custody in Britain and the USA', *British Journal of Criminology*, 31: 126–51.

King, R. D. and McDermott, K. (1995) *The State of Our Prisons*. Oxford: Clarendon

Kingdon, J (1995) *Agendas, Alternatives and Public Policies* (2nd edition). New York: Harper Collins College Publishers.

Kothari, G., Marsden, J., and Strang, J. (2002) 'Opportunities and obstacles for effective treatment of drug misusers in the criminal justice system in England and Wales', *British Journal of Criminology*, 42(2): 412–32.

Lart, R. (1996) *HIV and English Drugs Policy*. PhD thesis submitted to Charing Cross and Westminister Medical School, University of London.

Lart, R. (1998) 'Medical Power/Knowledge: the treatment and control of drugs and drug users', in: R. Coomber (ed.) *The Control of Drugs and Drug Users: Reason and Reaction?* London: Harwood Academic Publishers.

Lee, M. (1994) 'The probation order: a suitable case for treatment', *Drugs: education, prevention and policy*, 1 (2): 121–33.

Leech, M. (1997) *The Prisons Handbook 1997/8*. London: Pluto Press.

Lewis, D. (1997) *Hidden Agendas: politics, law and disorder*. London: Hamish Hamilton.

Lewis, R., Hartnoll, R., Bryer, S.,Davlaud, E., and Mitcheson, M. (1985) 'Scoring smack: the illicit heroin market in London 1980–1983', *British Journal of Addiction*, 80: 281–90.

Liebling, A. and Krarup, H. (1993) *Suicide attempts and self-injury in male prisons*. London: Home Office.

London Drug Policy Forum (1997) *Drug User and the Criminal Justice System: a report of the London Drug Policy Forum conference to consider the links between drugs and crime*. London: London Drug Policy Forum.

Lowthian, J. (2002) 'Women's prisons in England: barriers to reform', in P. Carlen (ed.), *Women and Punishment: the struggle for justice*. Cullompton: Willan Publishing.

MacDonald, M. (1997) *Mandatory Drug Testing in Prisons*. Birmingham: University of Central England.

MacGregor, S. (1989a) 'The public debate in the 1980s' in: S. MacGregor (ed.), *Drugs and British Society: Responses to a Social Problem in the 1980s*. London: Routledge.

MacGregor, S. (1989b) 'Choices for policy and practice', in: S. MacGregor (ed.), *Drugs and British Society: responses to a social problem in the 1980s*. London: Routledge.

MacGregor, S. (1998a) 'Pragmatism or principle? Continuity and change in the British approach to treatment and control', in: R. Coomber (ed.), *The Control of Drugs and Drug Users*. London: Harwood Academic Publishers.

MacGregor, S. (1998b) *Drug and social policy: policy frameworks and policy interests* – paper given at ISDRUTS closing meeting, Lisbon, 7–9 Oct. 1998.

MacGregor, S. (1998c) 'Reluctant partners: trends in approaches to urban drug-taking in contemporary Britain', *Journal of Drug Issues*, 28(1): 188–98.

MacGregor, S. (1998d) 'A new deal for Britain?', in: H. Jones and S. MacGregor (eds), *Social Issues and Party Politics*. London: Routledge.

MacGregor, S. (1999a) 'Medicine, custom, or moral fibre: policy responses to drug misuse', in: N. South (ed.), *Drugs: cultures, controls and everyday life*. London: Sage.

MacGregor, S. (1999b) 'Drug treatment systems and policy frameworks: a comparative social policy perspective', *European Addiction Research*, 5: 118–25.

MacGregor, S. and Ettorre, B. (1987) 'From treatment to rehabilitation – aspects on the evolution of British policy on the care of drug-takers', in: N. Dorn and N. South (eds), *A Land Fit for Heroin: drug policies, prevention and practice*. London: Macmillan.

MacGregor, S., Ettorre, B., Coomber, R., Crosier, A., and Lodge, H. (1991*) Drugs services in England and the impact of the Central Funding Initiative. ISDD Research Monograph Series No. 1*. London: Institute for the Study of Drug Dependence.

Maden, A., Swinton, M., and Gunn, J. (1990) 'Women in prison and use of illicit drugs before arrest', *British Medical Journal*, 301: 1133.

Maden, A., Swinton, M. and Gunn, J. (1991) 'Drug dependence in prisoners', *British Medical Journal*, 302: 880–1.

Maden, A., Swinton, M. and Gunn, J. (1992) 'A survey of pre-arrest drug use in sentenced prisoners', *British Journal of Addiction*, 87: 27–33.

Mallender, J., Roberts, J. and Seddon, T. (2002) Evaluation of drug testing in the criminal justice system in three pilot areas. Home Office Research Findings 176. London: Home Office.

Malloch, M. (2000) *Women, Drugs and Custody*. Winchester: Waterside Press.

Marsh, C. (1986) 'Medicine and the media: government campaign on misuse of drugs report', *British Medical Journal*, 292: 895.

Marsh, D. and Rhodes, R. A. W. (eds) (1992) *Policy Networks in British Government*. Oxford: Clarendon Press.

Marsh, D. and Rhodes, R. A. W. (1992) 'Policy communities and issue networks: beyond typology' in: D. Marsh and R. A. W. Rhodes (eds), *Policy Networks in British Government*. Oxford: Clarendon Press.

Martinson, R. (1974) 'What works? – questions and answers about prison reform', *The Public Interest*, 35: 22–54.

Matthews, R. (1999) *Doing Time: an introduction to the sociology of imprisonment*. London: Macmillan.

McLaughlin, E. and Muncie, J. (1994) 'Managing the criminal justice system', in: J. Clarke, A. Cochrane and E. McLaughlin (eds), *Managing Social Policy*. London: Sage.

McLaughlin, E., Muncie, J. and Hughes, G. (2001) 'The permanent revolution: New Labour, new public management, and the modernization of criminal justice', Criminal Justice, 1 (3): 301–18.

Melossi, D. and Pavarini, M. (1981) *The Prison and the Factory: the origins of the penitentiary system*. London: Macmillan.

Miller, P. and Plant, M. (1996) 'Drinking, smoking and illicit drug use among 15 and 16 year olds in the United Kingdom', *British Medical Journal*, 313: 394–7.

Morgan, R (1997a) 'Imprisonment: current concerns and a brief history since 1945', in: M. Maguire, R. Morgan, and R. Reiner (eds), *The Oxford Handbook of Criminology*. Oxford: Oxford University Press.

Morgan, R. (1997b) 'Are custody, control and justice compatible? The aims of imprisonment revisited', in: A. Liebling (ed.), *Security, Justice and Order in Prisons: developing perspectives. Cropwood Conference Series 1997*. Cambridge: Institute of Criminology.

Morgan, R. (1999) 'New Labour 'law and order' politics and the House of Commons Home Affairs Committee Report on Alternatives to Prison Sentences', *Punishment and Society*, 1(1): 109–14.

Morris, T. (1989) *Crime and Criminal Justice Policy since 1945*. Oxford: Blackwell.

Mott, J. (1977) 'A long-term follow-up of opiate users and their criminal histories', in: D. J. West (ed.), *Problems of drug abuse in England, papers presented to the Cropwood Round-Table Conference, December 1977*. Cambridge: Institute of Criminology.

Mott, J. (1994) 'Notification and the Home Office', in: J. Strang and M. Gossop (eds), *Heroin Addiction and Drug Policy: the British System*. Oxford: Oxford University Press.

Nichols, A. and Henderson, S. (1990) 'The implications for prison work', in: S. Henderson (ed.), *Women, HIV and Drugs: practical issues*. London: ISDD.

Padel (1990) 'HIV and prisoners' rights', *Liverpool Law Review*, 12: 55–68.

Parker, H., Bakx, K. and Newcombe, R. (1988) *Living with Heroin: the impact of a drugs 'epidemic' on an English community*. Milton Keynes: Open University Press.

Parker, H., Aldridge, J. and Measham, F. (1998) *Illegal Leisure: the normalisation of adolescent recreational drug use*. London: Routledge.

PDM Consulting Ltd (1998) *Evaluation of Prison Drug Treatment and Rehabilitation Services: executive report*. London: HM Prison Service.

Pearson, G. (1987a) *The New Heroin Users*. Oxford: Blackwell.

Pearson, G. (1987b) 'Social deprivation, unemployment and patterns of heroin use', in: N. Dorn and N. South (eds), *A Land Fit for Heroin: drug policies, prevention and practice*. London: Macmillan.

Pearson, G. (1990) 'Drugs, law enforcement, and criminology', in: V. Berridge (ed.), *Drugs Research and Policy in Britain*. Aldershot: Avebury.

Pearson, G. (1991) 'Drug control policies in Britain', in: M. Tonry and N. Morris (eds), *Crime and Justice: a review of research, Volume 14*. Chicago: Chicago University Press. pp. 167–227.

Pearson, G. (1992a) 'Drug problems and criminal justice policy in Britain', *Contemporary Drug Problems*, Summer 1992: 279–301.

Pearson, G. (1992b) 'Drugs and criminal justice: a harm reduction perspective', in: P. A. O'Hare, R. Newcombe, A. Matthews et al. (eds), *The Reduction of Drug-related Harm*. London: Routledge.

Pearson, G. and Gilman, M. (1994) 'Local and regional variations in drug misuse: the British heroin epidemic of the 1980s', in: J. Strang and M. Gossop (eds), *Heroin Addiction and Drug Policy: The British System*. Oxford: Oxford University Press.

Petersilia, J. (1991) 'Policy relevance and the future of criminology: the American Society of Criminology 1990 Presidential Address', *Criminology*, 29: 1–15.

Pierson, P. (1994) *Dismantling the Welfare State? Reagan, Thatcher and the Politics of Retrenchment*. Cambridge: Cambridge University Press.

Player, E. and Martin, C. (1996) *The ADT Drug Treatment Programme at HMP Downview – a preliminary evaluation. Research Findings No. 31*. London: Home Office Research and Statistics Department.

Pollitt, C., Harrison, S., Hunter, D., and Marnoch, G. (1992). 'No hiding place: on the discomforts of researching the contemporary policy process', in: J. Vincent and S. Brown (eds), *Critics and Customers: the control of social policy research*. Aldershot: Avebury.

Power, K. G., Markova, I., Rowlands, A., McKee, K. J., Anslow, P. J., and Kilfedder, C. (1992) 'Intravenous drug use and HIV transmission amongst inmates in Scottish prisons', *British Journal of Addiction*, 87: 35–45.

Power, R. (1989) 'Drugs and the media: prevention campaigns and television', in: S. MacGregor (ed.), *Drugs and British Society*. London: Routledge.

Power, R. (1994) 'Drug trends since 1968', in: J. Strang and M. Gossop (eds), *Heroin Addiction and Drug Policy: the British System*. Oxford: Oxford University Press.

Ralli, R. A. (1994) 'Health care in prisons', in: E. Player and M. Jenkins (eds), *Prisons after Woolf: reform through riot*. London: Routledge.

Rein, M. and Schon, D. (1993) 'Reframing policy discourse', in: F. Fischer and J. Forester (eds), *The Argumentative Turn in Policy Analysis and Planning*. London: UCL Press.

Reiner, R. (1991) *Chief Constables*. Oxford: Oxford University Press.

Reiner, R. and Cross, M. (1991) 'Introduction: Beyond law and order – crime and criminology into the 1990s', in: R. Reiner and M. Cross (eds), *Beyond Law and Order: criminal justice policy and politics into the 1990s*. London. Macmillan.

Research Bureau Ltd (1986) *Heroin Misuse Campaign Evaluation: report of findings*. London: Research Bureau Ltd.

Rhodes, R. A. W. (2000) 'Governance and public administration', in: J. Pierre (ed.) *Debating Governance: Authority, Steering and Democracy*. Oxford: Oxford University Press.

Rhodes, R. A. W. and Marsh, D. (1992a) 'Policy networks in British politics: a critique of existing approaches', in: D. Marsh and R. A. W. Rhodes (eds), *Policy networks in British Government*. Oxford: Clarendon Press.

Rhodes, R. A. W. and Marsh, D. (1992b) 'New directions in the study of policy networks', *European Journal of Political Research*, 21: 181–205.

Rice, G. (1997) 'The use of drugs in prison', *Forensic Update*, 49: 6–7.

Riley, D. (1995) 'Drug testing in prisons', *The International Journal of Drug Policy*, 6 (2): 106–11.

Roberts, J. V. (1998) 'The evolution of penal lobby in Canada', *Social Policy and Administration*, 32 (4): 420–37.

Robertson, R. (1994) 'The Arrival of HIV', in: J. Strang and M. Gossop (eds), *Heroin Addiction and Drug Policy: the British System*. Oxford: Oxford University Press.

Robertson, R., Bucknall, A. B. V., Welsby, P. D., Roberts, J. J. K., Inglis, J. M., and Brettle, R. P. (1986) 'Epidemic of AIDS related virus (HTLV-III/LAV infection among intravenous drug abusers', *British Medical Journal*, 292: 527–9.

Robins, L. N. and Reiger, D. A. (1991) *Psychiatric Disorders in America: the epidemiologic catchment area study*. New York: Free Press.

Robson, C. (1993) *Real World Research*. Oxford: Blackwell.

Rochefort, D. A. and Cobb, R. W. (1993) 'Problem definition, agenda access, and policy choice', *Policy Studies Journal*, 21 (1): 56–71.

Rock, P. (1986) *A View From the Shadows: the Ministry of the Solicitor General of Canada and the Making of the Justice for Victims of Crime Initiative*. Oxford: Clarendon Press.

Rock, P. (1990) *Helping Victims of Crime: the Home Office and the rise of victim support in England and Wales*. Oxford: Clarendon Press.

Rock, P. (1994) 'The social organisation of a Home Office initiative', *European Journal of Crime, Criminal Law, and Criminal Justice*, 2: 141–67.

Rock, P. (1995) 'The opening stages of criminal justice policy-making', *British Journal of Criminology*, 35: 1–16.

Rosenbaum, M, (1981) *Women on Heroin*. New Brunswick, NJ: Rutgers University Press.

Ross, M. et al (1994) 'Prison: shield of threat, or threat to survival', *British Medical Journal*, 308: 1092–5.

Ruggiero, V. (1995) 'Flexibility and intermittent emergency in the Italian penal system', in: V. Ruggiero, M. Ryan, and J. Sim (eds), *Western European Penal Systems: a critical anatomy*. London: Sage.

Ruggiero, V. and South, N. (1995) *Eurodrugs: drug use, markets and trafficking in Europe*. London: UCL Press.

Runciman, R. (1996) *The work of the criminal justice working group of the ACMD*, in: Home Office Special Conferences Unit, Criminal Justice Conference Report: Drugs and Criminal Justice, 28 Feb.–1 March 1996, Selsdon Park Hotel.

Ryan, K. F. (1998) 'Globalising the problem: the United States and international drug control', in: E. L. Jensen and J. Gerber (eds), *The New War on Drugs: symbolic politics and criminal justice policy*. Cincinnati: Anderson Publishing Co.

Ryan, M (1978) *The Acceptable Pressure Group – Inequality in the Penal Lobby: a case study of the Howard League and RAP*. Farnborough: Saxon House.

Ryan, M. (1983) *The Politics of Penal Reform*. London: Longman.

Ryan, M. and Sim, J. (1995) 'The penal system in England and Wales: round up the usual suspects', in: V. Ruggiero, M. Ryan and J. Sim (eds), *Western European Penal Systems: a critical anatomy*. London: Sage.

Ryan, M. and Sim, J. (1998) 'Power, punishment and prisons in England and Wales 1975–1996', in: R. P. Weiss and N. South (eds), *Comparing Prison Systems: toward a comparative and international penology*. Amsterdam: Gordon and Breach Publishers.

Ryan, M., Savage, S. P., and Wall, D. S. (eds) (2001) *Policy Networks in Criminal Justice*. London: Palgrave.

Sabatier, P. (1988) 'An advocacy coalition framework of policy change and the role of policy-oriented learning therein', *Policy Sciences*, 21: 129–68.

Sabatier, P. (1991) 'Toward better theories of the policy process', *Political Science and Politics*, 24: 147–56.

Samson, C. and South, N. (1996) 'Social policy isn't what it used to be: the social construction of social policy in the 1980s and 1990s', in: C. Samson and N. South (eds), *The Social Construction of Social Policy: methodologies, racism, citizenship and the environment*. London: Macmillan.

Scott, J. (1990) *A Matter of Record: documentary sources in social research*. Cambridge: Polity Press.

Seddon, T. (1996) 'Drug control in prisons', *The Howard Journal*, 35 (4): 327–35.

Shove, E. (1996) 'Constructing knowledge: commissioned research and the sociology of the environment', in: C. Samson and N. South (eds), *The Social Construction of Social Policy: methodologies, racism, citizenship and the environment*. London: Macmillan.

Sim, J. (1990) *Medical Power in Prisons: the Prison Medical Service in England 1774–1989*. Buckingham: Open University Press.

Sim, J. (1991) '"We are not animals, we are human beings": prisons, protest and politics in England and Wales 1969–1990', *Social Justice*, 18: 3.

Sim, J. (1994) 'Reforming the penal wasteland? A critical review of the Woolf report', in: E. Player and M. Jenkins (eds), *Prisons after Woolf: reform through riot*. London: Routledge.

Singleton, N., Farrell, M. and Meltzer, H. (1999) *Substance Misuse among Prisoners in England and Wales*. London: Office for National Statistics.

Skocpol, T. (1985) 'Bringing the state back in: current research', in: P. B. Evans, D. Reuschemeyer, and T. Skocpol (eds), *Bringing the State Back In*. Cambridge: Cambridge University Press.

Skocpol, T. (1992) *Protecting Soldiers and Mothers: the political origins of social policy in the United States*. London: Harvard University Press.

Smart, C. (1984) 'Social policy and drug addiction: a critical study of policy development', *British Journal of Addiction*, 79: 31–9.

Smith, G. (1992) 'Research politics, political pluralism, pluralistic policy and policy research', in: J. Vincent and S. Brown (eds), *Critics and Customers: the control of social policy research*. Aldershot: Avebury.

Smith, M. J. (1993) *Pressure, Power and Policy: state autonomy and policy networks in Britain and the United States*. London: Harvester Wheatsheaf.

South, N. (1998) 'Tackling drug control in Britain: from Sir Malcolm Delevingue to the new drugs strategy', in: R. Coomber (ed.), *The Control of Drugs and Drug Users: reason or reaction?* London: Harwood Academic Publishers.

South, N. (1999) 'Debating drugs and everyday life: normalisation, prohibition and 'otherness', in: N. South (ed.), *Drugs: cultures, controls and everyday life*. London: Sage.

Sparks, J. R. (1994) 'Can prisons be legitimate?', *British Journal of Criminology*, 34: 14–28.

Sparks, J. R. (1996) 'Penal 'austerity': the doctrine of less eligibility reborn?', in: R. Matthews and P. Francis (eds), *Prisons 2000: an international perspective on the current state and future of imprisonment*. London: Macmillan.

Sparks, J. R. and Bottoms, A. E. (1995) 'Legitimacy and order in prisons', *British Journal of Sociology*, 46 (1): 45–62.

Sparks, J. R., Bottoms, A. E., Hay, W. (1996) *Prisons and the Problem of Order*. Oxford: Clarendon Press.

Spear, B. (1995) 'A personal account', *Druglink*, 10 (5): 12–13.

Spector, M. and Kitsuse (1977) *Constructing Social Problems*. New York: Aldine de Gruyter.

Stares, P. B. (1996) *Global Habit: the drug problem in a borderless world*. Washington, DC: Brookings Institution

Stern,V. (1998) *A Sin Against the Future: Imprisonment in the World*. London: Penguin Books.

Stevens, B. C. (1977) 'Death associated with drug addiction in Greater London during 1970–74', *Medicine, Science and the Law*.

Stimson, G. V. (1990a) 'Research on British drug policy', in: V. Berridge (ed.), *Drugs Research and Policy in Britain*. Aldershot: Avebury.

Stimson, G. V. (1990b) 'Reviewing policy and practice: new ideas about the drugs problem', in: J. Strang and G. Stimson (eds), *AIDS and Drugs Misuse: the challenge for policy and practice in the 1990s*. London: Routledge.

Stimson, G. V. and Lart, R. (1991) 'HIV, drugs and public health in England: new words, old tunes', *Journal of The International Addictions*, 26 (12): 1263–77.

Stimson, G. V. and Lart, R. (1994) 'The relationship between the state and local practice in the development of national policy on drugs between 1920 and 1990', in: J. Strang and M. Gossop (eds), *Heroin Addiction and Drug Policy: the British system*. Oxford: Oxford University Press.

Stimson, G. V. and Oppenheimer, E. (1982) *Heroin Addiction: treatment and control in Britain*. London: Tavistock.

Stimson, G. V., Alldritt, L., Dolan, K., and Donoghoe, M. C. (1988) 'Syringe exchange schemes for drug users in England and Scotland', *British Medical Journal*, 296: 1717.

Stokes, J. (1996) 'The Outsider', *Druglink*, July/August 1996: 15–17.

Strang, J. (1998) 'AIDS and drug misuse in the UK – 10 Years On: achievements, failings and new harm reduction opportunities', *Drugs: education, prevention and policy*, 5 (3): 293–304.

Strang, J. and Gossop, M. (1994) 'The 'British system': visionary anticipation or masterly inactivity', in: J. Strang and M. Gossop (eds), *Heroin Addiction and Drug Policy: the British system*. Oxford: Oxford University Press.

Strang, J., Clee, W. B., Gruer, L. and Raistrick, D. (1997) 'Why Britain's drug czar mustn't wage war on drugs', *British Medical Journal*, 315: 325–6.

Strang, J., Heuston, J., Gossop, M., Green, J., and Maden, T. (1998) *HIV/AIDS Risk Behaviour among Adult Male Prisoners. Research Findings No. 82*. London: Home Office.

Sykes, G, (1966) *Society of Captives*. New York: Atheneum.

Tamlyn, R. and Billings, J. (1995) 'Prison halts drug misuse?', *Prison Service Journal*, 99: 28–31.

Tarling, R (1993) *Analysing Offending Data*. London: HMSO.

Tchaikovsky, C. (1994) 'Why drug testing won't work: the case against MDT for prisoners', *Release drugs edition: prisons special*, 4: 7.

Thom, B. (1999) *Dealing with Drink: alcohol and social policy: from treatment to management*. London: Free Association Books.

Thomas, P. A. (1990) 'HIV/AIDS in Prison', *The Howard Journal*, 29 (1): 1–13.

Thomas, P. A. (1994) 'AIDS in Prisons in England and Wales', in: P. A. Thomas and M. Moerings (eds), *AIDS in Prison*. Aldershot: Gower.

Tippell, S. (1989) 'Drug users and the prison system', in: S. MacGregor (ed.), *Drugs and British Society: response to a social problem in the 1980s*. London: Routledge.

Tizard, B. (1990) 'Research and policy: is there a link?', *The Psychologist*,10: 435–40.

Trace, M. (1990) 'HIV and drugs in British prisons', *Druglink*, January/February 1990: 12–15.

Trace, M. (1995) 'Blowing hard and soft on drugs', *Prison Report*, 31: 4–5.

Turnbull, P. J., Dolan, K. A., Stimson, G. V., (1991) *Prisons, HIV and AIDS: risks and experiences in custodial care*. Horsham, West Sussex: AVERT.

Turnbull, P., Stimson, G., and Stillwell, G. (1994) *Drug Use in Prison*. Horsham, West Sussex, AVERT.

Turnbull, P. and Webster, R. (1998) 'Demand reduction activities in the criminal justice system in the European Union', *Drugs: education, prevention and policy*, 5 (2): 177–84.

Turnbull, P. (1999) Drug Treatment and Testing Orders – interim evaluation. Research Findings 106. London: Home Office.

Turnbull, P., McSweeney, T., Webster, R., Edmunds, M. and Hough, M. (2000) Drug Treatment and Testing Orders – Final Evaluation Report. Home Office Research Study 212. London: Home Office.

Useem, M. (1995) 'Reaching corporate executives', in: R. Hertz and J. B. Imber (eds), *Studying Elites Using Qualitative Methods*. London: Sage.

Von Hirsch, A. (1985) *Past or Future Crimes: deservedness and dangerousness in the sentencing of criminals*. Manchester: Manchester University Press.

Walker, R. (1989) 'We would like to know why? Qualitative research and the policy-maker', *Research, Policy and Planning*, 7 (2): 15–21.

Wayne, P. (1996) 'Injecting trouble into the system', *New Statesman*, 13 September 1996: 24–5.

Weir, M., and Skocpol, T. (1985) 'State structures and the possibilities for 'Keynesian' responses to the Great Depression in Sweden, Britain and the United States', in: P. B. Evans, D. Rueschemeyer and T. Skocpol (eds), *Bringing the State Back In*. Cambridge: Cambridge University Press.

Weiss, C. H. (1977a) 'Research for policy's sake: the enlightenment function of social research', *Policy Analysis*, 3: 531–46.

Weiss, C. H. (1977b) 'Introduction' in: C. H. Weiss (ed.), *Using Social Research In Public Policy-Making*. Farnborough: Saxon House.

Weiss, C. H. with Bucuvalas, M. (1980) *Social Science Research and Decision-making*. New York: Columbia University Press.

Weiss, C. H. (1986) 'The many meanings of research utilisation', in: M. Bulmer (ed.), *Social Science and Social Policy*. London: Allen Unwin.

Weiss, R. P. (1998) 'Conclusion: imprisonment at the millennium 2000 – its variety and patters throughout the world', in: R. P. Weiss and N. South (eds), *Comparing Prison Systems: towards a comparative and international penology*. Amsterdam: Gordon and Breach Publishers.

Wildavsky, A. (1979) *The Art and Craft of Policy Analysis*. London: Macmillan.

Wilks, S. (1995) 'Policy networks in a changing world', in: J. Lovenduski and J. Stanyer (eds), *Contemporary Policy Studies, Volume II, Proceedings of Conference held at University of York, April 18–20 1995*. Political Studies Association, Exeter: Short Run Press Ltd

Wilks, S. and Wright, M. (1987) (eds) *Comparative Government–Industry Relations*. Oxford: Clarendon Press.

Wilks, S. and Wright, M. (1987) 'Conclusion: comparing government–industry relations: states, sectors and networks', in: S. Wilks and M. Wright (eds), *Comparative Government–Industry Relations*. Oxford: Clarendon Press.

Wilson, C. (2001) 'Networking and the lobby for penal reform: conflict and consensus', in: M. Ryan, S. P. Savage, and D. Wall (eds), *Policy Networks in Criminal Justice*. London: Palgrave.

World Health Organisation (1987) *Prevention and Control of AIDS in Prison: recommendations of a consultation*. Geneva: WHO.

Wright, M. (1996) 'Policy community and policy network', in: P. Barberis (ed.), *The Whitehall Reader: the UK's administrative machine in action*. Milton Keynes: Open University Press.

Young, A., and McHale, J. V. (1992) 'The dilemmas of the HIV positive prisoner', *The Howard Journal*, 31 (2): 89–104.

Young, J. (1971) *The Drugtakers: the social meaning of drug use*. London: Paladin.

Young, J. (1973) 'The myth of the drug taker in the mass media', in: S. Cohen and J. Young (eds), *The Manufacture of News*. London: Constable.

Young, J. (1986) 'The failure of criminology', in: R. Matthews and J. Young (eds), *Confronting Crime*. London: Sage.

Young, J. (1997a) 'Breaking windows: situating the new criminology', in: J. Young (ed.), *Writing on the Cusp of Change: essays in contemporary criminological theory*. Middlesex University. Centre for Criminology.

Young, J (1997b) 'Charles Murray and the American prison experiment: the dilemmas of a libertarian', in: C. Murray (ed.), *Does Prison Work?* London: IEA Health and Welfare Unit.

Index